THIS IS MY L·I·F·E
L·I·F·E · IS · Fullfilling · Eternity

A Profile On Me.

Name: Justin Heazlewood.
Age: 12 Years 1 Month.
Height: 150 cm.
Weight: 39 kg.
D.O.B: 12/6/80
Favourite:
Food: Pizza.
Drink: Coke.
Sport: Surf Lifesaving.

First published in Australia in 2018 by Affirm Press,
a Simon & Schuster (Australia) Pty Limited company
Bunurong/Boon Wurrung Country
28 Thistlethwaite Street, South Melbourne VIC 3205

Affirm Press is located on the unceded land of the Bunurong/Boon Wurrung peoples of the Kulin Nation. Affirm Press pays respect to their Elders past and present.

New York Amsterdam/Antwerp London Toronto Sydney/Melbourne New Delhi
Visit our website at www.simonandschuster.com.au

AFFIRM PRESS and design are trademarks of Affirm Press Pty Ltd, Inc.,
used under licence by Simon & Schuster, LLC.

10 9 8 7 6 5 4 3 2 1

© Justin Heazlewood 2018

All rights reserved. No part of this publication may be reproduced, stored in a retrieval system, or transmitted in any form or by any means, electronic, mechanical, photocopying, recording or otherwise, without prior permission of the publisher.

The moral rights of the author have been asserted.

A catalogue record for this book is available from the National Library of Australia

9781925584011 (paperback)
9781925475937 (ebook)

Cover design by Design by Committee
Typeset by J&M Typesetting in Bembo 12/16.5
Printed and bound in Australia by Lightning Source

The author wishes to thank: Will, Nicole, Coco, Caroline, Martin, Benjamin, Scot, Matt, Dion, Tammy, Billy & Mum.

Get Up Mum

By Heazy.

Starring:
Len Ken Justin
Edna Maureen
Nigel and Heazlewood.

1

'Lights! Camera! Action!'

I turn out the lights and get into position on the couch beside Mum, balancing a cup of tea on my knee. It's Friday night – slide night at Nan and Pop's. Mum and I have brought over the latest packet we got back from the chemist, and these are new slides that I'm in! The projector hums quietly, sending a beam of soft light through the lens onto the canvas screen. Speckles of dust float around the beam like eyelash insects. The warm air smells like old books and photo albums and Pop's dresser drawers. It feels like the olden days, before I was born, when my family were young.

Pop and I are usually the only ones interested in the slides but Mum is in a good mood and Nan's had a few home-brews. I've already got my tape recorder in position. While Nan was in the loo I planted it in the gap between the lounge and her single sofa chair. I rewound until I heard the tape smack into place, then I pushed down 'record' and 'play' on the right side of the double tape deck. I can see the small red light glowing in the dark. I'm capturing everything!

'When that red light goes out, I'll love ya.'

Bugger! I'm busted already. Nan's beady eyes scan me warily from her chair – she doesn't miss much. She usually knows when I'm recording. I know it bothers her but I can't help doing it.

'You love me already though,' I say.

I lean over and press stop. My trick is to show her I'm turning it off and then wait until she's distracted (which doesn't take long) and sneakily press record again. I'm trying to be more secretive because I've decided recordings are better when no-one knows they're being taped.

'And don't you spill nothin' on my lounge suite or I'll choke ya bottom!' Nan says with a drawl.

My job on slide night is clickerer. I press down on the square orange button. The projector makes a mechanical noise as the lever slides out and the canister shifts position. The white square on the screen is swapped with a rich fuzzy green. It's a crater surrounded by trees.

'How come we're going so far back into New Zealand!' says Nan in a high pitch.

Mum's testing the reel by showing some of the old slides. Nan and Pop went on a holiday to New Zealand in the seventies and took a LOT of photos from the airplane window. I hammer the button to skip through the scenery.

'Wait a minute dear go back, I want to look at that one,' says Mum.

I flick the switch into 'reverse'.

'I can't remember a lot of this,' says Nan.

'I don't think I've ever seen these ones,' adds Mum.

Press. Whir. Click.

A sign says: 'Te WaikoropupuūSprings.'

'Wake up. They're my springs,' jokes Mum. I love Mum in her silly mood.

Press. Whir. Click.

Get Up Mum

A Maori dancer is onstage leaping up in the air.

'That's Pop getting out of bed,' chirps Mum. 'Nan just pinched him on the bottom!'

Pop does an impression of a tribal warrior.

'Hoo wah wah!'

Good old Pop. His neat head of white hair is combed sideways and tucked behind his big ears. Pop's honest, hardly swears and loves a cup of tea. Sometimes we play crib together and watch the footy. He's the closest thing I have to a Dad.

Press. Whir. Click.

A bunch of sheep stand in a row in a paddock.

'There's Justin's school photo! Justin should see all these, he did a project on New Zealand.'

I did! I got an A for it.

Mum knows. Mum knows better than anyone.

A slide gets stuck. Pop calls for the tweezers but Mum tries to use her nails. They'll have to pull the lever out.

'Well push it in and pull it out,' says Nan. 'That's what I said to you on our honeymoon.'

I giggle.

'Did you hear that Mum?'

I'm excited and laughing and loving everything. Nan yells at Mum not to waste her time with the square cartridges. Her glass of home-brew tips and she spills beer on her precious new carpet. I'm yelling at Nan as she yells at Mum.

'NO! Maureen! Don't waste your time—'

'NAN! QUICK! It's dripping onto the carpet—'

'Oh shaddup!' says Pop, with a cartoon growl.

The timing is perfect. I crack up and vibrate inside. Hanging out with my family is like being in my own sitcom sometimes. Recording it makes it worth double because I'm going to be able to listen back later.

The slides are great for conversation because everyone has to work together to remember who's in the picture and what's happening. This way I get to hear the family history, which is better than just looking through the photo albums.

Nan and Pop had whole other lives before me. They were looking after kids and working on farms and getting sick and going to war. One of Nan's catchphrases is 'hard times, you don't know what hard times are'. Mum was just a kid growing up like me, except she had three brothers – Nigel, Ken and Max. I don't think Nan and Pop were around much because they were always working.

Next is a photo of Mum and Nan. Mum's around twenty and Nan's middle-aged. Nan's wearing a pink top and short denim shorts.

'Oooh. Who's that leggy piece,' says Pop with a grin.

Nan's always had good legs. We often see them when she shows off her latest 'badge' from the garden. Nan bruises easily. She always says she's 'no lady' and can be found 'head down, bum up' in the garden. She's very active for her age. When she retired she joined the Field Naturalist Club – it's a club full of old people who go on walks and look at flowers. Sometimes I join Nan and her friends for a bushwalk. She's always full of stories and sayings and lessons.

I stare at Mum's face projected onto the canvas screen. She was so pretty! She could have been a model in her flares and fuzzy red slippers.

'How long before I was born?'

'You were just a twinkle in my eye,' she says.

I like the idea of being a twinkle. Even though I wasn't born, I'm still part of the story.

'Justin, you're supposed to hold your little finger out when you drink with them cups,' says Pop. He's watching me try to sip my cup of tea. It's the first time I've used one of Nan's fancy cups. There's a picture of a lovely brown duck with green on its neck against a brown and white lace pattern. I'm still working out how to hold its dainty handle.

I shoot my pinky out straight. Pop's blue eyes sparkle as he laughs.

'You bend it a bit dear,' says Mum. 'It curls around like this.'

She makes a curve with her little finger. I try to copy but my finger doesn't want to bend.

'Elegancy!' laughs Pop.

I'm funny without even trying!

'Look at this bloody twelve year old. Likes his fine china for his cup of tea!' Nan says, delighted.

'And do you come to Britain often?' says Mum, doing her posh voice.

'Oh my word!' says Pop.

All eyes are on me now. I feel warm.

'I've always been a "cup of tea Annie",' I chirp

'He's always had his cup of tea,' says Mum. 'He has his coffee in the morning. I buy him the decaffeinated coffee. He has it for his breakfast, just like me.'

Mum spoils me. She gets me breakfast every morning and makes my bed. Other kids my age have to do it all themselves but I'm an only child and the only grandchild Nan and Pop see – I like being special.

The picture changes to a bright sports oval. Finally, we're onto the latest ones. The shots are from the inter-schools cross country race. There are blurry boys running but they're not me.

'It's hard when they're running,' says Mum. 'You don't know where they are.'

'Poor Justin huffin' and blowin',' says Nan. 'When you did that …'

The tape pops and there's the sound of scratchy static. The tape recorder shuts off. I slide my earphones off and take a big breath in. The voices are gone. The picture leaves my head. There is only quiet now as I breathe out. I'm in my bedroom in Burnie. It's dark outside. Shadows hover through the curtains. The wind rattles the back gate. I scan my ears. In the room next door, Mum's room, I can hear bed springs squeaking.

'Sssssst … sshhhhht.'

My chest freezes. It's so horrible, through the walls.

'Ssshhiiiiitt.'

I place my earphones back on. I lean over and fish the tape out of the deck. I flip it round and slot it back in and press down 'play'. I stare into the red glow of the stereo. The soft crackle of static returns, like a campfire in the distance. The sound rolls on, the voices return, Nan and Pop are with me again.

We only looked at the slides a week ago. Mum was fine then.

What happened?

PART ONE
1992: Grade Six

2

Today at school I made a mock cover of *The Advocate* with my best friends Nick and Paul. We made up our own disasters and world events: a nuclear meltdown happening in Los Angeles and treasurer John Dawkins saying the price of beer and cigarettes will go up by two dollars in the budget. I cracked everyone up with my Toyworld ad for a Michael Jackson doll with ten different noses to choose from. It's amazing when you laugh so hard you have tears in your eyes.

When the school bell rings we grab our backpacks and go our separate ways home. Lucky for me my house is on the same street as the school.

The clouds above the oval are spread out like fluffy butter. That's where the athletics carnival will be held soon – I'm going to kick butt! I trudge uphill with my thumbs hooked in the straps of my backpack, past the basketball courts and across the new fitness track. I hoist myself up and over the fence and head towards home. The street is quiet except for the tweeting of birds. The shadows of the houses stretch in long blocks across the road. I can smell cool woodsmoke as a plover squawks nearby.

I know all of this. This is Montello, where I've lived all my life. Everything I see is familiar. Across the road is Jeremy Dyson's place. He was the first kid to have a Voltron action figure. On the opposite side further up the road is the Dixons'. Mrs Dixon is on the parents and friends committee and their letterbox has a yellow safety house sign. Then there's the block with a small overgrown paddock – sometimes I spy a horse in the long grass.

The lines of the footpath sweep beneath my feet. There's a square of footpath with 'MOLLY 86' scratched in the cement. I wonder who wrote it and how they managed to find the cement when it was still wet. I step lightly over the square, to get the timing right.

'Tread on a crack, break your mother's back.'

I need all the luck I can get.

I cruise up to the red brick flats of Brooker Court and check our letterbox. We're number one, the first on the left. Barbara, Mum's closest friend, is in number two. Trudy and her daughters, Mandy and Linda, are in three. In the middle there's a long, sloping driveway.

Ray and Vurlie are in number five, on the opposite side. Vurlie is strict and has a perfect lawn that you're not even allowed to walk on. She tells me off for rescuing tennis balls from her garden. Elsie's in six. She's a little old lady with curly hair – I used to call her 'Mrs Dickie Bird.' I'm not sure who is in number four. It keeps changing but I think it's a young woman at the moment. Overall we have good neighbours. A few years ago Mandy and Linda and I put on a concert in the backyard. All the neighbours came and Linda did tricks with her dog while I told jokes holding my Kermit the Frog doll.

I knock on the door.

Mum takes too long. Hmm. Things aren't good.

Get Up Mum

I hear the thud of the bedroom door and her heavy steps. The front door opens slowly. Mum looks tired. Her eyes are bleary and dull.

'Oh, is it that time already?'

I step inside, looking at Mum closely. Her brown hair is greasy and ruffled. She glances at the clock above the kitchen table and scratches her head.

'I was just …'

'Are you okay?'

'Yes, I was just having a lie down.'

Inside everything looks normal. There's the TV and the brown modular couch, the cane stand with ferns, photos of me on the wall. But something's not right. Something's off.

As I walk into the kitchen I spot a mixing bowl on the bench. It's smeared with chocolate icing rings.

'Did you bake a cake?' I ask hopefully.

Mum plonks herself down on the couch.

'Oh Justin, you know what happened?' she says, her voice lowering. 'I started eating the cake mixture and then I couldn't stop!'

The room goes dark as the sun passes behind a cloud. My thoughts are foggy and slow.

'What! Did you eat the whole cake?'

'I couldn't help it,' she laughs weakly.

It could be funny, but it's actually pretty weird. I stare into the bowl.

'I don't know what gets into me,' says Mum, smiling into the distance.

There are two plastic shopping bags beside the kitchen bench. I start unpacking and putting things away.

'Mum, did you get my decaf coffee?'

'Oh, did I? Is it there?'

'No.'

'Damn, I forgot. That's okay, I'll get some tomorrow.'

She grins giddily on the couch.

'I've still got a damn headache. I think I might go and have a lie down.'

She wanders towards her bedroom, humming.

I feel an ache start to swell inside me. I go to my room and dump my bag. I need to have a little think. Through my window I can see the backyard, the back fence and trampoline. The lawn needs a mow but it's still too damp. I tend to my grass pet – a potato in a stocking with googly eyes and grass growing from its back. He needs a mow too.

'Hee, hee, hee!'

Mum starts laughing in her bedroom. She does that when she's not well.

I trim my grass pet and put water in his dish and plonk down on the edge of the bed. I pick up my nylon string guitar and beginner guitar book. I've been learning 'House of the Rising Sun.' It's a memorable old song with cool chords:

> Am C D F
> Am C A7
> Am C D F
> Am E7 Am

I sometimes hear it on 3MP on Pop's radio in the garage. I always stop and listen because the fingerpicked guitar is so dramatic and the organ is all wild and wobbly. The singer sounds upset and angry as he bellows the beginning of each line. I have no idea what it's about.

I'm finding the F chord tricky. It's like a C major except you cover the top two strings with one finger. It's not easy changing from D to F while keeping the strumming pattern (down, down, up, down, up). Nick's better than me and can do fingerpicking like Tommy Emmanuel.

I can't stop thinking about Mum in her room next door. She's just lying there, on top of the bed. I want her to get up and DO something! I put my guitar down and walk into the hallway.

Mum's door is half closed. Hanging on the knob is a porcelain clown decoration. It's dressed in silky yellow pyjamas and nightcap, lying back on an orange moon. Its pale face is decorated with red circle cheeks and a spot on its nose. It has lace around its neck and a little fringe poking out under its cap. Its eyes are black with a white dot inside, like a cartoon. They stare at me as I push the door open and poke my head in.

'Are you okay, Mum?'

'Hmm,' she says in a high pitch. 'I like your playing.'

She's lying on her side with her head resting on top of the pillow, staring into space.

'Mum, can you get up?'

'What for?'

'I don't think it's good for you to lie there.'

'It's okay dear. I'll get up in a minute.'

There are clothes scattered on the floor and piled up on her clothes horse. Mum usually keeps her room tidy.

'Five more minutes, Justin, I promise.'

There's not much more I can do. At least I've said something. At least she knows I'm worried.

I go back to my room and open up one of the top cupboards. Seeing the name in cement on my way home from school made me think about time capsules. Montello Primary made one in Grade Four. It was a big white cylinder and we each put a piece of work in. I contributed the cassette of my radio show. It won't be opened until 2010! I'll be thirty!

I made my own time capsule last year. I think I put it up here ... the top cupboards are dusty and jumbled and chock full of crap like bags of toys and schoolwork and blankets. I use a rolled-up finger painting like a sword, checking for spiders.

Up the back I pull down a white shoe box.

Justin's Time Capsule DO NOT OPEN!

Found it! I can't remember what's in it. I figure it's okay to check now. It's been nearly a year.

It's full of cool stuff. There's lots of little trinkets like my Carlton membership medal, Wal Footrot soap, Parliament House rubber, Alf toothbrush and a green plastic handle with 'JUSTIN' written on it that's meant to clip onto your can of Coke.

There's a letter inside too ...

To the Dude that's reading this,
Yeh, this is Jussy's Time Capsule!
I enclose a few of my silly possesions.
It 6.30pm on the 17th of November
1991!
The world is polluted! Our
government sux. And we are getting
heaps of American crap on our
T.V network!
Otherwise the world is okay!
I have the best Nan and Pop in the world!
But my Mum is having some probcems.
~~wether~~ whether or not she still is
now I don't know.
     Nick is my best friend!
Big Deal I hear you say.

I have quite a lot of stuff in my room!
Um... I have a nice cat Blossum.

I have 3 uncles (2 of them care
 about me - Ken and Nigel)
A can of coke costs $1.00!
My favourite song is "I'm too sexy!"
I almost have the whole collection
of Footrot Flats Mags!
I am going quite good at school!
        P.T.O

I play table tennis, football, cricket and I am in the Surf Life Saving club.
I won't bother tellin' ya what the stuff in my capsule is. You work it out for yaself. Oh well, better go now.. um if you find this come and tell Justin. if ya now him!
   By Dudes.
        From
          Justin
            Heazlewood

3

I'm a bit nervous coming home from school the next day. I don't know what sort of mood Mum will be in. I can hear rock music blaring from our house. I scurry up the steps and yank open the screen door.

My black tape player is on the table. It's turned up and distorting like crazy. Mum faces the table, dipping one knee then the other in time with the music. It's like she's dancing in a trance.

'Mum!' I yell.

I think it's Mum's new Jimi Hendrix tape but at this volume it's just one big scream. I reach for her shoulder. Her head jerks around.

'Sorry dear, I didn't hear you come in.'

'Mum, the whole neighbourhood can hear!'

'I didn't realise it was so loud.'

She doesn't seem worried.

I stare at my tape recorder. How long had she been going?

Mum goes to the couch and takes out one of her Benson & Hedges. She's started smoking again. Next to her are a Paddle

Pop wrapper and scrunched up packet of Thins chips. I don't like Mum eating junk food.

'Mum …' I want to say she'll put on weight, but it seems a bit mean.

'Oh, I don't do it very often,' she says, looking down at the wrappers. 'I'll have to go on a diet, won't I? How was school?'

'I finished a new *Montello Times*.' This is the school newspaper I edit – I'm also the cartoonist.

Mum squints her eyes as she puffs on her cigarette. No more words come.

'We did a story about the pulp mill strike.'

Mum stares forward, smiling at nothing. Did she hear me?

'Mum!'

Her eyes dart back to me.

'Oh, did you! I'll have a look at it later.'

I snatch up Mum's rubbish and walk towards the bin. The Paddle Pop wrapper smells like lolly banana. The wet stick reads 'Second Chance Draw.'

Our brown bin is overflowing. Mum didn't bother putting in a bread bag lining so I'll have to empty the whole thing outside. I pass the laundry and notice a piddly, tangy smell. Blossum's red litter tray needs changing. Mum stopped buying cat litter and just uses dirt from the garden now. She can't see how dirty it is so it sits there for ages. It's not fair on Blossum.

I open the back door near the laundry and tip everything into the garbage bin. Down the bottom is sloppy and putrid with juice. I hold my breath and blast it with hot water from the laundry tap. I scrub at the gunk with a brush and place the bin upside down to drain. It's gross but at least it's done.

When I head back inside I see Mum, grinning and muttering away to herself. She's in her own world. I hover by the laundry door and listen.

Get Up Mum

'Ahhh, get off me!' Mum whispers in a silly voice. She erupts into a huge giggle. I can't help but smile too. It's weird because I also know that all this is wrong.

'Mum, what are you laughing at?'

'Oh, nothing dear, silly things.'

She never lets me in on the joke. She springs up from the couch.

'What shall we have for tea? Fish and chips?'

I love fish and chips but Tuesday isn't takeaway night.

'Can we afford it?' I ask. I know Nan wouldn't approve. Mum's only on a pension and normally we have to be careful with our spending.

'Yes, I've got enough there.'

I think of the 'opposites sketch' on *You Can't Do That On Television*. They reverse the roles – in one sketch the kid really wants to go to school but his mum forces him to stay in bed. Sometimes my life with Mum feels like an opposites sketch, too.

Before we leave to pick up fish and chips, Mum does her stove checking routine. She holds out a hand and wiggles each finger as she marks off each hotplate knob. She also turns her head to make sure the power point behind her is off. She gets in a rhythm of waggling and turning.

'Mum, you haven't used the stove today.'

'I know dear, but can you check?'

I place my hand on each coil. They're cold.

'Mum, it's off.'

'Okay dear, I'll be done a minute.'

I go and wait in the car. We have a yellow Volkswagen beetle. Everything about it is loud, even the doors, which I always have to slam shut. The best way to impersonate the engine is to stick out your tongue and blow a huge raspberry. When Mum finally gets in the car we head up to Terrylands where the milk bar and takeaway shops are. As we drive through the quiet streets of Burnie I count the lights on in other homes. I imagine the normal families that are probably inside – mums and dads making chicken Kiev for kids with brothers and sisters.

There's no one else at the fish and chip shop. The TV in the corner is playing *Sale of the Century*. Normally I'd be watching it at home. I go to the fridge and get a can of Ninja Turtle soft drink. Raphael is my favourite. His colour is red so he gets the best flavour: cola. I ask Mum to order an apple turnover as well.

'We'll both get one, will we?'

Back home I nurse the warm packet as we climb up the stairs and Mum opens the front door. The smell of chips is something to look forward to. Inside I put the packet on the bench as Mum takes out two plates. She tears open the paper and starts gobbling up the chips.

'This'll be good, won't it!' she says giddily.

I open the cupboard and take out Nan's homemade tomato sauce. I miss Nan.

After tea Mum goes to lie down. We usually watch *A Country Practice* together but tonight Mum isn't interested. She's got a headache. Afterwards I turn off the TV and lock the back and front doors and leave the kitchen light on so I'm not alone in complete darkness. I switch the stove timer around to sixty minutes so that I know when it's bedtime. I hear the steady ticking as I head to the bathroom.

The toothpaste squeezer I got from the school fete is a dud. It has a metal pin that you're supposed to feed the toothpaste tube into, but it's too fiddly. I'll have to squeeze by hand. I lean over to drink fresh cold water from the tap. In the mirror I see a round head with a flat mouth and glasses. They are thick wire frames with square lenses. My hair is a straight brown bowl cut. I have a big dimple but it only shows when I smile. I take off my glasses and suddenly the whole room is a blur. I can't see my own face. I peer in with my nose against the glass. Now my eyes are in focus. A blue-hazel nebula.

I head to my bedroom and close the door. I pull out my favourite comic *Footrot Flats*. The dog is the narrator. At the start of each strip he sums things up, so it's easy to switch my concentration on and off, and I've read them before anyway. The dog's owner Wal is always in strife and getting belted and blown about.

Outside my bedroom window there's a gust of wind. It makes the clothesline creak. I wish Mum had given me a goodnight cuddle.

Wal and his greenie friend Cooch clomp around in gumboots. *Footrot Flats* is set in New Zealand and must be the only cartoon where it rains like real life.

I love that you can tell how a character is feeling by their eyes. If they're dubious then their eyebrows are slanted. If they are worried their eyes are more pointy on top and rounded at the bottom. The dog's eyelids droop, making him look sad and weary. I don't like seeing him like this.

In this episode he's waiting in the rain. Hundreds of streaks fill the frame and little droplets hang from his head.

'What a miserable, miserable day. There are days when your nose is blocked, the fleas are holding a nip-athon on your back, dinner is four hours away and you wonder if it's worth going on.'

I start to feel sleepy. I put the comic down and turn out the light. School tomorrow, another day.

Mum's bed springs squeak.

'Ssssssht!'

Icicles and lightning. I can hear her swearing through the walls.

BRIIIIIIIIING!

The alarm timer! Ha.

I like the surprise. It's a trick I play on myself.

4

Today was a pretty good day at school because I got to talk to the girl I like! Tennille's from New Zealand. She is very pretty and smart but also shy. She chose me in 'Heads down, thumbs up'. Even though I had my eyes closed I knew it was her. But as I walk home, skipping over the cracks in the footpath, my excitement fades away and my tummy starts to feel muddled. My ribs clench as I wonder what I might find when I get home. When Mum gets full blown sick it lasts for ages. Some of her symptoms really upset me like the swearing and hissing. It sucks because sometimes she isn't that bad and other times she's REALLY bad and I don't really know why. I just have to work on staying strong, like Nan always says. But Nan isn't here through the week.

Our neighbour Barbara is working in her garden. I go over to say hello. She's a friendly old woman with a high voice.

'How's school?' she asks. 'You'd be busy finishing up grade six!'

'Yep.'

'Not long to go now is it? Gosh. Doesn't time fly. It seems like only yesterday that you were heading off to kinder.'

I remember the photo of me standing by the old tractor tyre in the backyard on my first day. I had my little grey satchel and a nervous smile.

'Are you excited about going to Parklands?' asks Barbara.

'Yeah a bit.' Parklands is the high school I'm enrolled in for grade seven. It's a lot bigger than Montello and a little further away. I'll have to catch the bus there and back.

'It's a good school. And you always do well,' says Barbara.

I do! In surf club I have three gold medals from beach flags and from school I have eight 'Advocate Achiever' certificates. By grade two I was so far ahead in my reading that the teachers asked me to help others. The principal Mr Blazely told Nan and Pop I had leadership potential.

'And how's Mum?'

I gaze down at the garden gloves in Barbara's hands. I'm never sure what to say.

'She hasn't been real good has she?'

'Nah,' I frown. The sun bounces off Barbara's plants. The white blooms glare like lamps.

'I know she's not well when she stops coming round for a coffee. Has she been to see her doctor?'

'She went a while back. I don't know if she tells the doctor everything.'

Barbara makes a noise.

'Well I'll just keep an eye on her. If it gets real bad you come and let me know.'

I nod but I know I won't – I don't want to worry anyone.

I wish Mum was out tending to our garden. I can see where weeds are starting to sprout up as I say goodbye to Barbara and walk towards our flat. I pick my favourite flower 'Starry Eyes.' It's a white daisy with a purple centre. I pluck the petals and wish for Tennille.

Get Up Mum

This year.
Next year.
Sometime.
Never.
This year.
Next year.
Sometime.
Never.
This year!

Blossum's stretched out on the bottom step, basking in the sun. I can see his brown fur beneath the black. He makes a meow when he sees me. I stroke the top of his soft head. I got Blossum when I was seven. I poked my finger through the kitten cage at the pet shop. Blossum was the first to come over and nuzzle it. I'd already named him by the time I found out he was a boy.

Mum opens the door warily. Her eyes are low and mean. She is wearing the same T-shirt as yesterday – a baggy pink one with a low neck. She hitches the sleeves up around her shoulders and kicks the doorstop into position. I can smell her sour B.O. – I know she's been in bed all day.

I plonk my bag down inside. Mum moves to face the kitchen bench. She leans her face up, like she's trying to threaten someone before a fight. I watch a ripple of anger move over her face. She forces her mouth together so hard that her jaw quivers and her teeth make a crunching sound.

Crack!

Like little bird bones, snapping. I'm instantly upset.

'Mum! What's wrong?'

She turns to face me.

'Oh I'm just sick of Barb and the way she carries on.'

I close the front door. Mum sneers as she impersonates Barbara.

'"How's your mum and dad? Where'd do you go for lunch? What did you order?" She always wants to know every little detail!'

'She's just being friendly.'

'What did she want outside?' Her eyes narrow.

'She was just asking about school.'

'You see? She sticks her nose in all the time. She's always interfering. I can't go two days without her knockin' on the door wanting something. It's enough to drive a person mad!'

Mum glares in the direction of next door and yells.

'What sort of toilet paper did ya use to wipe your bum!'

Mum's joking is embarrassing. I'm the only one who can hear.

Barbara feeds Blossom on the weekends and gets the washing off the line for us when it's raining. She brings over biscuits she's made with jam in the middle and hundreds and thousands on top. She does ask lots of questions but only because she cares about us. We're lucky to have a neighbour like her. Why can't Mum remember that?

When Mum gets sick she thinks Nan and Pop are bad people and that Barbara was planted there to spy on her. In grade four we almost moved house.

'And then she ...'

'Mum!' I raise my voice. Her eyes flicker and seem to growl at me. I'm not scared. I know Mum would never attack me.

On the way to the backyard I notice a stale smell in the laundry. I lift the washing machine lid to find it still full of grey murky water. Mum's undies are floating in it. I close the lid and wander into the fresh air.

Get Up Mum

It's quiet in the backyard – just the whoosh of the breeze through the shield of trees. Little brown birds are fluttering near and far. The lawn is rich green with thick tufts of clovers. I like hunting for four leaf clovers but they're darn hard to find. I find Blossum curled in a soft circle under a rosebush. He pops his head up as I squat down and massage his neck. Blossum purrs so I know he's happy and he loves me.

Leaving Blossum I peel off my shoes for a jump on the tramp. I'm higher now and can spring up and see in any direction. I can see over the fence into Barbara's backyard or over our fence into the church carpark or onto Bird Street or the back of the house and bathroom window. My legs are springs and my arms are wings. The wind lifts my hair and my weight brings me down.

'Ssstinking … SSHHIIT!'

A horror wave hits. It's Mum! She's having a shower while she's swearing to herself. The bathroom window is open so I can hear her from out here.

'Trollop! Sssstinking … bag of SSHIIIIT!'

It's such a savage sound. Such ugly words. She's so angry in her cave.

'Bitch! Sssssss … TROLLOP!'

The backyard is where I come to get away. I can't let the anger get me.

I jump off the tramp. There's a sting rising inside me as I storm past the gate and the car and the dried worm on the oil stain shaped like a question mark. I walk fast because I'm the fastest. I can solve this problem quickly. I'm ready to get away, across the road, up the street, near the school.

My heart's beating fast with worry. I'm a bit light-headed. There's a prickly, tickly feeling under my skin. It's a feeling I get sometimes after I've been running around. I get so wound up and famished and all I want to do is demolish some bread and biscuits and scull sweet green cordial from the fridge. My body and my head aren't completely connected. My head is a cloud. My body wants fuel!

I glance around the street. There are no cars and no people. I see traces of smoke from chimneys. The sun is hidden behind rooftops. I look back at our fence, pale green and rickety. I hold my breath. Thump, thump, thump. I can't hear anything except the sound of my heart.

I wait against the school fence.
I've got nothing to do.
No money or ball.
I have nowhere to go.
I imagine a brother. He looks worried.
I feel … no one.
No one is coming for me.
I wait.
I stare down the road. The sea and the sky.
The smell of pine and distant burn off.
I step forward.
There's a bird on its side in the gutter.
Its feathers flutter in the breeze.
A soft, black vegetable.
I tear inside.

5

She said yes! Nick's mum said I can stay over on the weekend!

I'm packing while I wait for Nick and his mum to come pick me up. Mum walks out of the hallway rubbing her head like she just woke up. It's 4pm on Friday.

'Okay and when will you be back?'

'Sunday.'

'Oh. Aaaaaand …'

Mum thinks of questions she might need to ask. 'When do you need the permission form for Arm River by?'

Why does she want to talk about this now? We had all week to plan this stuff.

'On Monday.'

Mum sits down at the table and picks up a pen and drags a notepad across.

'And what would you like me to get from the supermarket?'

'Mum, Nick'll be here in a minute.'

'Have you got everything? Have you got your toiletries?'

I hear the toot of Nick's car.

'Yep and my pyjamas. Okay, bye Mum.'

'Yes, bye dear.'

We reach our arms out and hug loosely. Her cheek is hot and soft. I yank my bag onto my shoulder, swipe past Blossom and hurry down the steps and out to Nick's mum's white car.

I sling my bag in the boot and climb into the back seat. Nick's younger brother Danny sits in the front.

'Wait till you see what we're having for dinner!' Nick grins.

'Pizza!' yells Danny.

The car smells clean and fragrant. It's normal and wonderful in the back. The engine is quiet and doesn't advertise to the whole street that we're going.

Nick's mum looks up at the rear view mirror. I see her clear, bright eyes.

'Hello Justin!'

Nick's mum is a bit younger than mine. She's skinny with long brown hair and a sharp face. She's quite casual and in control of things. We never really say much and it's sometimes hard to know if she likes me. She's usually in the background while Nick and I play computer or watch TV, but if we fight with Danny she gets upset. She gets along well with Nick. She has a smart personality and they laugh and joke together. I get jealous sometimes because I'd like to do that with my mum.

Okay, forget about Mum, concentrate on Nick and having fun. It's my favourite thing ever knowing I get to relax and sleepover and join in on Nick's life – even if it's only for the weekend. I take a final glimpse of our house as the car pulls out of the driveway. Mum's lace curtains are open. What will she do all weekend?

The car accelerates with a heave. I feel a pang of guilt.

Get Up Mum

Nick's my best friend. He came to Montello in grade four from the mainland and I could tell straight away he was a cool dude. He had dark blond hair that was long at the back and short at the front (a style I've always wanted). He wore a 'Rip N Tear' windcheater with hood, silkie Adidas 'enforcer' pants and chunky Aerosport shoes.

I offered to show him around and we realised we had quite a bit in common. He loves table tennis and WWF wrestling and his parents are divorced so he doesn't have a dad either. He's clever and funny but also a bit crazy like me.

We pull up to the steep drive of his house on Colgrave Road. The light is dimming and the air is sweet. I know I've got nothing but yummy food and laughing ahead of me. Friday night is 'surprise night' where Nick's mum brings home a treat like Chomps or musk sticks or Malteasers. The guest is always included in 'surprise night'.

I've never had my own computer so getting to play on Nick's Commodore 64 is the best thing ever. He has a huge container of discs. Some of them have hidden games so it's exciting because we get to work them out together.

While we wait for pizza, Nick loads up a brand new game called *Future Knight*. He flicks his fringe out of his eyes and flexes his long skilful fingers. I rock myself gently on the cane kitchen chair. A shape whizzes by my head and bounces off the desk. It's a yellow nerf dart. I hear Danny's giggle behind us.

'Danny, rack off!' yells Nick.

I like how Nick protects us both. He's on my side and I've got him all to myself.

'Hey Nick, is it okay if I record?'

I reach around and slip a tape into his white ghetto blaster on the floor. Nick speaks in a quick, jittery fashion.

'Yeah, it'll be funny to listen back to.'

In *Future Knight* there's a pink spaceman who wanders around a grey factory shooting pink balloons, and avoiding pink blobs on the ground and a hovering vacuum cleaner robot thing that is also pink. I wiggle the joystick. I have no idea what I'm doing or where I'm going.

'Oh, so what do you do, you go that way!'

Nick is often sarcastic.

'You didn't say which way,' I yelp, waggling the joystick. 'I better get me bum wigglin'!'

Nick giggles.

The spaceman in *Future Knight* has a bubble butt, a bit like Nick. If I shift the joystick up and down at the top of a ladder, it looks like he's flashing a moon.

'Wiggle moon!'

This keeps us more entertained than the actual game.

'You boys gonna watch the football? It's about to start now.'

Nick's mum appears with reports from the real world.

I love footy but I want to stay here with Nick. I'm not done playing.

'Justin are you going to be warm enough in a sleeping bag tonight?'

I run into a balloon with a face on it, taking 200 points off my energy. It's not a good time to discuss bedding.

'I haven't got a doona for that bed yet,' she adds. 'How come this curtain's wet?'

'I dunno,' says Nick, trying to concentrate on shooting the pink balloons.

'It's saturated.'

'I didn't pee on it.'

Nick's mum lowers her voice and laughs.

'I didn't say you did …'

'Danny did.'

Get Up Mum

'Ah, NICK! Do you mind?'

'Sorry Mum.'

Nick's mum can get cross and stressed. We're not very good at conversation and I get shy around her. At least I'm never in trouble.

'Justin, I'll give you a blanket as well.'

I'm avoiding the main vacuum cleaner shaped sentinel baddie.

'Justin?'

'Yep.'

'Look. Blanket as well as a sleeping bag there.'

'Right.'

I don't look.

It's Sunday afternoon, the end of the normal weekend. I ring Mum to ask her to come and get me. She takes a long time to answer.

'Hull-oo?'

The notes are odd. The 'o' goes down and up the way a little kid says 'Muu-u-um!'

'Hi Mum, can you pick me up at five?'

I wait for her to reply.

'At Nick's?'

'Yep.'

There is a long pause.

'Okay.'

It's a different voice. The timing is off.

'I'll come now then?' she says flatly.

'No, in an hour, at five?'

'… at five.' she repeats.

I hang up. I don't want her to come.

Nick's mum is chopping things for tea – the kitchen is full of the sweet smell of soup. Nick and Danny are fooling around in the hall. The lounge is empty. Yesterday we watched cartoons while eating breakfast. I was safe in Saturday and in between the fun.

Nick gets out his acoustic and electric guitars.

'Let's practice "Unforgiven",' he says, handing me the acoustic guitar.

I feel nervous. I don't know if I want to hear it today. It's so sad and it's Sunday and I'm about to leave.

Nick and I started learning guitar last year. Last month we performed a Spanish guitar duet up at Parklands High School. I was so nervous but we didn't stuff up. Nick's way better than me and can do proper fingerpicking and power chords and licks. Our current favourite band is Metallica. Their cassette cover is black except for a snake that is black as well. Nick plays the tape so we can remember how the guitar bit goes.

'The Unforgiven' is a long serious song. It starts with a horn, like a ship arriving at port. It swells in volume and is broken by a drum punch. Now there's only guitar, the prettiest and moodiest guitar I've ever heard. The notes pick me apart at the ribs. The snare does a military-style drum roll. It could be a funeral procession.

The sun goes behind a cloud as Nick's room grows gloomy. I rest my chin on my hand and focus on the carpet. The song tells the story of an old man who tries to please everyone but people are cruel and interfere so he ends up dying alone. I am pushed deep inside my feelings. Time moves slowly as big thoughts close in. The singer is gentle and sorrowful. He dubs the man 'unforgiven'. The chorus keeps repeating with 'Never free … never me.' After an eternity it fades into the distance.

'Cool song!' says Nick.

He sets me up with his acoustic and we go over the backing.

Get Up Mum

Nick leans over close, his hands helping mine find the right place on the frets. It's a simple riff once you get the timing of the picking. Nick has the reverb turned up on his amp so it sounds just like the tape. I pluck away at the backing while Nick chimes in with the opening riff. It's better to be playing the notes. It feels more comfortable. Now I'm inside the song. I can control it.

'Justin, your mum's here!' Nick's mum yells from up the hall.

I put the guitar down and gather my bag. I thank Nick's mum for having me.

'See ya tomorra,' says Nick, shaking his fringe.

I walk down the steps. Our yellow Volkswagen waits in the sun. Mum stares ahead from the driver's seat. Face frowning. Lips snarling.

Nick waves from the stoop. I wait until we pull away, then I stare hard and wide out the window as an ache creeps up my throat. The engine roars to life. Electric guitars thrash in my head.

I'm alone again
with Mum.

6

I don't want to get out of the car. I don't want to go into the house.

Mum's swearing. And she's crunching.

'Mum!' I whine.

All the good fun is gone. Now I'm annoyed.

Mum can't get the key in the door.

'Buggar ya!'

Her jaw clenches.

Crack!

The worst sound of all. A bullet in my ear.

'Mum!'

'I can't help it.' She looks dumb and desperate. She scratches her head and throws the keys on the table.

The house feels so hollow. I turn the TV and the heater on. I pull the curtains closed. The screen door rattles like faint thunder. That's Blossum's knock. I let him in and get his food out of the fridge.

'Mum you shouldn't leave the spoon in Blossum's cat food like that, Nan says it could cause metal poisoning.'

Get Up Mum

Mum doesn't care. She's too busy hissing at the vegetables.

I hate you. The thought scolds my mind. I shouldn't think like that but I can't stand it. I'm sorry. I'm angry. I'm confused.

I take a can of Jelly Meat from the cupboard and open the door to the porch. Blossum follows me like a happy shadow. His bowl, tucked away in a corner near the porch railing, is covered in ants. They've made little cities out of each cat biscuit leftover.

'Blossum, wait!' I imagine he understands.

I put the can down, pick up the bowl and take it into the laundry, trying not to let the ants use my arm as a highway.

'Ssssshhht!' I pass Mum's swearing back. Her right arm leans against the top cupboard, forming a crook for her forehead to rest in. Her face glares down at the bench. In the other hand she grips a pair of tongs like a weapon. It's a weird position, as if she can't support the weight of her own head.

Chops sizzle away behind.

'Sssssstinking bag of ...'

'MUM!' I yell.

There's a slash of shock across my stomach. The sword of Mum's sound.

In the laundry I blast the bowl as best I can. I dish up half a can of cat food and chop it with the spoon. Blossum's head butts my hand as his sharp little teeth gobble away. I don't mind. At least he's happy.

There's a blunt shout from the kitchen.

'Tr-ollop!'

When Mum gets going she repeats the same two swear words over and over. She hisses the s's in 'stinkin' and shooshes the 'sh's in 'shit'

From a distance it sounds like: 'ssssss ... ssssshhhhh ... ssssss ... ssssshhhhh ...'

This is what I hear through the walls at night.

Lately she's been adding 'trollop!' in the pattern so it's more like: 'ssssss ... sssshhhhh ... TR! ... ssssshhhhh ... TR! ...'

It hurts me. Every time.

'Slut!' Mum whispers at the wall. 'Slut' is a new one.

I yell at Mum to make her stop. I say anything.

'Mum! You've got to stop!'

I have to get my annoyance out.

I have to stop the horror getting in.

'Mum! Who are you swearing at?'

'Sorry dear I'll stop.'

'Is it me?'

'No, it's nothing to do with you dear. It's just anger that I have to get out.'

Hmm. Anger she has to get out. What does that mean? How can you be angry when there's no-one there to be angry at? It makes no sense.

I ruffle my beanbag and plonk it in place in front of the TV. *Beyond 2000* is on. I love the opening titles with a robot pushing a girl on a swing and a space car flying into a futuristic city.

At least Mum's making tea. Everything could be okay if she'd just stop swearing. I can handle Mum lying on the bed and laughing to herself. It hurts to think about how close we are to being normal. I can imagine being able to relax and enjoy myself. But those crazy sounds! They attack me so I can't think. They ruin everything.

I can't stop them, so I concentrate on TV.

Mum hands me my plate of chops and spuds.

'There you go Justin. I'm sorry, I'm a bit tired. I'll be better after a sleep tonight,' she smiles weakly.

Mum's a good cook when she's well. She does baked lamb shanks and homemade apple pies. These chops are charred and the spuds are underdone – it's like biting soap. My heart plummets.

Get Up Mum

Mum lies down on the couch behind me. She's not even watching TV, she's just carrying on. I swivel round to see her hiding her face in the crook of her elbow. She's like a little kid playing peekaboo. She hisses into the space.

'Can you not sit like that!'

Why can't she sit up on the couch like a normal person? Why can't she rest for half an hour so I can watch my show?

In the ad break, she leans forward and glares at the screen, dark and mean. Her eyes are little brown bombs. Her mouth is squashed and horrid. Her cheeks squirm as her jaw clenches.

I hate that ugly face.

Crack.

'MUM!'

'I can't help it.'

I try squashing my teeth together. I power my jaws and jam my teeth together. I feel my cheek muscles bulge. I increase the tension. My neck vibrates. I draw more force into my back teeth. My teeth shake but there's no friction. I don't know how to make them crack like Mum does.

Crack!

The butterflies in my stomach catch fire.

'Mum! Please,' I plead.

'Sorry, I can't help it.'

'Maybe go to your room then?'

I'm so sick of it. I just want to watch my show and relax.

'Yes, I think I might go to bed. I'm overtired.' She trudges towards her bedroom.

Suddenly the lounge feels lonely, especially with laughter on TV.

Justin Heazlewood

It's so strange at first
because for a split second
I've forgotten who I am.

I can't remember
what it even is
to live my life
It's dark and I'm somewhere
in the middle of nothing.

Then I get a fright
as the shock pours in
and my blood runs electric.

I don't know how long
it's been going
but it's wrong
and I can't get up
but I have to get away.

I was away
before,
all forgotten and hidden.

With the sound turned down
the colour came clear
I liked it there.
Tucked in the deep

                          asleep

                          new i n v i s i b l e o u t l i n e s

Get Up Mum

There were pieces of a story
I didn't know.
Some people I needed.

It goes away now,
as everything comes back.
My life.
All at once.

'OWOOOOOOOOOO!'

I'm worried
inside my electric chest.

I listen to the nightmare
and miss being asleep.

7

My eyelids fill with a soft blue glow as morning light creeps into my room. I wriggle my toes. I pick my nose with my thumb. Last night my fingers were in my ears.

'RAA! RAA! RAA!' says the alarm. It's 8am.

I rewind the worried memories. It's okay though. I'm safe and the morning is friendly.

Still, there's worry in my heart – things are getting worse.

I step into the shower and close my eyes and let the wet fog slosh down over my face. I concentrate on the rain pattering down onto my brain.

I get out and dry my back with a new technique. I hold the towel behind me by the corners and swivel it back and forth. I slide into my Montello Primary green and gold uniform. I'm ready to trot off to where I belong. A full day of school with lessons and friends!

Mum makes me breakfast and flicks through her handbag to give me money for my lunch order. She seems a bit calmer.

'I'm sorry about last night,' she says.

I hand her my glasses.

'Can you give them a clean?' Mum takes out a cloth and spray. I let my tired eyes relax in the fuzz.

'You should go to your doctor, Mum.'

'No, I'll be alright. Don't you worry about me.'

I walk out the door and into the cool sun. The road is coated in a wet sheen and the grass is twinkling. The sky is smoky, as though the world is under a blanket.

I see that all our neighbours are home. Their cars are in the carports. I wonder if they heard Mum crying last night?

A snail is crawling into the middle of the path. I feel sorry for it – so small and going so slowly. Nan calls them 'shellbacks'. She hunts them down and fills up her home-brew tin. Then she pours salt on them and closes the lid and sometimes I find them sitting by the bin and wished I hadn't opened the lid. I make sure not to tread on this little shellback. There's nothing worse than feeling a crunch underfoot.

When I reach school I find Nick and Mr Burgess huddled around the Macintosh playing *Scruffy*. It's a platform game where you are a small dog who has to find bones and avoid killer turtles and robots. We found out a cheat where you can skip levels but made up a rule that your go doesn't count if you use the cheat. I've still got the top score.

'Hey Justin-time!' Mr Burgess calls. 'So Carlton play Collingwood this weekend! Are you ready to concede defeat?'

'We're ahead of you on the ladder!'

'We've got Daicos back.'

Mr B has a wispy brown moustache and receding hairline. Today he is wearing a black and white jumper with a collar and tie underneath. He's the coolest teacher ever. Mr B often feels more like a friend than a teacher. He not only lets us play games on the new Mac (the only one in the school) but he gets as excited about them as we do. He has his own fun inventive teaching style and somehow manages to get us excited about maths! We have running competitions and he's very supportive of the *Montello Times*. Best of all he often laughs at my jokes.

'What about Hawthorn? Who do they play?' asks Nick, his eyes on the screen.

'Bye, Nick!'

'Huh?' says Nick, flicking his hair.

'I'm saying bye.'

'Whaddaya mean … oh, right, we've got the bye.'

'Alright Justin, whoever loses has to do as many laps of the fitness track as the points margin. Let's do a run now.'

Most mornings we start class with a run around the fitness track. It's crisp but a bit slippery outside. I pump my arms and pound my legs and suck in cold and blow out heat, engines burning at full throttle.

I catch the rear end of Elvis. It's a sight I'm used to – his red shorts and blond bob bouncing up and down. Elvis is the cheekiest kid in school, which often makes him the funniest too. If there's something naughty that needs doing you can always dare Elvis. He's also one of the smartest kids and the fastest long distance runner. We can be teammates at table tennis but rivals in maths. It's mostly a friendly competition, depending what mood he's in. One thing's for sure, there's no-one like Elvis.

Mr Burgess surges up next to me. I glance over at the side of his head, backed by the oval and bushland and sea in the distance. He's like a big kid in a light blue T-shirt. We pound the track down to the bottom of the playground towards the fence that overlooks a brambly paddock. We're shrouded by gumtrees now and the bright morning air flushes my face.

I'm coming third. I'm used to this. My nickname at surf club is 'Justabout.' It started in the Under Eights. I guess I looked funny in my bathers and cap and thick glasses with elastic on the back. Even though I struggled sometimes I'd always bust a gut and 'just about' get there, but more often than not I'd come third or fourth. Our coach Mr O'Gary nicknamed me 'Justabout' and it caught on big time. I took it as friendly teasing. I liked standing out because I was generally shy. 'Justabout' made me feel like a mascot.

'Go Justabout!'

'You Justabout got there!'

The final stage of our morning run is around the toilet block and uphill past the oval cellar. Now my legs are heavy and my chest is burning. All I want to do is stop. I won't win. Elvis is too good, again. Now I'm split in half and buckled over and heaving in breaths. Air hits the back of my throat like dry blades. My heart's pounding like a machine.

'Good race,' Mr Burgess puffs. He flashes a smile then returns to his exhausted grimace. Elvis walks with his hands on hips and tongue hanging out. We're the frontrunners. I don't pay attention to the rest. Nick doesn't try that hard and Tennille, well, she's jogging slowly with her friend Melissa. I hope she's impressed by me.

After lunch Tennille comes up to me as we're walking into class. She opens up her pencil case and reaches in.

'This is for you.'

Her tanned, dainty fingers are holding a green clover. I take it from her carefully, by the stem. It has four circles.

'You said you wanted one. I found one in our backyard.'

'Oh, thanks!'

I try to think of something else to say but she's already walking away, talking to Melissa. I sit down and slip the clover inside my desk, next to a fresh packet of choc buds. I feel my face heating up.

Mr Burgess is at the front of the class. This is my favourite time of day – Supertest time! You have twelve minutes to answer as many questions as you can. If you pass, you move up one level. Mr Burgess designs the tests at home on his Macintosh with cool graphics. First it was the characters from Ninja Turtles all the way up to Splinter. Elvis, Nick and I have raced so far ahead that Mr B has to make up new levels just for us! Elvis and I have just entered 'Sai' which is the weapon used by Rafael.

I pick a speck of sleep from my eye. I'm still a bit groggy.

Crack!

I feel a flash of panic. But it's just Nick cracking his knuckles.

'Heads down and go!' calls Mr Burgess.

All my excitement burns inside. My hands tremble and my mind goes all funny. When I'm under pressure I start by panicking but then I remember how smart I am and I start to relax and focus. My mind goes into a calculator zone where I reach for the answers like my mouth reaches for words. This level is hard because we have to add up three numbers instead of two.

Eight seven and three is sixteen carry the one.

Eight one and one is eleven carry the one.

Two and one and one is four.

Four hundred and sixteen.

I can hear Elvis' pencil scratching like crazy. His head is almost touching the desk as he hunches over with his free hand cupped around the paper so no-one else can cheat.

'Okay and stop.'

There's a loud clang of pencils and the classroom is suddenly filled with the sighs of relief and laughter. Mr Burgess collects up our tests. He'll mark them tonight and hand them back tomorrow.

'Has anyone seen my ten-colour pen?'

'It's there, behind you.'

'Haven't you got eyes in the back of your head?' says Mr Burgess.

'People in Chernobyl do,' I pipe up. 'They've got legs in the back of their head.'

No-one else gets it but Mr Burgess does.

'You have a very clever sense of humour,' he says, coming up to my desk.

I can tell he really laughed and is impressed with me. I beam with brightness inside.

He tells me about a new game on the Macintosh that he and his son have been playing. I study the black hairs on his hands and the silver watch on his wrist. His son is lucky to have Mr Burgess after hours.

There's an ad on TV that goes: 'My dad picks the fruit that goes to Cottee's, to make the cordial, that I like best!'

So someone made up: 'My dad picks his nose that goes to Snotty's, to make the boogie juice, that I like best!'

It makes me remember I don't have a Dad.

I've never met him. He and Mum never married. They went to school together and Mum said he was a good runner, which is where I must get it from. She sat behind him in class and had a bit of a crush on him. She's always said if I ever have any questions I'm free to ask but I don't really. His name is Geoff and he's an electrician who lives in Wynyard with his own family.

A few years ago Nan and I were at the supermarket when she introduced me to an old couple. I thought they paid more attention to me than most of Nan's friends. She told me later on that they were my other grandparents. I guess they don't want to know me.

I wouldn't mind the idea of Mum meeting someone. Her last boyfriend was Jamal who was a Malaysian sailor she met when

Justin Heazlewood

I was about six. They wrote letters for a while and she'd always send him photos of us and he'd say he loved us.

I don't miss having a dad because I don't know what it's like. If I did have one I'd want him to be just like Mr B.

8

Mum won't stop crying.

It started while she was making tea. I'd been in and out of Mum's room begging her to come and get tea ready. Finally she rose from the bed. Then I thought she had a cold because she was sniffing as she got the pan out. Then I noticed her cheeks were glistening. She was crying quietly to herself.

I went up to her and put my hand on her shoulder. I wanted her to stop. She said she needed to cry.

Now I'm sitting in my beanbag eating spaghetti bolognaise in front of *I Love Lucy*. I don't really like old shows, especially when they're in black and white. Mum's gone back to lie on the bed. I'm full of worry about what's to come. But for now I can enjoy eating tea. I scrape and scoop and slurp up the slippery tangles.

I switch the TV over to the ABC news. I need normal things now more than ever. They're making a big deal out of Paul Keating putting his hand on the Queen's back. The English press have dubbed him 'The Lizard of Oz!'

I change the channel again and *A Country Practice* comes on. Blossum slinks over to me. He peers over the edge of the beanbag with needy green eyes. I like how serious he takes getting comfortable. He hops up and works out where to put his feet. Once he's steady he starts massaging my legs with his paws. He turns round and walks himself into a ball and settles down with a groan. Now I'm protected by a warm furry weight.

'Awoooooh.'

NO! Mum's mournful howl. Always loud.

Tonight's going to be bad, I can feel it.

'Awooooooh.'

If I can hear then surely the neighbours can too. I've got to stop Mum before she really gets going.

I put my fingers under Blossum's soft body and gently lift him up. He knows what is happening. We can both go from rest mode to fully alert in a second. I hurry into the hallway.

The lights are off. The air is thick with grief.

'Mum, what's wrong?'

'I have to cry, dear,' she says weakly.

The streetlights cast shadows through the open curtains and onto the outline of Mum on the bed. Mum is lying half on her stomach and half on her side. Her head is raised to talk to me. One leg is folded up. It looks like the recovery position we learned in surf club.

'The neighbours will hear.'

'No, they won't.'

I wander back in the lounge and turn the volume up on the TV. If she's going to cry then I don't want to hear it. Blossum steps over to me, his green eyes full of concern.

'Awwooooooooooo ...'

I want to turn Mum down. I want to slow down my heart.

The sound of crying fills the room, drowning out the TV.

I have no idea what to do. Mum's moaning in agony. No-one cries like that. It's making me crazy inside. I can't keep listening.

Get Up Mum

'Awowoooooooo.'

I stare at Mum's bedroom door. Behind it is a haunted cave. Mum at her worst in the centre of the bed. A volcano of ghosts, floating towards me.

I storm through the door.

'Mum, please stop! I can't take it.'

Her voice is a wet whisper.

'The doctor says I need to cry.'

'Why?'

'There's pain from my past. If it doesn't come out I get sick.'

You are sick!

I'm frozen in the moment, stuck in this dark house where nothing makes sense and everything is weird and I'm worried and alone.

'Can you do it quieter?'

'I'll try, really.'

There's a twinkle on her cheeks where the light meets a streak of tears. She flops her head back down.

I go back in the lounge as the crying starts up again and that's when I …

'Awwooooooooooo.'

… and that's when I know I really can't take it any longer.

I go to the kitchen table and I reach for the phone, squashing the receiver to my ear and pressing the numbers. I jam a finger in my other ear.

'Hello?'

NAN!

I pour myself through the line.

'It's Justin. Mum won't stop crying.'

'Oh gawd.'

My voice wobbles. Tears coat my eyes. The world goes fuzzy.

'It's really bad.'

I tilt the receiver towards the wailing. I want them to hear.
'How long's this been going on for?'
'All night. She's been bad all week.'
I hear a voice talking to Nan on the other end of the phone.
'… Maureen is it?'
POP!
I imagine being by his side.
'Don't be upset matey. I know it's hard,' says Nan.
I close my eyes. My heart stomps with pressure. I'm not sure whether to ask …
'Can you and Pop come and get me?'
I ask because I'm desperate. Nan doesn't respond straight away.
'Hold on lad …'
She talks off the phone.

I have it worked out. I could pack a bag in the half hour it would take them to drive to pick me up. I'd wait out on the step and they'd pull into the drive. I'd climb into their car and we'd go, away from the noise, away from the pain. They wouldn't have to come in. It wouldn't matter if Mum didn't realise I was gone. She probably wouldn't notice straight away.

'Justin,' Nan's voice brings me back to the moment. 'I think it's too late for us to come over there now. Your mum might not like us interfering.'

I hear the words. My mouth is open because my nose is clogged.

'We might end up making it worse. How about you go and put her on? I'll try and talk some sense into her.'

I blink and squint, trying to squeeze the tears down.
'I don't think I can take it!'
Nan sighs.
'I know darling, I can hear it in your voice. It breaks our heart to hear you so upset. Really. You know we'll be over there on

Get Up Mum

Friday. You be strong and try and hold on till then. You're a man now. You go and tell her she's got to stop!'

I sniff and wipe away the tears. Nan's talking sense.

'Now you go and put your mum on.'

I place the receiver on the hook, being careful not to hang up. I can hear their tinny voices through the holes.

'… can't go on like this,' says Pop.

'… taking them bloody tablets …'

Mum's bedroom door is less scary. She's gone quiet.

'Nan wants to talk to you.'

'I didn't hear the phone ring!'

'I rang her.'

Mum sits up with a jerk. Her voice is high.

'You did! Why?'

'Because you wouldn't stop crying.'

'Oh,' she sniffs.

I hover in the hallway while Mum talks to Nan. That's right, I told on Mum.

Mum puts the phone up and returns.

'Justin, Nan again,' she says casually.

That was quick!

'She seems a bit calmer there now,' says Nan. 'She knows how much it upsets you when you've got to get a good sleep and be ready for school.'

'Okay.'

'She promised she won't carry on anymore tonight.'

'Okay.'

'You just try and forget about it and concentrate on doing well at school so you can get ahead in life and be a success!'

'Okay, thanks Nan,' I stammer.

'Your Pop's standing here and he's very worried as well. We both think the world of you and love you very much.'

My tears return. My heart aches to bursting.

'I love you too.'

I'm so lucky to have Nan and Pop.

I hang up and gaze at Blossum, perched in front of the heater. I like how neatly he sits, with his paws pressed together. He looks me in the eye and blinks very slowly. I wonder if it's a signal. Blossum knows.

I grab a tissue and have a big blow. Mum comes out and puts her arms around me weakly. She's warm and sweet with B.O.

'I'm sorry that I upset you dear, really I am.'

'This can't go on!' I say.

'Okay I'll stop it really, I didn't realise it was upsetting you so much.'

She speaks quickly while I stare ahead. My thoughts are so tired.

'I don't know what gets into me sometimes.'

Mum wanders off. I close my eyes and think about bed.

There's a wind up car on the table. A little orange Volkswagen. I pull it back and wind it up until the back wheels start to SNAP! SNAP! SNAP! SNAP!

I hold the car in place and aim it at the couch. The car zooms forward and flies off the edge and rolls across the floor.

There's credits on the TV.

I've missed *A Country Practice*.

I've missed everything.

9

In the morning Mum makes me breakfast as usual. When I walk into the kitchen after my shower she hands me a bowl and goes out to the swing seat to have a cigarette. She's been calm since her big cry.

I eat my Weet-Bix with warm milk and sugar while watching *Astro Boy*. He's a robot boy with big eyes and black spiky hair and jetpacks coming out of his red boots. I love the opening titles. The song matches the colours perfectly and there is a chorus of voices creating an exciting atmosphere. He's normally gentle and curious but kicks butt when he gets mad.

Uh-oh! This is the sad episode about the baby elephant. Mean hunters are shooting at robot animals in a park. A baby elephant is bathing with its mother. The mother tries to protect its baby but the hunters come and shoot the mother. She crashes to the ground. The baby elephant is wailing and the mother has tears in her eyes as she's dying. I feel tears well up in my eyes. I feel sad but that's okay. It helps release the pressure in my chest.

The hunters are about to steal the baby. Astro appears, ties their guns in a knot and rescues the baby elephant.

I've seen this episode before – there are always repeats of cartoons on TV. I remember how upset it made me when I was little. I couldn't stop crying. The same happened when Mum and I saw *Bambi* at the Burnie cinemas. The mother dies in that one as well.

I've always been very upset seeing animals get hurt in movies, even more than when people are hurt. In *Turner & Hooch* the dog gets shot and keeps crawling along the ground, trying to protect its owner. In the *NeverEnding Story* the white horse sinks into the swamp of sadness, even though Atreyu screams at it to keep going. Animals are so beautiful because their eyes say everything.

When I arrive home from school in the afternoon I see a tan Subaru parked in our driveway.

BK 1481. It's Nan and Pop!

Mum seems well behaved. She's often able to pull herself together if the phone rings or someone knocks at the door. It confuses me – if she has the ability to pretend to be normal, why not use it all the time?

Nan and Pop have been working out in the backyard. Pop's mowed the lawn and Nan's weeded out the back garden. She doesn't touch anything inside because it tends to upset Mum.

'I'm an independent person!' Mum always says. She fights anyone who tries to help her with chores but then doesn't do the jobs herself. This is Mum at her most annoying.

I'm going over to Nan and Pop's house in Wynyard for the weekend. Mum's not coming until Sunday lunch, which I'm happy about. I load my gear in the boot of the Subaru and settle into the backseat with my electronic tennis game. Soon it's just the drone of the engine and the cars swishing past outside the window. I have Nan and Pop all to myself. Everything feels cosier the closer we get to Wynyard. It's prettier than Burnie with more trees and less traffic.

We drive with the sea beside us. Table Cape looms in the distance. It's lovely when the sun starts setting below the clouds and the sky turns orange. The cape watches over the sea like a guard. It has a lighthouse on its head, which makes me think of Inspector Gadget's siren inside his hat.

Nan and Pop's is a mustard weatherboard beside a huge tree. Straight away the garden greets me with colour. Pom poms of red and white and yellow spring from their beds like a cheer squad. Clusters of roses wait in full bloom. My favourite is one called 'Taboo' – it has rich dark red velvet petals. They gather in a cluster. I want to bury my face into it like Nan's powder puff. I take a swig of the fresh perfume.

Nan's garden amazes me every time. There are chirping birds and wafts of sea breeze and soft grass underfoot. The lawn is keyhole shaped and surrounded by shrubs and daisies and vines and trees bursting out in every direction. There's a bird bath and canary aviaries and a veggie patch and hot house. Nan and Pop's is like a little farm. There's life everywhere – even inside, where the pet budgie Sparky is perched in his cage, prattling away.

Every time I visit the first thing I do is go for a walk around the garden. I crush a few lemon verbena leaves in my hand and bring my palm to my nose. Wow! Such sweet soothing freshness. Nature's Vicks VapoRub. It cleans my mind out and brightens my mood. I close my eyes and think of all the good memories of Nan and Pop's. Barbecues and ball games and blowing bubbles. I open my eyes to the soft green lawn and blue sky. A gentle jungle of tree tops and soapy buds. My legs are fresh, the breeze ruffles my hair. I can stop worrying!

I'd better do my chores. I fetch a bucket, fill it with water and top up the birdbath. Inside are some of my old marbles, which Nan put in to attract the birds. They also attract me. I like the metallic gold one that has reflective coating like the latest wraparound sunglasses.

I pad back towards the house and head into the garage. The home-brew barrel is wrapped up in its electric blanket (to keep the temperature even). Pop's radio hangs on a hook beside it and beside that is the canister of fish food. The flakes smell salty and I always want to nibble some. Nan built a big fish pond in the garden by the swing seat. I sprinkle a pinch onto the water. Spit is first on the scene. He is the king of the pond. His eyes bobble as his funny mouth gobbles up the fish food. Food is magic because it makes animals come whenever you want.

Okay, my work is done. Now for a reward! I follow the back path towards the strawberry patch, past the marigolds and flowers that look like spaceships – sometimes I pick the flowers and pretend I'm in a video game. The strawberries are between the hot house and the veggie garden. I flip through and find a plump lolly jewel that a bird hasn't pecked at yet. It's scented from the day's sun and the warm juice is ripe as it bursts onto my tongue. It's so sweet and runny and beautiful. It's as though it was nestled in amongst the leaves, waiting just for me.

'We've GOT to get her back on those tablets.'

Nan and I are parked on the swing seat on the patio. The air circles my bare legs as I massage my feet on the patio tiles. This is where we come to sit and talk before tea. The birds are tweeting. The plants are nodding their heads. Nan's garden is better than TV. The patio is full of orchids in beer bottles and hanging buoys that Nan collects when they wash up on the beach. They remind me of old diving helmets.

Nan usually does most of the talking during these chats. I like listening. Nan knows a lot about a lot of things and has an opinion on everything. She often ends her views by saying 'That's in my book' and I remind her that she'll have to actually write the book. Right now we're talking about Mum. Nan's upset seeing our house the way it was.

'The state of that laundry, Justin, was shocking!'

I look down at the cobbled patterns of the bricks. I feel bad.

'That poor cat having to use such soiled litter, I ask you. And the washing machine water stank to high heaven. Justin how long have those clothes been sitting there?'

I try to keep this stuff from Nan – she gets too worked up. I hope I haven't let her down. Was I supposed to do those jobs?

'Mum's been bad for a while.'

'Well I wish you'd let me know earlier, we could have been over there and seen to it. But you know what she's like, she wouldn't let me do any vacuuming or look inside the fridge.'

Nan does her impression of Mum, vague and high pitched.

'I'm alright. I'll do it. I've just been having headaches.'

Nan turns to me with her wide eyes and downturned mouth.

'Justin, I know she'd not left that bed all day!'

She faces forwards again and takes a sip of beer.

My head feels full. I don't know what to say in these conversations. I don't have many helpful answers.

'I emptied the bin and washed out the cats bowls,' I say.

Nan holds up her heavy hand and slaps it down on my thigh. I think it's supposed to be tender but it hurts a bit.

'Good onya man. You're old enough now, you can get in there and make sure some of those jobs are done. You make sure she's taking them damn tablets. Do you watch her take them?'

Hmm. I don't really know. Not every day. I often hear the rattle of the bottle. I figure she takes them.

'I think so.'

'But do you see her take them? Do you see that she's swallowing them?'

My heart is racing, I don't want to let Nan down.

'I'll make sure she does.'

'You ought to get in there and say "Excuse me Mum, but have you swallowed your tablet."'

Nan softens her voice for the impression of me.

'You never know, Justin. I don't know if she's hiding them under her tongue. I don't know if she spits them back out after or what.'

When Blossum needs to take a worm tablet Mum hides the tablet inside a ball of mince. I could make a joke but it's all too serious. We'll have to go in soon for tea.

Nan tells me I have to be strong.

'The strong survive, the weak … they fall.'

Nan says as long as I talk about my problems I'll be okay – it's no good bottling things up.

'Unless it's home-brew …' I say quietly, but Nan doesn't catch the joke.

'This is part of your mum's problem, she keeps things to herself. I'm forever trying to get her to open up. "Maureen, if something's bothering you then please just tell me." But she won't. She keeps herself bottled up until she gets to screaming point and by GOD, has she let Dad and I have it over the years.'

A lot of family stories take place when I was either a baby or not born yet. Mum had to stay in the psychiatric hospital when I was a baby. No-one ever talks about this – all I know is that she didn't have a very good time.

'Your mum hasn't liked psychiatrists in the past. They don't do a bloody thing except dish out tablets. She's a wonderful woman your mother … when she's well.'

Nan says things I already know. She gets bogged down as we go round in circles. I've heard it over and over. I think of school and Tennille and Nick and surf club. I think of each thing until I think of nothing.

'She seemed a bit better today,' I say.

'Yes, I noticed her eyes were a little brighter. A little.'

10

'I dunno if you're comin' walkin' or not, but it's five o'clock!'

Nan's at the door. She's my alarm.

Okay, okay. I'm up! It's 5am and I'm up!

The layers of thick dream clear away like wisps of cloud. It's the end of sleep mode and time for real life. I sit up, blink and let my mind begin to whir into life like the slide projector.

I'm young Justin! I love waking up at Nan and Pop's place in Wynyard. I'm in a special separate zone. My eyes are still bleary and groggy but my heart's wide awake. There's a special atmosphere that I want to be a part of. It's Morning Walk time and I'm ready.

I'm already sneaking around the house. I avoid flushing the toilet so I don't wake Pop. The curtains are open but it's still dark outside. It's so early but it's not night and the day hasn't started yet. The world is on pause. Everything is set like jelly inside a fridge, waiting to be dug into with a spoon. For now it's soft and gentle.

Nan is like a native animal you have to get up very early to catch. She gets up so early she's already managed to have breakfast and now she's whipping around the kitchen preparing porridge. I've never seen her tired or yawning, she just speaks a bit quieter. I try to look sharp. I'm part of Nan's walking crew and I want to impress her with how alert I can be.

Nan dishes me up a steaming ladleful of the white gluggy stuff that looks like Clag glue. I'd prefer Coco-Pops but I know how serious Nan is about porridge. Talk about boring. Oh well, this is the only time I eat it, as long as there's plenty of sugar on top.

'It's good roughage. It'll get your bowels working.'

Nan thrives on porridge and talking about roughage. She's been up since sparrow's fart and done a poop already. I know this because she tells me. I don't really know when I'll do a poo. I don't need to think about my bowels.

Nan's watching the clock and scanning the sky outside for the weather while checking I have everything ready for the walk.

'Merle'll be here soon, go and put your boots on please.'

Nan's wearing her set of professional bushwalking gear. Japara, purple windcheater, gloves, blue long johns under parachute shorts, bum-bag full of tissues and lollies. Nan recently retired and started getting serious about walking. She bought an expensive tent and sleeping bag and joined the North-West Walking Club and the Field Naturalists Club. I go on walks with her as much as I can. Being in nature is one of my favourite things to do.

Nan's friend Merle arrives with her gigantic Siberian Husky called Chelsea. We stride out together on the hard road. I feel good. There are no cars around. My nose is excited. I can't see much but I smell everything. Crisp, sweet, dewy, smoky wonder. I breathe it in like fuel for my thoughts. Rich, earthy, overnight air. It's drifted down from the trees. It's wafted out of a chimney to greet me. Adventures at dawn. All my favourite motions and atmospheres in a sprawling morning course. This is the time I feel the most me.

Oh, the stars! My wonderful twinkle friends. There's not much to do but gaze up and wonder. Where did they all come from? Where do we all go?

We'll walk down through the main Inglis road out past Gutteridge Gardens then along to Wynyard beach and back. Sometimes Nan and Merle go out to Oldina Pines in the thick bush. That's more of an operation and they have to carry torches because it's pitch black (no streetlights). I think I prefer this route. You get to see the sunrise over the sea and the sky turn from black to blue.

'There's Venus, out to the North,' Nan points with gloved finger.

'So it's a planet and a star?'

'Yes and it's the first one out in the morning and the last one to disappear at night.'

I want to be an astronomer or a vet. I've been fascinated by space since I was little. In grade two I made up my own project that wasn't even part of schoolwork. I borrowed a book from the library and created a colourful page for each planet in the solar system. Saturn looked so cool with its rings and Mars was all scary and red. Neptune was mysterious and blue while Jupiter was eleven times bigger than earth! Nan is still impressed. She says I inspired her to start taking notice of the sky.

Nan has different moods. At home during the day she is Work Nan, which is the scariest. When she's Work Nan she storms in while Pop and I are reading the paper and demands to know why something hasn't been done. After five when she knocks off and has a couple of home-brews she turns into Relaxed Nan. She says she's 'just in the mood' and tells stories and has a giggle. This is definitely preferable.

Downtown or at the bowls club she's usually on her best behaviour. She speaks more formally and is a bit kinder towards me and Pop. Walking Nan is similar but it feels more natural. Nan seems most herself – she can still get flustered if it turns wet or I get too cold but is also genuinely happy to be out in nature. I like how her face lights up when we reach a summit or walk through a leafy ballroom.

Left, right, left, right. Our legs are in rhythm, even the dogs. Merle is firm with Chelsea and says 'Heel' in a stern voice. Chelsea sits there puffing away with her long, hammy tongue hanging out.

'Sometimes Merle walks Chelsea and sometimes Chelsea walks us!'

Merle is Nan's best friend. Merle is a bit more prim and proper than Nan. She plays croquet and goes to church on Sundays. Merle worked with Nan at the Spencer Clinic for the aged. Nan was a geriatric attendant there, which is one step down from being a nurse. She wanted to be a nurse but her father talked her out of it.

We walk past where the new slot car track is! There are milk crates outside the cafes with cartons of milk. The paperboy is picking up stacks for his route. The main street is bathed in a soft glow. The day is warming up. I feel heat beneath my clothes instead of cool. The sun rose so gradually I hardly noticed it wasn't dark anymore! The sky above us is a rich royal blue, like a king's cloak.

We walk by Guttridge Gardens, which is a grassy embankment next to the Inglis River. This is where they hold the Christmas carols each year. Soon we'll pass the jetty and wharf where the fishing boats are. I drift in and out as Nan and Merle yaffle away.

We approach Wynyard beach. My chest unfolds with feelings as I soak up the memories. This is where Pop and I would come walking when I was little. The endless runway of snowy sand.

The distant cheer of the tide going out. I'd stamp my prints into the sand, holding Poppy's big hand, so warm and safe.

We'd walk for ages, in the golden light, as far as the pipes. These were submerged cement cylinders with shaggy green creatures on them. They marked the end of the beach where we'd sit and have a spell. On the way back I followed our footprints like breadcrumbs. If I got too tired I'd end up on Pop's shoulders. Everything was better up high. I was king of the beach.

At the end we'd get a Dixie. It was the meltiest, creamiest vanilla ice cream in a paper cup. It came with a little wooden paddle. Pop told me that a Dixie was what they called the cup soldiers were given in the army. I don't think that one came with ice-cream.

The sun is out now and everything looks wonderful in the new light. The horizon is tinged pale blue and gold with pink clouds blooming over the cape. The molten globe of the sun wobbles over the horizon. The morning is awarding us gold, silver and bronze. It's our prize for being the first out of bed.

We come across a charred circle on the sand. There are beer cans and singed chip packets.

'Why can't they take their rubbish with them,' Nan frowns.

There are hoodlums about. Scary teenagers with Iron Maiden shirts and crew cuts. They hoon around in old cars and rip flowers out of their beds. Merle shakes her head.

'Undesirables.'

We head back the same way. Now it feels like a whole different walk. The gardens are bathed in colour. Birds call out and the last two stars have a shoot out by the moon. My legs are fit and streaming ahead. I'm more relaxed and less worried about being shy around Merle and the dog.

Soon we'll be home. Nan and Merle will go out on the swing seat on the patio to have their all-milk coffee. I'll make some toast and watch *rage*. It's Saturday morning! I've got nothing but (hopefully) clear skies and a relaxing weekend ahead.

I've bought eight 'C' batteries so I can run my recorder without the cord. I like the idea of outdoor recording and capturing some of our swing seat highlights. I wanted to try interviewing Nan but I get shy. She's back to Work Nan, chopping lettuce for a salad.

'It'll probably go flat while you're waiting for me. Have you cleaned your teeth so they're nice and pearly white?'

'No, but I did it this morning.'

'Yes, but you've had breakfast since then. Go and do them again.'

Outside the canaries are chirping away with their laser whistles. In the kitchen the radio plays 'I Still Call Australia Home'. I carry the stereo up the hall and catch Pop in the bathroom combing his hair.

'Combing me plurry hair,' says Pop.

'It's not just any hair, it's plurry hair,' I laugh. Another one of Pop's funny old words.

Sometimes I look at Pop and I'm amazed how old he is. His nose and ears are grand old things that keep growing. Pop has a deep voice. Sometimes it gets so low it gets lost in a gurgle. Pop's 73 now so we all worry about him dying. Nan says she lays awake some nights just to make sure he's breathing. He's slowing down a bit but still has a drink and a laugh and an argument with Nan.

On Saturday afternoon we head down town. Pop puts the lotto in, picks up a prescription and calls in on his mate Lenny who works at the cheese factory. Pop and Lenny have worked out a system where Lenny collects the cans from the workers and Pop takes them down to Camalco to be recycled. I end up with the pocket money!

I help them load five hessian bags into the boot of the Subaru. They're tied up loosely with black string and have a stale beer smell that I don't mind. There are some instant win cans of Solo – I'd love to look inside but we don't have time. At the recycling warehouse a bloke takes the bags and puts them on a scale. We end up with $23.65!

We head back home to watch the Carlton game on TV. Carlton lead seventy-eight to seventy-one at three quarter time, but they only kick one goal to Collingwood's five in the final quarter. Every roar from the Collingwood crowd punches me in the guts. Now there's a hollow feeling as I realise Carlton won't make the finals. This was our best season in ages. I followed them through every game. Now it's over. A cartoon magpie flies onto the screen and prances off. Mr B is going to give me crap on Monday.

'What sort of peaza will you get for dinner?' asks Pop.

At about 5.30pm I ring up Mamma Rosa's and order a ham and pineapple to be delivered. It costs twenty dollars, which is a lot of money so I don't ask very often. Nan says she could make savouries that are just as nice for a fraction of that.

The Gulf War is on the news. They show footage of an air strike on an enemy base using night-vision. There's a black screen with green laser sighters and an eerie flash of green light. It could be a movie.

'Why do we have wars?' I ask.

'I don't know Justin, I've asked myself that question,' says Pop.

Nan's worried someone might let off an atom bomb. America

dropped one on Japan once. *Terminator Two* has a horror scene where Sarah Connor sees the world getting wiped out from a nuclear explosion. A playground catches on fire and she rattles the fence as her skin gets blown off. She's a screaming skeleton …

DING DONG!

The doorbell rings. Pizza! I collect it from the delivery boy and run back into the kitchen to move the slices from the box to a plate. Nan and Pop won't eat until they've finished their beer, so I put theirs in the oven. There's a rush of water to my mouth as I breathe in the steam of the first salty, fruity, cheesy, mouthful. After a few bites I'm so thirsty that my whole insides are aching and itching and the only thing that will do is a cold slurp of sweet, fizzy Coke.

'Aaaah' I gasp. A rainbow swirl of oil from my lips floats in the black.

Hey Hey It's Saturday comes on. My favourite show.

I love weekends at Nan and Pop's.

11

Sunday mornings always feel like a special occasion. I wake to mist on the window and frost sparkling on the lawn. Ice clings to the blades like the liquid nitrogen in *Terminator Two* (such an excellent movie!). My skin crawls at the sight. I'm a little caterpillar, still in my jammies, toasty from bed and tiptoeing to the toilet. The toilet roll doll stares at me. Next to her is a garden gnome, holding tools behind his back.

I don't like to sleep in too long on Sundays. I don't want to miss out on the cosy atmosphere. In the kitchen I'm met with the steamy tang of soup bubbling away on the stove. I lift the lid of the pot to find a frothy cauldron of orange islands, teardrops of steam cling to the lid. The fan heater blares and the air slinks around my legs like a cat. Pop stands at the kitchen bench beside a marmalade jar with the lid off. He's just made breakfast, cutting the toast into fingers, which I do now because it tastes better.

'Mornin'' he greets me groggily. 'Looks like a good frost out there!'

The radio plays Pop's favourite show, *Australia All Over* with Macca. People call in from all around Australia. They are often camping out and having a cup of tea somewhere in the bush. Glenda is camping at Bermagui and enjoying the birdlife. I like being a part of everyone listening in together.

I open the cupboards to find … a new kind of Weet-Bix! Hi-Bran! How does Nan manage to make everything healthy? I slip my finger under the tab and unstick the lid. I unfold the thin plastic like a present and slide my hand down the side to find the 'collect-a-card.'

No. 12 'Phobos – The Martian Moon.'

Deimos and Phobos are the two moons of Mars. I pull out two crisp bricks and splash them with boring light milk and (healthy) brown sugar. I park my bowl next to Pop. He dabs at the toast crumbs on his plate, slowly lifting a finger to his tongue.

The doorbell does its two-note 'ding-dong.' The paperboy! I whizz past the fridge and grab the eighty cents sitting on the deep freeze. There's a tall teenage boy in a japara at the door. I like the smell of all his papers – it's calming. I put the money in his hands and grab the smooth new *Sunday Examiner.*

'Thanks.'

That's all we ever say.

The first thing to do is to check the bingo numbers against the card we got last week. Then Pop passes me the sections as he's finished reading them. I head straight to the comics. It has *Footrot Flats* (brilliant, but I've usually already read them in my books at home), *Garfield* (funniest), *Snake* (sometimes funny) and *Fred Basset* (dumb).

I wander up the hall to see what Nan's up to. Through the crack in the door I can see her sitting up in bed with a book. There's an empty plate and cup on the bedside table from where she got up at sparrow's fart but went back to bed: Nan's version of a day off.

I watch *Couch Potato* and *Wide World of Sports*. I have my shower and potter around. I'm starting to feel restless. I look at the clock then peer out the front window. Then I hear it …

The engine of the yellow Volkswagen. Mum's here.

My throat feels tight. I don't know where to look. What sort of mood will she be in?

I hear the engine stop. A pause. Then Mum opens her door. Not too long in between. Part of me doesn't want her to get out of the car. I hover by the hallway. I want things to be good.

'Hi Mum.'

'Hello,' she says with a croak.

Mum's wearing her glasses and purple windcheater with white pants. Her mood seems okay, she just sounds tired. She puts her bag down and sits at the kitchen table. Her shoulders are hunched and her eyes are lowered. She has a faint smile that's out of place. I don't mind this. Anything but swearing.

I tell Mum about my morning walk and can collecting with Pop. But silence soon sweeps in and fills up every moment. We run out of things to say. Mum doesn't need to talk. She sits with one leg over the other. Her bare foot taps up and down. She often does this, tapping away with her foot. It's quite hypnotic.

'Hello Maudie,' Nan appears in the kitchen. She sounds careful, her voice is lower.

'Hello!' Mum says weirdly. Nan walks over to hug her but Mum doesn't stand. She barely moves as Nan leans down to put her arms around her.

'Was there much traffic between here and your place?'

'No. Never is,' says Mum.

Nan's good at making conversation. She talks and talks. She works hard to involve Mum.

'That rotten jasmine's broken down all the trellis work. Do you keep your jasmine trimmed back Maudie?

'No, it's alright.' Mum says flatly. She hardly ever plays along. It makes me sad to watch Nan try so hard.

At least there's a positive: for lunch we're having roast chicken! Nan's roasts are my favourite. The beautiful brown bird appears on the kitchen bench. Spuds are sizzling in juices from the pan – they're Nan's Dutch creams she dug up yesterday.

Mum offers to cut the meat. Nan harps on about the electric carver.

'No, I'm right!' Mum snaps.

'Okay, okay, I'll stay out of it,' says Nan.

'Yeah, go on, you stay out of it,' Pop jokes.

I don't take my eyes off Mum.

'Justin, how many potatoes?'

She dishes up without too much fuss.

'Woah, not too heavy for me,' says Pop. He can't eat much because of his tummy.

I have a chicken leg and a wing, coated in gravy. Caramel steam dabs at my nostrils. This is the best time, when the whole meal is ahead of me. I spear a spud onto my fork. Ow, too hot! I lean forward and let it roll out of my mouth. I don't want to wait. I scoop up some soft pumpkin instead. Now I squash down on smooth, doughy sweetness. These are the best vegetables, the ones that taste good with every bite. Unlike peas which are hard to get excited about.

'Did you say Barbara has a new lawnmower, Maureen?' says Nan, through a mouthful.

Mum's head is down. She gobbles non-stop when she's sick. She barely looks up.

'Hmm? Think so.'

My head is down too. I'm in chicken heaven. I attack the flesh and bones from every angle. The meat is juicy and tender, the skin is crispy, the flaps are fatty, the parson's nose is … funny.

'Justin, did you tell your mum about where we went for our walk yesterday?'

'Yep,' I sigh. I glance at all our plates. Mum is finished, I'm nearly finished, Pop is halfway and Nan has barely made a dent.

'You going for a walk tomorrow with Merle?' Pop croaks.

'You know I am,' she frowns.

I collect mine and Mum's plates and carry them to the sink.

'Mum and I'll wash up,' I say. I wouldn't normally volunteer but I want to keep her off the bed.

After scraping down the plates I present Mum with the wish bone. We have a tradition where we hold it thumb to thumb, trigger fingers round the skinny bit. She seems happy that I remembered. She puts her fingers around and counts us off.

'One. Two. Three.'

I snap off the little piece, leaving Mum with the base. She hides the bones inside her hand. I have to guess which is the bigger piece.

I guess right.

'Make a wish!'

I close my eyes. A computer maybe … Carlton to win the premiership …?

For Mum to get well.

Sunday afternoons are hard when I'm sad. The outside grows quiet while inside I feel every emotion twice as much. All the memories of the hard times seem to collect. My mood is heavy and I feel more alone. I ache for everything I miss and everything that can't be fixed.

Mum and Nan are having a lay down (Mum snoozes, Nan reads). Pop and I are splayed out in front of the Swans game. The atmosphere at the game seems bleak. There's a red and white cheer squad with a couple of old ladies waving pom poms. Sydney are bottom of the ladder and losing, so even when they get a goal hardly anyone cheers. The players don't even smile.

I don't care who wins but I don't want it to end.

By five Mum and I are packed up to leave. Nan wraps up vegetables and meat for us to take home. Soup is in a milk carton with the top pressed flat.

'We won't want all that.'

'Yes, Maureen, it'll help get you through the week,' says Nan sternly.

Ugh. The week. Don't remind me.

This really is a horrible feeling. I miss Nan and Pop already – I haven't even left yet! I pack the mood down and carry it around because I have to stay strong.

My first bad memory is from when I was six. Mum was sick and got agro at Nan and Pop. I think she told them they'd never see me again. I remember her dragging me to the car. Nan and Pop were upset. They didn't want Mum to go. I had to leave without saying goodbye. I was bawling as we drove off. That's where the memory ends. It was a Sunday afternoon too.

'Drive carefully, won't you Maureen?' Nan says as we walk towards our car.

'I always do.'

I load up the car and climb inside. Nan and Pop stand by the front door. The sun hovers low above the garage. The engine starts up like a small plane. Mum starts backing out. Nan takes a step forwards and kisses her fingertips. She holds her fingers out flat and blows. I kiss my hand and do the same. Invisible kisses flutter through the air.

Mum reverses onto the road. I crane my neck to see Nan and Pop. They are a small waving blur. The car heaves forward. The scene ends. They are gone.

The car shakes and swerves left, down the main road I walked along with Nan and Merle on Saturday. Now I'm stuck inside the car, watching it rush by. A spud rolls from a bag in the back and clomps onto the floor.

Same old Wynyard whizzing past. The main street is empty. The shops are shut. We pass the wharf and jetty and YT's fish and chip shop and the little pool where I learned to swim. It has a fence around it and is always closed.

I fix my gaze and let the lump swell and pain fly away. Words and noises and memories swirl. This is it. Mum and me again, in between, quiet.

I make the most of my thinking. I let all my thoughts float at once. I don't need them to make sense. I speed and skim and soar my eyeline across the blur of the waves in the distance as I spring off the horizon and scatter my attention. There are apricot-orange clouds stretched out like space ships. It's like an artist has painted a battle scene out of smoke.

Fuzzy, hazy, fairy floss solar flares morph into slipstreaming stealth bomber turbo cruisers. It's a busy scene with opposing fleets of starships mid-warp, firing photons and fanning flames and fumes and jet trails and blurred ships. I see a long main cruiser with jagged wings and tailfins swerving and smoking to avoid the plumes of silver fire. Tiny fighter ships gather on the edges as shields deflect shrapnel and damaged ships dive-bomb.

There are fluffy white clouds along the horizon. They have a dark outline on top and are lit from underneath by the low sun. It resembles a glowing wall of white water. A broken tidal wave, ready to wash us all away. I imagine what we'd do if it were real. How it would feel once it hit? If I held my breath would I stand any chance? Our car would get thrown and bobbed like a cork …

Mum flicks her lights on. She stares ahead, her hands gripping the black wheel. I relax my eyes for a while. As the sun sets the neon lights come to life.

Traffic lights look like electric lollies.

Alien suns!

What if there was a blue one?

On the hill to the right is a red blinking light. I love it because I don't know what it is. It could be a satellite or a cyclops or a distress signal. It could be something friendly and magical. I imagine sitting on the hill by myself. I'm next to the tower, nestled in the long grass. The only sound is the soft blink of the signal. A clock radio hum. I look out over the ocean road, waiting for the moonlight.

It's the loneliest thought but it's an exciting one. I'm in the last place on earth, separate to everyone and surrounded by trees. What happens in the hilltops in the middle of the night? Do I get any sleep? Can I dream? The red light on the hill. Mother Nature watching over me.

I twist the dial for 7BU. The radio bar glows green.

Mum flicks on her high beam. A blue light appears on the speedo.

A sad and mysterious song comes on. It has floating guitars and a thick drum pattern. The singing is high and mournful. Something about the sea on the tide. It has no way of turning. The music shifts the mood. The music is spacey and matches the twinkle and sparkle of the shopfronts and traffic lights.

'… there is nothing …'

The atmosphere matches how I feel. I sit back and wonder how it might all fit together. Mum the way she is. Me trying my best. Never knowing what's going to happen.

'… more than this.'

I expand inside, enjoying the ache. The music makes the sadness fit together. The blinking lights and the thinking inside. I know my feelings are special.

All of this is important.

I really love Mum.

'Who was that song by?'

Mum's face is faint.

'Bryan Ferry with Roxy Music. I've always liked that one.'

Mum knows about music.

'Hey Mum, tomorrow can we …'

'Don't distract me while I'm driving dear, I might have an accident.'

The Volks lurches up steep View Road. I feel the shudder of the engine, the tyres drag hard on the bitumen. The final corner is the steepest of all. Mum has to stop accelerating to change gears and just for a second the car feels like it might roll backwards. The car steers left and glides over a rise. The road flattens out. Right onto Bird Street. Our house.

Mum pulls into the carport and switches off the key. We sit for a while, staring ahead. I don't mind. I'm not in a hurry. The cooling engine ticks out of time. Mum bursts into laughter beside me. A high-pitched giggle, out of nowhere. It's all over her face. Her shoulders shake as she cackles.

I stay still and calm.

It's Sunday night. Mum is laughing at nothing. I'm waiting.

I stare hard at Mum. I record her giddy, leering face. Her flushed cheeks. Her faraway gaze.

I'm going to remember this for the rest of my life.

12

Okay, today is a dumb day. I slept in, then the toast slid off my plate and landed Vegemite side down. Then when I got to school Elvis blew a spit ball that landed on my neck. I chased after him but he got away. Then I failed Supertest on Tyrannosaurus level while Nick got 46/50 in five minutes! I don't know what went wrong. It's good for Nick but annoying for me.

Then at recess I checked the *Montello Times* competition box and there were NO ENTRIES! Not even one. At first I thought Elvis might have nicked them. We ran a competition to celebrate our 30th issue. The question was 'How many editions of the *Montello Times* have we made since it was created?' I even made it multiple choice. Mr Blazely let us put an announcement over the PA to remind people to enter. We said there'd be 'great prizes.' I can't believe no one entered!

Three editions ago we had a readers' poll and asked what students and teachers might like to see more of in the paper. When we went round to collect the polls and deliver the next issue most of the teachers didn't know what we were talking about or said they hadn't done it.

I don't get it. We make a newspaper that is entirely about the school and the students and sometimes it's as if no-one cares. I put so much work into it but it's getting harder to find other people to write articles. Sometimes it feels like I'm running the whole thing by myself. Why do I bother?

I started the paper last year with Damien Quilliam who was in the grade above me. We wrote the articles ourselves, scooting around classrooms, quizzing teachers, and getting the scoop on why the spook house was shut down during the fete and investigating Mr Blazely's 'wet grass gauge.' Our regular columns were Class Snippets (2/3B are doing work on shadows), recipes (pizza snacks) and football scores (Acton 197, Montello 24).

My favourite bit of the *Montello Times* is the cartoon section (where I draw all the cartoons). Under my nickname Heazy, I do 'Mac and Jack, the Montello Mates'. Mac is the trouble maker, always mouthing off and refusing to take off his trademark baseball cap. Last year I could only draw characters side on and I always avoided drawing hands. But I've just finished a cartooning course at Adult Education in Devonport so now my creations are a lot more detailed. I still avoid doing hands by keeping them in their pockets.

It's frustrating when the students and teachers don't appreciate all the work I put in. I wonder if it's worth it as I try to write the editor's report for our October edition: '1992 has been a good year so far for the *Montello Times*. But it has had its setbacks. We really wonder if anyone reads or cares about our paper after all the effort we put into it.'

I type 'we' but really I mean 'I.' Nick and Paul were supposed to be the deputy editors but lately even they've lost interest. Damien went onto Burnie High this year so I've been basically doing the paper single-handedly. Luckily Mr B lets me work on it in class and helps me learn shortcuts on the Mac. The paper is half the size and looks way more professional now with better graphics.

I show Mr B the report and he says it sounds a bit negative. Behind me Paul and Tennille are working together in a group. They've got their heads down, concentrating on something. I'm a bit jealous. I don't like the idea of missing out. I want to join my friends but I also have to finish the computer games top ten. The paper is a big responsibility and if I don't do it no-one else will.

ENDLESS QUESTIONS...

I write as neatly as I can. So far so good. There's only been a couple of stuff-ups.

This will be the final page where I make my conclusions. The Universe is my final project for primary school. This year The Frilled-Neck Lizard, The Platypus, The Wedge-tailed Eagle, Mars and The Olympic Games all got As.

I write 'Gravity' and rule underneath in red. I copy over the notes I've made.

'The only force that keeps all planets throughout the universe from flying off into space, is gravity ... the bigger the object, the more the force.'

'How big is the Universe?'

'The part of the universe we can see extends for about 160000000000000000000000km. But no one knows if it goes on beyond this.'

It's late afternoon. Mum comes out to make a drink.

'What's that dear?'

'My universe project!'

'Oh and how's it going?'

Her voice has a croak. It's been a while since she's spoken.

'Pretty good. I just have to do the drawings and I'm finished. Maybe you can check the spelling later?'

'Yes, okay, I will after my coffee.'

Her eyes are bright and her face is more relaxed. I watch as she makes her drink and even that seems more normal. She dings her spoon and takes a slurp of her coffee as she sits down beside me. I slide her my project book. She moves her head back and forth as she reads. I think of a cartoon character pretending to read the newspaper when they're actually spying.

She points a finger on the page.

'Is that how you spell whether?'

I lean over, reading upside down. I've spelt it without 'h.'

'Hmm, I get confused by that, when it's not w-e-a-t-h-e-r.'

'That's okay dear, make a note and we'll fix it up later.'

'What's that number?' she says.

'Um. Sixteen million, million, million, million, million, million kilometres. That's how big the universe is … that we know.'

'Golly,' says Mum with a soft laugh.

'Only one "g" in "beginning",' she says.

Damn! I'll have to use Tipp-Ex.

I found out that scientists have used fossils to date the earth's age at four billion years. The religious theory is that god created earth in seven days but astronomers have found quasars that are ten billion light years away!

'Perhaps god constructed the universe to appear old to baffle humans?' I say.

Get Up Mum

Mum says she isn't sure but she thinks God should have a capital 'G'.

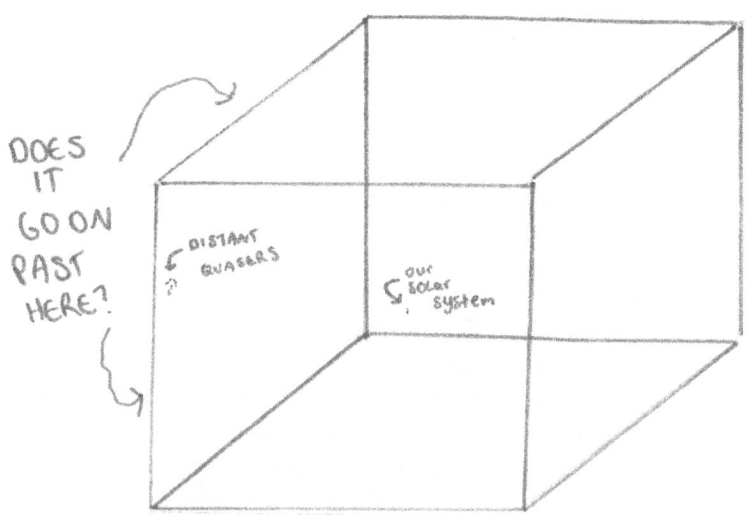

The next day I come home after school to the whine of the vacuum cleaner. The front door is open. Blossum is nowhere to be seen.

I step inside and drop my bag down. There are fresh flowers in a vase on the table. The house looks lovely.

Mum switches off the vacuum as I walk into the lounge.

'Hello dear,' she grins.

Her friendly face, so young and pretty. Clear eyes looking at me.

'How was school?'

'We did Each One, Teach One. Nick and I taught two grade two boys how to play table tennis.'

'Oh I bet they'd love that.'

I head to the kitchen. I take out the things for a chocolate thickshake. I'm smiling to myself. I'm happy but still wary.

'How are you feeling?'

Mum walks up behind me. She breathes out as she answers.

'A lot better thanks Justin. I had a really good sleep last night. I'm sorry I haven't been myself lately. It's horrible when I get like that.'

She puts a hand on my shoulder.

'I've vacuumed your room and put fresh sheets on your bed.'

'Great, thanks!'

A cool breeze drifts in from the kitchen window. I pour the topping and milk into a cup followed by a dollop of ice cream. I sit the cup underneath the whizzer and give it a blast. It stirs, purees, creams, whips, mixes and liquefies.

I take a straw out of the drawer and skewer the thickshake. I lock my lips around the straw and work my breath forwards and reverse. Thick, slow bubbles glug from deep inside the shake. They form a popping froth as I suck on the straw. Cool, creamy sweetness fills my mouth.

'Fish for tea okay?'

'Yeah great. Thanks Mum. And chips?'

'Yep. I've got chips to do in the griller. I bought some really nice rainbow trout fillets.'

My favourite!

The sun casts a yellow cloak over the trees outside. The mood is peaceful.

Mum came back.

13

Mum was born in 1954 or 1956 (I get them mixed up, but she's thirty-eight.) Apparently she was born so close to midnight that if the hospital's clocks were wrong her birthday could have been a day later!

Mum is the second youngest, with three brothers. Uncle Nigel and Mum were close growing up. He used to follow her around like a puppy dog. As kids they didn't see a lot of Nan and Pop as they were always at shift work. Uncle Ken and Uncle Max were five years older than Mum and Nigel was five years younger, so Mum had a bit of space to herself.

When Mum was a teenager she was sitting up in a tall tree with her best friend Anne when she laughed too hard and fell thirty or forty feet. Luckily a branch broke her fall and she was okay. Mum and Anne were hippies who used to get up to mischief. They'd dress up in lairy outfits and take the mickey out of things. Mum was good at doing characters and would put on silly voices. At school Mum's best subject was English. She left school in grade ten (which was normal in those days.) You either went to work in a shop or a factory.

I think Mum and Nan used to clash a bit. Apparently Nan was even more highly strung than she is now! Once Mum snuck over the fence to visit a boy she liked and when she came back Nan belted her with the kettle cord.

Mum's only smacked me once. We were next door at Barbara's and all the neighbours were there. Around the kitchen table I told them how sometimes when I was in Mum's bed she'd pop off. I showed them the actions of how Mum moved the covers up and down (like a jockey pulling on the reigns) to clear the smell away. This was a joke between Mum and I so I thought it would be okay to share. But Mum was very embarrassed and when we got home she was angry with me.

She took out the small metal broom and hit me with the handle. I cried for her not to and put my hands behind me to protect my bum. I caught the blow across my knuckles and they stung for ages. Mum felt bad afterwards but I guess I was being pretty cheeky.

I like hearing stories about Mum as a young girl. Apparently she was a really funny storyteller. She used to have everyone in stitches with her tale about blowing the candle out. It's a physical actions joke about a family all trying to blow a candle out and they each have a silly way of huffing and puffing.

'Oh gawd we'd laugh till we had tears streaming down our faces,' says Nan when she tells me the story.

Nan asks Mum to retell it but she gets shy.

'I don't do that one now.'

Mum just tells the last part of the joke, when the family have exhausted themselves trying to extinguish the candle, the young girl licks her fingers and snubs the flame out.

I like pinching out candles. The heat sizzles the spit but your fingers don't burn.

I wish I'd been there to see Mum at her best.

Get Up Mum

Mum made me laugh a lot as a kid. Our favourite story was about two toy rabbits called Rumbles and Tumbles. They go to England to see what real rabbits look like. We also loved *The Book of Nonsense* by Edward Lear where he makes up lots of crazy words.

'The Pobble who has no toes

Replied, "Fish, fiddle-de-dee!"'

Mum would read them out in her silly voice. We'd laugh until we had tears in our eyes. This is the Mum I love – when we're joined at the funny bone.

'There was a Young Lady of Norway,

Who casually sat in a doorway;

When the door squeezed her flat, she exclaimed, 'What of that?'

This courageous Young Lady of Norway.'

When Mum was twenty-one she met a Norwegian sailor called Kjell (pronounced 'Gel') and went to visit him. She travelled on a huge boat called the QEII (pronounced 'Kewy too') and even called into Tahiti on the way (I know from the postage stamps in her collection).

Mum stayed with Kjell and his family at a town called Grong. In summer it was only ten degrees and in winter it was minus twenty! They had the 'midnight sun' where the sun never fully sets and Mum got to see the Northern Lights ('Aurora Borealis').

She ended up being over there for about six months. She says it was lonely at times because Kjell's family didn't speak any English. Also she fell down some stairs and hit her head and that's why she sometimes feels a burning sensation on top of her head.

In the end she and Kjell parted ways. Mum says it wasn't hard because she wasn't too deeply involved. Sometimes she says he was more of a penfriend but it sounds more like boyfriend and girlfriend to me.

Nan has a different version of the story where Mum rang her up from Norway to say she had some very exciting news.

'I never got to find out what that news was. I have my theories.'

When Mum finally returned she didn't look well at all. Nan thought she was a ghost.

'I'll never forget that face until the day I die. It wasn't my daughter, it wasn't my Maureen. She was ever so skinny.'

She holds up a single finger.

'And pale! Oh she was dreadful looking!'

Nan says they both hugged and cried. She gets upset just talking about it. At the time they had a cockatoo called Rocky. He was the star family pet.

'When your mum first came in, I'll swear if that damn cockatoo didn't whip round on his perch and say 'Hello Maureen, and lovely to see you too!' Well your mum and I had tears streaming down our faces.'

There are often a lot of tears in my family stories.

At Christmas time we always decorate the tree with reindeer boots that Mum bought in Norway. She also hangs a Christmas stocking that she made. It's dark brown with a pointy end and little bell at the bottom. It features a house and a northern star made out of thin golden wood shavings. At the bottom there's a candle with tiny dashes around the flame. I like seeing something that Mum made. She was creative, like me.

14

She said yes! Tennille said she'd go with me.

Nick asked his girlfriend Kristy to ask Tennille's friend Amanda to ask Tennille out at the sock dance. It's a disco where you take your shoes off so Nick and I spent the night sliding around the polished tiles of the utility room where we have our assemblies. I met Tennille outside and told her how Mrs French wouldn't let me put on 'Let's Get Rocked' by Def Leppard because the lyrics were 'suggestive.'

'Mrs French is a dag! I had to get away from Amanda dancing to "Achy Breaky Heart".'

'Yeah, how is that song still number one?'

Then we stood in silence … then we said goodbye. Now I'm lying in bed and my heart feels like a race car. I've never had a girlfriend before. It makes me nervous.

She likes me!
She likes me!
She likes me!
I have a girlfriend! I have a girlfriend?
Now what?

Tennille came to Montello at the start of the year. She's from New Zealand. She was quiet but very pretty with a dimple like mine that shines when she smiles and clear blue eyes like the lakes in old photographs. Her hair is black and shiny and cut short in a stylish bowl. Her skin is quite tanned so she seems exotic to me. She has a cheeky laugh that comes out when I make fun of her accent and how she calls milk bars 'dairies.'

Now it's Friday and our first day together as a couple. In the morning we push our desks together. I'm not always sure what to say but I like having Tennille next to me while I work. I've never been this close to a girl for this amount of time.

At recess we slip away from our friends and go for a walk by ourselves. The Montello playground is very hilly with lots of trees so there are gumnuts and acorns scattered on the ground. I tell Tennille about my bushwalking with Nan. She tells me how she went 'tramping' on the South Island of New Zealand.

'Close your eyes,' she says. 'Hold out your hand.'

I stand with my eyes closed, listening to the shrieks of kids playing. I can smell the sun evaporating the dew. I feel a small weight in my hand. I open my eyes to see a flat skimming rock.

'My grandpa in Christchurch used to give me stones like this that he'd polish up. I'd put it under my pillow and make a wish.'

I thank her and ask her if she has any brothers and sisters.

Tennille tells me about a time her sister wet herself and her mum made a big fuss. Tennille decided to wet herself on purpose and got in trouble. She says I'm lucky it's just me.

'Are you spoiled?'

'Yeah Mum still makes my bed.'

The bell goes. I like it down here by the trees. I wish we could stay longer. In class we work together on an experiment. It's about finding out what colours make up other colours. We use the brown dye from a Smartie, blue biro and Texta ink. We put the colours on chromatography paper and place that in a beaker with methylated spirits.

The colours creep up the paper! Green breaks up in a blue streak, leaving behind yellow. The blue Texta has some red in it. The brown Smartie is made up of lots of different colours, mainly pink and blue.

We conclude that most colours are made up of a mixture of other colours.

Later at lunch we sit in the sun against the side of the toilet blocks. I leave my hand by my side with the palm facing up. Tennille does the same. My heart is pounding. I really want to hold her hand. I'm shy about anyone seeing, but once our little fingers touch Tennille moves her hand on top of mine. My heart feels wrapped up tight.

Tennille fidgets and her soft, skinny fingers come apart. I slowly slide mine in between hers. Now it doesn't matter what else happens. I'm happy to just sit here like this. The air is warm and I can relax. I just have to figure out how to eat a Le Snak with one hand.

15

Everything feels good at the moment! On the weekend I do a lap of the garden picking a sample of my favourite flowers. There's the small white beady one and the red frilly one and lavender and starry eyes and a yellow and black pansy. My hands are full so I open the screen door with my elbow.

Mum is on the couch, drinking a beer. I hide the posy in the sink and secure it with Alfoil. I clutch it behind my back and walk up to Mum.

'Close your eyes.'

She puts her beer glass down and sits up.

'Okay, open.'

I watch Mum's face go from curiosity to delight.

'Oh, how lovely. Thank you Justin.'

'Thanks for being such a lovely Mum,' I say quietly.

On Sunday Mum and I go for a swim at Healthglo indoor pool. She appears on the deck in her frilly bathers – sea green flowers on white. They're like normal bathers but with a little skirt around the waist. I like Mum in her bathers. They make her seem more girlish.

'Oooh it's chilly!' she squeals.

I'm wearing my new prescription goggles. They're not as strong as my glasses but they do the job. The only thing is they stick out a bit so I've been nicknamed 'Blowfly' at surf club.

I slip in the warm water, fill my lungs and dive under, scuttling along the bottom as far as I can. We use kickboards in surf club training so my legs are strong. I'm an excellent swimmer and have always felt like a natural in the water. I spread my legs like a frog and then twist around like a dolphin. The pool bottom wobbles with white diamonds of light from the window.

I paddle about, practicing breast stroke. I'm still getting used to the rhythm of stroke and kick. Freestyle is definitely my favourite. Backstroke is a pain. I don't like not seeing where I'm going.

'We've got the place to ourselves.'

Mum's voice is an echo. I see her head, floating in the deep end.

Mum doesn't really swim. She twirls her arms and paddles herself around, sort of like a dance. Her favourite thing is to sit in the spa, bubbling away. I join her after a while. With my goggles off and the steam engulfing me everything becomes a blur.

There's usually a blue cover on the spa. Once I slipped my hand under and felt around and the bottoms of my fingernails started to sting. I still don't know why. Were there lasers in there? Did I have an injury of some kind? It's just a weird thing that happened. Not funny enough to tell but too interesting to forget.

I take a breath and slip my head underwater. It feels like breaking the rules. Underneath it's like I'm inside an earthquake and a volcano. Everything is black and bubbling. I imagine this is what it might feel like if you were invincible and could fly and stuck your head inside the sun.

The worst part of Healthglo is getting out. On the walk from the pool to the showers and change rooms you have to pass the squash courts, which are huge dark caves of cold air. The carpet here is freezing and the draft nips at your feet. I hop from one rubber mat to the other like Frogger.

I fumble around for a twenty cent piece to drop in the box to turn the showers on. The coin hits the metal pile as the shower bursts to life. Whoever used it last didn't turn the hot water tap off! I thaw inside the warm waterfall.

The money runs out and the water snaps off. I'm back into the cold. I make sure to turn the tap off for the next person. I wait for Mum in the foyer, next to the racks of bathers and video game. I love the fresh feeling after a swim. My insides are lighter. I'm hungry now. I feel like hot chips.

Mum appears, smiling. We peek into the gym where they're doing aerobics.

'Have you ever thought of doing aerobics Mum?'

'I'll have to lose a bit of weight first.'

The crisp air boxes my face as we crunch along the gravel towards the Volks.

Get Up Mum

Mum knows
I like my carrots raw.

Mum knows
I like my back scratched.

Mum knows
I used to say 'lello' instead of yellow.

Mum knows
because she loves me.

Mum knows
I love the moon.

Mum knows
Nan carries on.

Mum knows
I need my toast cooled.

Standing in the kitchen,
waving her arms like an air traffic controller.
'Do Do' are her sound effects
and I laugh
and she laughs.

Mum knows
about my grommets
and my growing pains
and my scars.

Justin Heazlewood

(Chickenpox, a mole removed,
The plastic shape Stephen Fleming threw
and my lip bled.)

Mum knows
how to spell
Suc-cess-ful
and rec<u>ei</u>ved.
I before e
Mum beside me.

Mum knows
I hate meat pies
and I like to push the button
and I've never had a blood nose.

'Haven't you dear?'
Maybe she didn't.
But now Mum knows.
Because she loves me.

16

On Sunday night Tennille and I talk for three hours on the phone! It's the longest I've talked on the phone and the longest I've ever spoken to a girl before. At first Tennille is quiet and shy. I make her laugh by doing impersonations of our PE teacher Mr Townsend. He has a big nasally voice and some boys made up a song where they swapped the letters in his name: 'Tussel Rownsend! I've got a tussel for a teacher.' Tennille's laughter makes little explosions in the ear piece.

We talk about our favourite music and movies – time races away. At the end neither of us wants to be the first to hang up. We have to count to three and hang up at the same time.

The next day I make her a personalised cassette tape. On Side A I record myself doing a mock news report about school. On Side B I dub some nice instrumental songs from *The Synthesiser Album*.

Recording is definitely one of my main hobbies now. I've built up a collection of five tapes of my family and Nick. I also have five bought tapes including Tommy Emmanuel and The Twelfth Man and the latest one by Pearl Jam.

Tennille loves the tape and slips a letter inside my desk. It's my first love letter!

On Wednesday our class heads off for a camp at Arm River, between Cradle Mountain and Mole Creek. We learn how to make damper, walk through Marakoopa Caves and watch a feller buncher cut down two trees. I'm still quite nervous about how much time I should spend with Tennille.

Amelia tells us to pose for a photo. We're standing side by side.

'Put y'arm around her!' Amelia yells. I put my right arm up as my fingers rest lightly on her shoulder. She feels small. Tennille reacts by putting her arm around my back. I like the feeling of being held. I wouldn't mind staying like this for a while.

Tennille has a cool white windcheater with blue and gold cats on it. I have my black Adidas top with bright green logo. We both have small parts in the middle of our fringe. Mine's off to the side because the wind keeps blowing.

'SMILE!' yells Amelia.

It isn't hard.

At dinner I'm between Tennille and Nick and opposite Mr Burgess. All my favourite people! Nick wants to know what the hell 'chicken a la king' is while Mr B tells us about the new Mac game *Captain Magneto*. Nick teases Kristy about how freaked out she got by the possum skins inside the trappers hut. He's overly gruesome, as usual. Tennille sits quietly and I can feel her elbow touching mine.

She taps me on the shoulder.

'Amanda says I have food on my face, do I?'

Tennille is so pretty. Her brown skin is incredibly smooth. Her eyes are soft and bright and kind. I feel shy looking at her mouth.

'Ooooh, lovers!' The girls don't miss much.

Tennille blushes, as usual.

After dinner we meet in our 'couples's gang.' The plan is for each pair to wander off behind the rec room for five minutes and 'do whatever they want'. There's a movie and spotlighting due to start at eight. It's nearly dark now and I've got my jacket on. The smell of cool, wild forest is in the air.

I don't look at Tennille. I feel a bit sick. Too much butterscotch pudding! Nick and Kristy go first, but it's not a big deal for them. I know they already practice pashing. Nick's pretty bold and Kristy is the first girl in class to have boobs.

They return with fingers linked. Kristy's cheeks are pink and she smiles at the ground. Nick has a dazed smirk and keeps his mouth closed. He seems more grown-up. At last year's camp we spent our free time in the rec room playing quoits and table tennis. It's different with girls around – we have to act like we're sensible.

'Okay Tennille and Justin, your turn.'

We walk away from the others, behind the trees. An outside light makes spindly shadows on the walls of the cabin. Tennille stands with one leg bent and her arms by her sides. She stares off to the side, shyly. Now we're alone, for the first time.

Something is supposed to happen, I'm quite sure.

How exactly it's going to happen, I'm not quite sure.

I'll probably have to do something, but I wonder if I'll know when that is?

Okay, I'm thinking about it. I'm staring down at Tennille's shoes. They're simple white canvas ones.

Now I don't feel very good and I'm waiting and I'm wondering. I don't like it much, this feeling.

I look up hoping Tennille will look at me but she's looking downwards and doesn't seem sure so that makes me wonder what the right thing is to do. I know we're supposed to kiss but when does it start? I could lean in but I can't move. I feel very still.

I don't want to move.

So I don't do anything.

I stare and wait as Tennille does the same.

I'm sort of used to it now.

I'm so shy.

And so is she.

And she's waiting.

And so am I.

There's a tightness in my chest.

I'm scared.

I don't know Tennille that well.

'Let's go back,' she says.

That night I have a lot more fun with the boys in our cabin. We keep shining our torches and flashing moons and cacking ourselves in our sleeping bags.

When we head back to school on Friday Tennille and I start out sitting together on the bus but she spends the whole time talking to her friends. Back at school Mum picks us up in the Volkswagen. She offers to give Tennille a ride home. She climbs in the back seat. I get in the front seat because that's where I always sit, but then I wonder if that's the right thing. The car pulls away and I'm relieved because I can't change my mind.

I'm embarrassed by our noisy car.

I see Tennille in the rear view mirror. She doesn't seem happy.

I realise we haven't spoken all day.

17

'Justin! Come on! You'll be late for school!'

Mum comes flying out of the hallway in her nightie. She scurries to the kitchen and pulls out the bread. I'm in my beanbag in front of the TV watching *rage*.

'Quickly dear, I've slept in! Go and have a shower!'

'Mum ...'

'It's nearly nine o'clock!'

'Mum, it's Saturday.'

She's freezes and looks at me like a dopey owl. Her eyes soften as she laughs, embarrassed.

'Oh, here I was thinking it was Friday.'

She clicks her tongue.

'I must be going mad.'

Mum sits at the table, jotting things down. I look up to find her staring out the window, smiling.

'Mum?'

She takes a moment to respond.

'Yep?'

'You'll be okay for the parent–student race next week?'

Mum's eyes widen.

'What time is that again?'

'It's at the end of the day I think. It's just a fun one.'

'I hope it doesn't look too silly. Me flopping along the track like a big elephant.'

I laugh.

'No Mum, you're not even big.'

'When do you need the money for Camp Clayton?'

'Mum, that's ages away, towards the end of January.'

'It'll soon come round Justin. It's already December. Nigel will be here in a fortnight. That reminds me, I'd better get his Christmas present today.'

Mum's in planning mode. She sorts through the drawer, looking for some high school form. She seems worried.

'I've got to organise your bus pass for next year.'

'Mum, it's Saturday, worry about it later.'

'And how much is your table tennis dinner again?'

'Thirty dollars. It's a rip off.'

The 'Friends For Life' song from the Olympics has been finally knocked off number one. Effie and Norman Gunston did a funny take-off of it on *Hey Hey It's Saturday*.

'I might have to ask Mum and Dad to help us out for that one,' she says, gazing out the window. 'I don't know Justin, no sooner does money come into my hand than it flies out again.'

Once a fortnight Mum does ironing and housework for two ladies down the street. But we're always running low on money. Mum often borrows from Nan and Pop. Sometimes she borrows from me. In grade four it got so bad that we had to get a box of charity food from Vinnies.

The end credits of *rage* comes on. It always makes me feel a bit sad. I don't like things ending. Mum's eyes are in a strange squint. She holds the pen in her mouth like a thermometer.

Get Up Mum

'Mum?'

'Yes dear?'

'You're okay? You've done all the Christmas shopping?'

'Yes, most of it,' she says softly.

Her face forces a smile.

'We'll have a great time with Uncle Nige, won't we?'

I watch her warily from my beanbag. She's sitting at the table, doodling. Mum often draws patterns and boxes with crisscrosses. When I get home from school I can see where Mum's been daydreaming.

'I might go and have a little lie down,' she says.

'Are you alright?'

She scratches her head and frowns.

'Yes I just slept a bit funny, that's all.' She wanders towards her bedroom.

I get up to see what she's been drawing. There's an old postcard for the Burnie Inn. I once wrote to the World Wrestling Federation about a match I'd like to see. I never got round to sending it.

Now the blank half is crowded with Mum's doodles. There might be fifty.

BURNIE INN – BURNIE, TASMANIA
the building restored at Burnie Park is the
original Birnie Tavern, seated then and now
on beachstone foundations and two hard-
wood floor bearers the size of telegraph
poles.

I LIKE TO
BE SEEN –
PLEASE don't
send me in
an ENVELOPE.

Published by Douglas Souvenir
Distributors – Tasmania
(004) 31260

DS 117
Colour Photography and Copyright
by Robert Schram.
Printed in Australia

To WWF,
The match I'd love
to see is a
Jake "The Snake" Roberts
v Brutus "the barber"
how could Damien
cole with thishears and
how could the sleeper
hold match th DD+?
From Justin Hazlewood
Tasmania

I'm excited because tonight Nick's staying over at my place. In the afternoon we rent videos including the new Wrestlemania. Nick got me into WWF wrestling in grade four. It's so wild and cool and over the top. The Ultimate Warrior is my favourite. He's incredibly muscly but also has tonnes of energy. He sprints out to the ring and shakes the top rope like crazy. He has a mask and long hair and he doesn't follow anyone's rules. The other wrestlers hit him but he just shakes it off. The commentator thinks he's a nut.

'Whaddaya expect, he's crazy! A crazy man feels no pain.'

At bedtime we set my mattress up on the floor of the lounge with Nick on the couch. I mention my Universe project and how the Big Bang created everything. But what I want to know is what was there before the Big Bang.

'Imagine there was nothing,' I say, staring up in the black.

'So no stars or planets,' says Nick.

'Yeah, but not even a universe. There wouldn't even be black because that'd still be something.'

'Woah, I see what you mean.'

It's impossible for my mind. I take away the black and it's clear for a moment. I shrink it down to the size of a pinhead, but the space starts filling with detail.

'Let's play profiles,' says Nick.

It's a game we made up where we go through each girl in our class and give them a rating out of ten. We give them a score for looks, personality, humour and dress sense. Kristy and Tennille get automatic tens.

'Hey, when you went behind the cabins at Arm River, did youse pash?'

I picture Tennille standing there, looking at the ground. I miss her now.

'We didn't really do anything.'

'Was she frigid?'
I'm not sure how to answer.
'I think we're ... shy.'
'Kristy and I French kissed.'
'What's that?'
'Where you open your mouths.'
'Have you ever given yourself a hickie?' I say.
'Yeah, where you suck your own arm and it leaves a mark.'

In the morning Mum makes us breakfast. She's always been a good host, setting the placemats and putting out the plastic toast rack. Nick's always impressed. It makes me proud.

'Thanks Mrs Heazlewood! You've gone to a lot of trouble.'
Crack!
Was that Mum's teeth!? No wait, it's her ankle.
When I get to school the next day Kristy is standing outside the front door. Kristy and I don't normally talk. She looks serious.
'Tennille says she's sorry but you're dropped.'
When I get into class Tennille has already moved her desk.

18

Finally, it's here. The athletics carnival! And the last week of school. There's so much to think about. My mind is racing as soon as I wake up. The day is bright and fresh and I can feel the excitement in the air. Only metres down the road they'll be preparing the school oval with running lanes and markers and house sections. I love living so close to school. When I'm home sick I can still hear the bell and the kids playing at lunchtime.

I'm a fast runner. At surf club I used to be the fastest. I won the gold medal in the beach sprint in Under Eights. Then each year the Devonport boys kept growing and they eventually overtook me. At least I can still beat them in the beach flags. I'm still one of the fastest sprinters at school and Elvis only beats me at long distance. My best chance of winning is in the hundred metre sprint. I want to go out on top.

I jump out of bed and head for the kitchen, passing Mum's room. She's still in bed.

I've started getting my own breakfast some mornings. I shake Nutri-Grain into a bowl. It's my new favourite cereal. I still call it 'Grant Kenny' because he was the surf lifesaver on the ads.

Suddenly Mum flies into the kitchen in her nightie.

'I'd better make your lunch dear.'

I tell her there's going to be a barbecue. Her eyes are tired and worried. Her cheeks are puffy.

'Right, well I'll come down a bit later. I've just got a bit of a headache for some reason. When is your first race on?'

'About eleven.'

I stare down into my bowl. I'm worried about Mum.

The sky is a perfect blue with bright puffs of cloud and streaks of white. Behind me there's a yellow banner with a picture of a giraffe. I catch a whiff of cut grass, steaming in the sun. I've got sweet fluoro yellow zinc on my nose. Paul, Jeremy, Rhett and all my other mates in Gold house are gathered together on an unzipped sleeping bag. The teachers hand out gold stickers with our names on them.

Mrs Cleary's daughter strolls by with a camera.

'Everyone in Gold give me a big cheer?' I thrust my hands in the air.

'Woooooo!'

A group of girls in front of us stick their streamers and mascots in the air. There's a Garfield, a Snoopy doll in a yellow T-shirt and a leopard with a Richmond jumper. Nick's in the Green team (along with Mr Burgess) so I won't get to see him until lunch. Luckily Paul's in Gold (and goes for Hawthorn, so he can wear his cap) but I found out he's going to Burnie High next year so we won't see each other as much. Tennille's in Red but I haven't seen her so far.

The day starts with the preps and kinders running novelty races. First they do the 'Grand Prix' where they're given a hula hoop for a steering wheel.

'Drivers, start your engines,' says Mr Thompson through the megaphone. Mr Crawn holds his air horn skyward and blasts a toot. It reminds me of the gameshow *It's A Knockout*. The kinders are very cute, scurrying along circling their arms back and forth.

'Well done Thomas. He's scored more points for Red house, so let's give him a big cheer!'

The kids wander off, being fussed over by teachers and parents. I feel a strange panic as I remember that this is my last week of primary school. The kinders are at the start of school and I'm at the end.

'Go Anna! Go Anna!'

Our cheer squad is in full swing. We start cheering 'goanna.' The girls turn around with grins.

In the middle of the oval is a huge thick rope for the tug of war. For now it lays dormant, like a snoozing snake. Mr Thompson updates the big chalk scoreboard.

RED 82
GREEN 50
GOLD 15

Yeesh! We're not doing well at all.

'Grade six one hundred metre finalists to the marshalling area please.'

'Go Heazy! You can do it mate!'

Pressure swells in my chest as I walk to the start line. I'm a bit worried about my running shorts. They're very short. I hope no-one will see my undies.

I jiggle my legs and jump about. This is the hardest part of a race – the waiting. My heart's like a balloon pumped full of static.

'On your marks ...'

I step up to the line. Have I trained enough? I've got to get a good start. There are boys either side of me. Threats and competitors! I know I have what it takes.

'Get set …'

I'm holding my breath and my position and I wonder suddenly if I haven't stuffed everything up.

TOOT!

And I'm off. The grass is hard. My feet are bare. I'm fast and I'm pumping and I'm pounding. I can hear other people's breathing more than my own. Someone sucks in puffs and then hisses out exhaust through their tongue. *Hsst. Hsst.* It's an aggressive engine. I find it unsettling. Blue above, green below, white line ahead. I'm one of two in the lead. A green T-shirt, neck and neck. As I reach the white finish line I stick my head out like Linford Christie. Come on! I did enough, surely?

Mr Townsend jogs over and hands me a red peg.

I'm puffing but I'm standing. I'm fit and I deserve to win.

I look at the peg.

It has a number two on it.

I find Mum up the back of the Gold area. She's sitting by herself with her sunglasses on. She has one leg crossed over the other and her arms folded.

'Hi Mum,'

She looks up at me. Her mouth is a tight line.

'I only came second.'

'I think Gavin put his head down ahead of you at the end.'

What a crud feeling. Beaten by Gavin, one of the daggiest kids in class, with his thick eyebrows and goofy smile.

I'm more well liked. Winning is wasted on him.

I pull my hat toggle all the way up to my chin and tear open a muesli bar.

'Hello Maureen, I thought that was you!'

A woman with short red hair and a white top comes over. She's holding a program folded in half.

'Do you remember me, Vicki.'

Mum nods shyly and laughs.

'Yes.'

The lady talks quickly, turning to me.

'Gosh Justin, you're going well. I knew your mum when we were in marching girls. We used to call her Dormy!'

'That's right,' says Mum, clearing her throat. 'I used to sing Frere Jacques, Frere Jacques, Dormez-vous.'

'They used to make you sing it in school didn't they?' says the lady.

Mum looks ahead. She doesn't take off her sunglasses. The lady doesn't seem sure what else to say. She looks at me.

'She was a larrikin your mum in those days. I can see where you get it from, with your cartoons in the *Montello Times*.'

I smile, unsure what to say.

'Anyway, I'll let youse go. Enjoy the day. It was good to see you.'

She wanders off, saying hello to several others. It's a relief.

'That was Loretta's mum.'

'Oh.'

Mum has a few people who used to be her friends. I'm glad someone reads the *Montello Times*.

The last race for the day is the parent–teacher race. It's funny having Mum at the marshalling area.

'Are you ready Maureen?'

Mr Thompson knows Mum well. She used to come once a week for 'mothers help' from Prep to grade five. I loved having her there by my side. She'd help us make papier-mâché baskets for our Easter eggs and clay Santa decorations with cotton-wool beards and red felt hats at Christmas. Last year she read out kids' stories while they typed them up on the computer. I think she misses it now I'm older.

'I just hope I make it to the end,' she laughs.

The race has a handicap system so Mum and I are starting last. I see this as a challenge. The horn blasts and I'm away like a shot. I don't think anymore, I just run. There's no pressure because it's just for fun and I pass everyone easily. Only Jonathan in his green shirt and pale skinny legs is ahead. He looks back for his mum so she can catch up.

I don't look back. Now there's no one around me. There isn't even anyone at the finish line. I finish first by miles. I put my hands on my hips and wait. That was my last race. It feels good.

I check for Mum. She's jogging in my lane. She bites her lip in concentration. Her fists are clenched and her arms move carefully back and forth. At least she's not coming last!

'Well done Mum!' I cheer.

'Oh Justin,' she laughs, out of breath. 'You left me for dead!'

'We won though!' I say. I pinch the neck of my shirt and pull it up to my nose.

Mum is dazed. Her face is serious. She stops and leans on her knees, then stands up.

'It's been a while since I ... ran that far,' she puffs.

The shadows on the oval have grown long. The students and teachers are packing everything away. Cordial lids are screwed on. Stray yellow streamers wriggle on the ground. Mr Thompson announces the final house points.

Get Up Mum

RED 456
GREEN 420
GOLD 400

Last! How lame.

I put my track pants on over my shorts. My legs feel tired now. I turn to Mum, by herself leaning on a chair. Her face is a faraway frown.

Nick and Elvis wander past singing 'Amigos para siempre.' I want to laugh but it's a joke I'm not part of. I wave bye to Nick and go over to Mum.

'Are you okay?'

She looks up and makes a smile.

'Yes dear, just tired.'

The birds are nesting in the trees above. They sound like alarms.

On the last day of school I do my rounds delivering the Christmas issue of the *Montello Times*. It's always a good excuse to get out of class and roam the corridors. It's quiet and peaceful because everyone's still in class. Teachers are playing games or watching videos. I can smell the waft of ham and pineapple from the canteen below.

Clinton, one of the naughty pov kids, roams towards me. He's short and skinny with ratty brown hair. His eyes are wide and wet.

'You're all leaving me Heazy!' he says.

Clinton won't be going to high school. He has to stay back and repeat grade six.

'How am I gonna see all my friends?'

Most people think Clinton's a pain.

I'm not sure what's going to happen Clinton.

Everything is changing.

In the afternoon Mr Burgess presents us with our scrapbooks. These are a memento of our time at Montello, with a piece of our best work from each grade. We have a fun hour swapping books and cracking up at our finger painting and silly poems. I flick over my space shuttles and time machines and trees and animals and Aboriginal art.

At five to three the final bell goes. Mr Burgess lets us go.

'See you all next week, I mean next year, I mean, never. Have a very relaxing and safe Christmas and a fantastic year at high school next year.'

I wait until everyone else clears out. I want to walk down the maroon staircase for the final time. I want to do it slowly and dramatically so I'll have a good memory of it. I squeeze the cool black handrail. Each step feels important.

Get Up Mum

I pass the boys toilets and turn left towards the basketball courts. On the bank up from the oval there's the row of young trees that they planted when I was in grade four. We were each assigned our own tree. Mine's in the middle on the end. The only other one I know is Elvis'. His is a different species, a round ghost gum among the tall dark eucalypts.

There's no doubt about it – mine's the tallest.

At home the key is in the front door. I find Mum crouched on the floor in front of the hallway. There's a cassette beside her with brown ribbon spilling out. At first I think she's repairing it. She presses her thumbs down on the cover until the plastic snaps.

'Mum, what are you doing?'

She looks up. Her eyes are dumb and distant.

'There were some evil spirits, Justin. I think Keith Richards has the devil in him. It was coming through to me in his music.'

Mum presses her thumb down again, hard. She cracks another broken piece.

I put my bag down and stare.

Mum's sick again.

PART TWO:
School Holidays

19

Christmas morning has a soft haze about it. The atmosphere is quiet and still like a Sunday but with the excitement of a birthday. I wake up in my bedroom at Nan and Pop's place, happy and relieved. There's a wonderful weight on my feet and for once it's not Blossum but my Santa sack! I sit up and drag the pillowcase full of presents towards me. This is the heaviest it's ever been. I pull out lots of little trinkets and stencils and Furry Friends and bouncy balls and fluoro socks. The biggest present is a Surf City waterslide with a Wahoo Bump!

I wander up and down the hall greeting family members as they emerge from their rooms. Mum's in the bathroom doing her hair. I can smell the perfume and powder she's used. I see her eyes brighten as I look in on her. She smiles kindly and gives me a soft hug.

'Merry Christmas.'

'You look pretty,' I say.

Uncle Nigel walks by and ruffles my hair, mumbling and looking bleary eyed. I'm so excited to have him here for Christmas! I hung out with him a bit two years ago when Nan and I went to Canberra. We were there for my birthday and Nigel came down from Sydney and gave me a remote-control car. It required fourteen AA batteries (eight in the car and six in the remote) and we spent the whole afternoon whizzing it around the carpark.

Uncle Nigel is a good-looking sporty bloke with wavy brown hair and a cheeky smile that reveals his stained teeth. He loves cricket and a beer and has already shown me how to cook the perfect steak. He is always up for a game whether it's croquet or cards or cryptograph (a maths pattern game that Nan's bushwalking mate invented).

Walking into the kitchen I see that Nan has transformed the table into a festive buffet of formal ornaments and glowing bon-bons waiting to be ripped apart. There's a Santa centrepiece with a blue-eyed reindeer, fancy napkins in rings and pats of butter on little plates. The Heazlewood Christmas tradition is a ham and pineapple breakfast with champagne. Pop takes a sip and shivers.

'Whew. That's a bit sharp first thing in the morning.'

I pour some fruit juice into the tall thin glasses – somehow it tastes better like this.

Mum puts on a record with warm, thick organs – it really sets off the special festive atmosphere. The day often seems to buck her spirits and she's able to get through most of it without swearing (I think the champagne helps). There's a program of formal dining, orchestrated by Nan. She's more positive and if she's stressed she doesn't show it as much. Again, the champagne helps.

After breakfast I coax everyone into the present opening arena. I take my place on the floor, in front of the tree, right next to the treasure. I love playing Santa, swivelling around and delivering presents. I try to wait until each person has opened their gift before I give out the next one. Nan takes about an hour carefully unpicking the sticking tape – she wants to save the paper for next year.

Nan and Pop got me a computer! The only catch is it's a V-Tech Precomputer 2000 so it's more like an educational laptop. It has a tiny screen and maths and word games. It's not exactly what I had in mind but I would never let on. It probably cost a bit of money and it's the thought that counts, right? At least I have something new to play on and 'Letter Zapper' sounds alright.

Nigel is my favourite uncle because he's funny, and he thinks I'm funny too. He's like a comedian when he tells a story. He gets totally carried away, raising his voice and waving his arms around. Sometimes he has to stand up like he's performing for an audience. In the afternoon on Christmas Eve we were having a drink on the swing seat when Nan told a story about how she sat on the loo in the middle of the night and the top seat was down. Nigel inserted himself into the story.

'At four o'clock I opened the toilet door and WOOSH! All this water, it forced me back. I probably woke you up Justin.'

We were in stiches. I haven't seen Nan and Pop laugh so hard since we watched *Mr Bean*. I like how Nigel included me in the story. I think his excitement takes a bit out of him. Afterwards he had to sit down and catch his breath because of his asthma.

'I'm having too much fun!' is his favourite saying. Nigel hasn't been home in years but he's back for his high school reunion.

Nigel brings my silliness out and backs my craziness up. He makes fun of Nan and Pop so it's like having a friend inside the family. He's going to be a star recruit for my recordings over the holidays. I don't even bother hiding my recorder from him.

When he smashes a home-brew bottle I rush to the scene like a reporter.

'Look at it on the door Tony,' Nigel says, doing an impression of Michael Holding, the West Indian cricket commentator. I love doing accents as well.

'Did ya run into the door did ya?' asks Pop.

'It came at me. I think Justin pushed it as I was coming in.'

For a second I was hurt because he was lying but then I knew he was joking and it was a way of saying he likes me.

I love my uncle.

It's late at night and the party animals are raging while the fuddy-duddies have gone to bed. I've got Nige all to myself. He's got his fingers in his eyes, taking his contacts out. He slowly pinches off the flimsy films and places them in a dish sitting on the deep freeze. He fills each dish with sterile saline. I tell him not to spill his precious sterile saline and suggest a prank of filling up the water jug with saline when it goes out of date.

'Nah. I still use it. It costs too much.'

'Do ya? But it says replace after … two seconds.'

'Nah, well you don't.'

Fair enough. Nigel also has his grown-up side.

I study his face as he works. His brow has very deep creases with tiny dents from when he had bad acne. I can hear his breathing. It's thick and loud because of his asthma and probably because he smokes. He switches between his nose and his mouth. In between words it's a whole other language. He laughs with a soft snort and thinks with a long suck in through his mouth.

We've promised to get up and go for a walk with Nan in the morning, which is now in … four and a half hours!

'We're not gonna be in very pleasant moods are we?' I laugh.
Nigel puts on a low grouchy voice.
'What walk? Who cares about that bird over there?'
I'm off into hysterics. It feels good to laugh like this.
He does an impersonation of Nan.
'Nigel did you hear …' he gives her a light, airy voice.
I'm laughing so hard I'm out of control.
'What bird?' he says in a zombie voice. His face goes wide eyed and flat.
It's so late and I'm so tired and delighted. I'm just shaking and cackling. I'm a hot air balloon with an outboard motor.
Tomorrow after our walk with Nan we're set to play ten pin bowling in Cooee and then go over to my place to help Mum with the lawn.
'Let's look keen,' says Nigel. 'Dad'll want to go over and help Maureen out. It'll be nice if he does those couple of things.'
'Mum needs it,' I say seriously.
'Your mum sounded a bit better today … I mean yesterday.'
'Bit. Yeah.'
'So, maybe she'll be cool. I'm just leaving her alone at the moment.'
'Yeah,' I let a big slow breath out.
'Cos I don't want to …' Nigel breathes in and out slowly. 'I don't want to upset the apple cart.'
My stereo is sitting up on the deep freeze next to Nigel's contacts. I show him a trick where you record yourself talking very slowly and then play it back on high speed dubbing. If it works then your voice comes out all high and strange.
Nigel has a few goes but doesn't get that he has to lower his speed as well as his pitch.
'I've got to go longer do I?'
I like that Nigel has patience for my games.

Yahtzee is my favourite game. Our set has been around since the seventies and still has the original scoresheets. Uncle Nigel must have been scorekeeper when he was younger because he's written 'Mummy' and 'Daddy' for Nan and Pop and there's people like Ritva who is Uncle Ken's old girlfriend. I've studied the family games and can see Nigel was reigning Yahtzee champion. I can't wait to take him on.

We're bunched up around the kitchen table as the Boxing Day Test plays in the background. The scratch of the bowler's feet is followed by the crack of bat on ball – the Windies are one for twenty two. This morning was fine but now the day has turned grey and drizzly. The garden is a soggy bundle of mud and leaves. I've got my tape recorder positioned strategically underneath the table so Nan can't see.

'Twos twos twos.'

'I need threes. I need heaps of them.'

'We're warming up now, one two three four six!'

I like how all talking in Yahtzee is number talk. There's a running commentary as each player shares their strategy. Nan's had a few and her only strategy is to rattle the cup as hard as possible and scatter the dice far and wide.

'Look, I hate to be a party pooper but get 'em on the table, Mum!' says Nigel.

They always end up on the floor, which puts pressure on whoever picks them up. Nan gets suspicious when the scores don't go her way.

'That was rigged!' she says.

The rattle makes Pop's ears ring so we have to take the cup off her. Nan's new solution is to shake the dice in her hand and slap them down hard on the table. It's not a proper roll and I don't like it. Eventually Nigel brings over the yellow beaker we use to fill the iron.

'It's got a better tone.'

'You gave me a nil. You gave me a nil!' Nan cries.

'Neil,' I cackle. Nan's so funny because she doesn't understand the game and uses old fashioned words like nil and ruddy and sod and then slurs them a bit, which means she makes up entirely new words that makes me laugh even more.

'Is that your card or mine?' she says, referring to her scoresheet.

'Cardial!' I giggle.

'Cardial arrest,' she says. 'Too much excitement.'

'You're hypertensive today,' I comment.

'I'll have a stroke tonight mate,' she says matter-of-factly.

There is excitement when Pop's going for Yahtzee.

'Here we go! Here we go!' Pop holds his dice cup up high and does tribal chants.

'Hoo-waa-waa-wa! Hoo-waa-waa-wa!'

'No!' I urge. Nigel and Pop are challenging my score.

'Yahtzee! Yahtzee!' sings Pop.

The lone dice flips and skids. Pop's face goes from giddy to grumpy.

'Oh you shit arse!'

We all crack up.

'I hope you got that on tape,' says Nigel quietly.

Pop's famous for not swearing.

'I did and I got everything you said before too!'

'Look out,' says Nan. 'That'll be the end of it.'

I roll five ones giving me Yahtzee bonus (two yahtzees in one game is a bonus hundred points). I don't celebrate as much because I'm used to high scores. When Pop finally does get his Yahtzee we all wail like sirens.

'Yaaaaaaaaaaaaaaaaaaaaaa!'

'Aaaaaaaaaaah not fair!'

Nigel comes in with a screamer over the top.

'Wheeeeeeee!'

'I will not put my bit in there,' says Nan. 'Wow wow wow wow wow!' She slams the table with each 'wow.'

'I hope this is just a passing phase for this family,' says Nigel dryly.

It's the perfect line.

Mum drifts into the kitchen carrying home-brew bottles and puts them in the fridge. I feel a jolt – I'd forgotten about her during all the commotion! Her expression is blank and distant.

'Maureen you should be here, you're …' Nan trails off to concentrate on her dice.

Mum makes a coffee. She stabs the spoon into the sugar bowl.

Nan rattles her dice carefully. I'm in a ring between her and Nigel.

'Maureen you're champion at this game, why aren't ya here?'

'I'm not playing it right now.'

Mum speaks in a high pitched voice. A shy little girl.

There's a quiet over the table now. I can hear all our different breaths going in and out. Tense silence.

Mum pours the water and holds the mug over the sink while she stirs. It's a propeller inside a bell.

Ding!Ding!Ding!Ding!Ding!Ding!Ding!Ding!Ding!Ding!Ding!Ding!Ding!

The spoon hits the sink with a clank.

My heart gives a kick.

I can sense the tightness.

Nan groans. Nigel sighs.

I don't mind. It's nothing new to me.

There's a roar from the TV. Boon took a classic catch!

The shadow of Mum passes.

20

It's New Year's Eve and Nan and Pop are hosting the Field Naturalist Club's party. It's a group of old people who go on short bushwalks and look at flowers, so there are lots of grey hairs in our backyard. I'm at the bottom of the lawn with a few of the old folk standing next to a tower of wooden blocks, a big backyard version of Jenga. I'm running my stereo off batteries for the first time so I can capture the atmosphere of the big night.

There's a small crowd gathered to watch us play. Ladies in cardigans and floppy hats and grey haired blokes with collared shirts. I like the attention. I use my thumb to carefully prise and slide a block away from the right side of the stack. The tower rocks gently as I create a space. I feel a thrill followed by relief – the tower stands! The pressure is back on the next player.

Finally the tower falls. At least it wasn't me! From behind I feel warm hands grab me. They clutch my legs and support my back. Now the grass is the sky and the blood's in my head and there's cheering and laughter.

Barry's got me! He's the scout leader who's always up to mischief. Whether we're on a walk or a barbecue you can tell where Barry is because of his raucous, gravelly laugh.

'Haw haw haw!'

I've watched his face and even when he's listening, even when the conversation is a sad one, his eyes are still cheeky and his mouth is slightly upturned, ready to spring into a grin. He wears bus driver shorts with long socks and a beard like a garden gnome. Wherever Barry is, it's the centre of the action.

Barry's holding me upside down and I'm worried my glasses could come off.

'Let's dunk him in the pond!' cries Barry.

He carries me over to where the tadpoles are.

'No-o-o-o-o!' The air is forced out of me as I laugh. I can feel whiskers on my arms. Strong hands clutch my calves.

Barry spins me round. It's so silly and out of control.

'Alright that's enough. I might put me back out!'

I'm returned to earth, whizzed up like a milkshake. It's been a while since I was upside down and spinning around.

I'm surprised to find that I'm the only kid at the party. Usually there's at least one other kid my age on walks with the Field Nats. I thought Nigel and I would end up spending more time together but he's busy talking to the only two young women here. I've combed my hair and put on my smartest button up shirt. I was secretly hoping someone might bring along their niece or granddaughter. Sometimes there are girls at family gatherings and they're usually friendly to me.

There are groups of people sitting on fold out chairs by the barbecue. On the table is a huge bowl of orange punch that Nan made and Nigel slipped some gin into!

Mum's been inside all night playing records. Nan and I have tried to get her to come out but she says she doesn't want to. We don't want to upset her so we've all just left it. No-one else really knows her or asks anything so at least we don't have to explain.

I head to the loo and find her crouched down by the entertainment unit. She's done her hair and put on makeup (Nan's suggestion). The brown cupboard where all the records are kept is open and there are several covers fanned out on the floor, beside a glass of wine.

Part of me wishes Mum would come outside but then I'm glad she's doing something and not just lying on the couch. I guess a party needs music and no-one else is going to bother with it. I tell her that Billy Ocean was a good choice because it got Nigel doing a barn dance.

'Did it? That's good,' she smiles faintly.

I go back out to the yard to fill in more time before midnight. Having a conversation with this crowd isn't easy because old people never seem to take me seriously. I'm actually quite smart and very mature for my age but a lot of them seem either too hard of hearing or totally uninterested in talking to a kid.

The only other youngish guy is David. He has a soft English accent and grey curly hair. I overheard that he's into computers so I mention the laptop Nick's mum bought and my knowledge of the computer programming language BASIC. David tells me about his computer – a desktop with an Intel 486 processor and Windows 3.1, which is the latest system. I ask if there are any games on it but he reckons only Solitaire.

I try to think of more to say but David mutters something and wanders off. I wait and watch him but now he seems to be talking to someone else. I feel a bit crappy. I have an idea that I should use the memory of this feeling to remind myself what it's like to be twelve. If I remember every year, when I'm a grown-up I'll still have a good knowledge of what it's like to be a kid and how interesting they can be. Someone should remember, why not me?

I wander down to the bottom of the lawn. The round pumpkin globe of the sun slips behind the horizon. The grass is cool beneath my feet. I watch members of the Field Nats tottering around Nan's garden. Their voices are high so I can tell they're impressed. I'm proud on Nan's behalf. The Field Nats know the scientific names of plants and which birds are attracted to which flora. I need to go to the loo again. Normally I'd wee under the lemon tree. I head down by the barbecue, listening in on the conversations. Nan's talking about numerology and tea leaf reading. Pop's explaining the rules of Yahtzee. I think Nigel's gone off somewhere with Nicole, one of the women he was chatting to before. I sit down by myself and watch the flames for a while.

Just before midnight we gather in a circle by the barbie. About half the old fogies have left by now. I'm clutching my tape recorder by the handle. I take a big breath in and scream to the stars.

'HAPPY NEW YEAR NINETEEN NINETY THREE!'

One of the ladies points at my stereo and asks if I can put Auld Lang Syne on. I tell her I don't have it but she says she means the radio. I flick the switch onto 7BU and they're playing it. I feel a moment of panic because it means I can't record us singing Auld Lang Syne as well.

Nigel was able to coax Mum out for the countdown. I give her a kiss on the cheek and say Happy New Year. She folds her hands in front of her and looks shyly to the ground. Now the radio's off and it's quiet.

'Shall I go and put a record on?' asks Mum quietly.

I panic. I don't want the others talking to Mum.

'What? Nah, silence is good.' I blurt. Maybe it's a bit late for music now, I don't know. I just want her to be calm.

'I like the night now,' says Nan.

'Speech!' jokes Barry.

Nigel ends up addressing the group.

'Let's all have a good year,' he says. 'Let's do some good walks. Some walks we haven't done before.'

He's only been with the club for a day.

'The main thing is let's just sort of get out there and enjoy life. I know all you guys do because you do your walks and stuff like that and that's great. Especially you younger ones with the white hair.'

Everyone laughs. Nigel is a natural.

'Hey, let's have a good year!' says Nigel.

'Why not,' says Pop. 'It'll be our own fault if we don't I 'spose. We will try anyway.'

'He'll really try,' says Nan. 'He's a goer, this fullah at heart.'

It's formal Nan! I've never heard her talk so lovingly about Pop.

The party is winding down.

'We've got nothing to take home, only ourselves.'

Nan goes out the front to fuss and see everyone off because that's what the hostess is supposed to do.

Nicole's going home with her dad, Barry. Nigel is hovering around trying to get her number. He whispers to me to grab a pen from inside. Nicole is incredible daggy with a squawky laugh and puffy white face. I'm not sure why Nigel likes her. I race inside to fetch a pen, happy to have something to do. Mum's back at the record player playing Dolly Parton.

I race back down to the barbecue, making an engine noise with my mouth. It's cool that everyone's leaving now. I think we were all under pressure to be on our best behaviour. Now we can cut loose and be silly. There's an orange glow from the barbecue and the red dot from the stereo. I've left it running with no-one around. The listener on the tape might be lonely so I pick it up and speak to the red dot.

'Well that's it guys, everyone's packed up and gone. Hope

you've enjoyed the recording of New Year's Eve and I hope I celebrate many more with you. Chow dudes.'

… but wait! Nigel and Nan are sitting back down at the barbie! I grab the tape deck and hurry down, narrating as I go.

'Party's not over yet. It's only just started dudes.'

Nan has the fire stoked up. Nigel's leaning next to it munching on a sausage. Pop's about too! Nigel's in a great mood and declares that we should 'do a Heazlewood.'

'Nigel, would you like to do something for me?' asks Pop.

'What? Do a Heazlewood?'

'Do a Heazlewood!' I growl.

I don't know what 'Do a Heazlewood' means but I like the sound of it.

'I'm gonna stick on the Pearl Jam!'

I scamper towards the house. I find Mum on the couch staring into space. The John Farnham special is on TV with the sound down. She seems tired and sad now.

'Mum, can I put on my Pearl Jam tape?'

'They might be a bit loud now.'

'Okay. You should come outside.'

'I might.'

I race back outside. I don't want to miss a second.

There's a high moon partially covered by wisps of cloud. A lovely smoky heat lands on my knees. I'm bright and awake and ready by the fire. I check the red light is still on.

'Hey where's my sister, go and get my sister.' Nigel says.

'I've told her to come down.'

'No, leave her alone, she won't come,' Nan says briskly.

'No no go …' says Nigel quickly.

'NO!' Nan blocks.

'I'll go. I'll go ...' he concedes.

'Don't bloody start it,' says Nan, scowling. She's back to her usual self.

'Yeah, bring her out,' says Pop cheerfully.

I don't mind as long as I don't have to do it.

'If they don't want to come then that's it,' mutters Nan.

There's something about the night that still doesn't feel right. There's a tension in my throat, like hiccups.

'Why didn't anyone bring their kids?' I ask.

'You enjoyed yourself ...' says Nan, 'AND did you hear all the comments Leonard. About the lovely garden and home.'

Nigel returns with Mum. He stands next to her like a new student being introduced to the class.

'Look at Dad here. He's brought his chair out right on the fire and he's being a Heazlewood.'

'Poor old Pop!' Pop chuckles.

'Look at Mum.'

'... hands in the bloody pocket. Draw your chair round here Maureen, go on, get into it,' says Nan happily.

'And look at your son ...'

'Why doesn't anyone bring their kids?' I ask, my voice rising in a whine.

'He's just ... a total dickhead.'

I laugh.

'Yeah, why didn't they bring their kids?' says Pop.

'They bring them to the Sunday walks. I'm stuck with a bunch of boring adults ...'

'No, didn't you realise what you were? You were the number one scene,' says Nigel.

'I was the number one party animal,' I agree.

We have our own private New Year's celebration with a kiss and cuddle.

'Happy New Year Maureen. We hope we have a happy new year don't we?'

Nan uses greetings to send messages to Mum. I wish we could act normal sometimes, just for a second.

It gets too late for Mum and Pop and they soon wander off to bed.

I'm with my two favourite people by the fire. I have the tape rolling and thought it'd be better. I'm not that keen on the conversation.

Nigel seems pretty drunk now and keeps repeating himself. He and Nan spend ages talking about him and Nicole. It's all a bit grown-up and boring.

'If she's still a virgin then you leave her a virgin.'

'What have I created here? What have I created?' stammers Nigel.

'A nan lecture,' I say quietly.

I ask again why no-one brought their kids. I'm annoyed about that. Someone should be talking about me more.

'Pretty bad eh?' says Nigel.

'What are you saying Justin darlin'?' Nan has a puzzled look.

'They didn't bring their kids.'

'Tonight?'

Nan looks like she has no idea what I'm saying.

'Yeah,' says Nigel. 'There should have been someone around Justin's age.'

'As I've told you before, you're the greatest little walker and that's why all these walkers respect you.'

'Why be a legend when you've got nobody to show it to?' says Nigel.

21

School holidays mean sleeping in and barbecues and swimming and cricket and daylight savings and staying up late! I love that it's still bright outside at eight o'clock. The scent of Christmas pine hangs in the air.

I never know what day it is during the holidays. I just wake up and wander outside where there's fresh pollen in the breeze and clothes fluttering on the line. Sprinkler mist nips at my knees as I get a barefoot massage from the grassy carpet. I don't bother wearing a watch. It's lunch when Pop lights the barbie. The cricket is either on or not on. Mum's either well or not well.

Uncle Ken arrived yesterday so we're heading off to Crayfish Creek to set up the caravan and camp for four days. It's the first time the whole family has been together and I'm very excited to tape all the commotion. There's the whole process of getting ready and packing the car and picking out the site and winding up the caravan, which usually involves a lot of arguing between Nan and Pop. At least with Uncle Nigel and Uncle Ken here Nan is slightly better behaved. Even Mum hides her swearing under her breath.

Ken is Mum's older brother by four years. Ken has dark grey hair and a white beard similar to Kenny Rogers, but doesn't like being compared to him (or being called Kenny). He's a country and western musician who lives in Canberra and travels around playing in clubs. He made a small record called *Ol' Blue* that I sometimes play at Nan and Pop's. In grade five he helped me pick out my first guitar.

Once we're all set up at the campsite I slide my stereo down at the end of the couch inside the caravan, half covering it with a jacket.

'Turn it off, you don't want that on,' says Pop. He's resting on the grey chunky sofa beneath the canvas window. Bugger! I'm sprung already. Now I need to come up with a reason to leave it on that doesn't reveal the real reason.

'No, leave that on for the …'

'What for?

'Playing music in the morning …'

'In the morning?'

I feel heat in my cheeks. Nigel, Ken and Nan are squeezed around the kitchen table. I feel eyes on me. I'd better make a joke.

'For me to get up and play Pearl Jam at three o'clock in the morning. That can be our alarm clock.'

'I'll shove ya out that window there if you do,' says Pop.

'Who's he want to play?' asks Ken, yawning.

'Pearl Jam.'

'Who?'

'Pearl Jam.'

'Who?'

'Pearl … Jam.' I say it very slowly.

'Pearl … Jam,' Ken repeats, equally slowly. 'Is it good music or just a bunch of crap?'

'Bunch of crap,' mutters Nan.
'Good music! Nigel'll tell ya,' I chirp.
'Nah, it's good music.'
'I'm pleased to hear that,' says Ken.

Pearl Jam is a cool rock band from America with a great song called 'Alive.' I just bought their tape *Ten*.

Ken's into daggier country stuff and The Beatles. We've always gotten along but not like me and Nigel. Ken's serious and reserved but once he's had a few drinks he definitely comes out of his shell and acts silly.

I want to show him how far I've come on guitar so I get out my guitar pick collection and fan them on the white laminex table. There's a white one with flames and a red 'Tortex' brand with a turtle on it. He inspects each one and declares whether they're too soft or too hard for him.

My favourite is black with a skull and crossbones on it.

'Cos I'm a rough and tough dude.'

'Rough and tough dude,' he smiles. 'Hold onto them, they're all good. They're all worth something in their own right.'

It's dark outside now. I'm nervous and excited and hovering around. The caravan feels like a cubby, especially with the furry brown carpet. Everything is compact and designed to convert into a sleeping area. There's a little gas stove that Nan makes the toast on and a sink where you pump the tap up and down. There's a little wood panel fridge, foldaway kitchen table and plenty of sliding cupboards for storing matches and torches and trowels. On one cupboard is a little cartoon sign:

Justin Heazlewood

They must think I'm a mushroom because they keep me in the dark and feed me bullshit.

Nan hasn't brought any chocolate, so I make a peanut butter sandwich.

'Has he got the worms?' Nan mumbles.

'Who … me?' I say through a mouthful.

'You'll end up like Elvis Presley if you start eating stuff like that,' says Ken.

Nigel laughs heartily. I don't get it.

'I said have you got the worms?'

'Nah he's camping. He's earnin' an appetite.'

Yeah. Nigel gets it.

The rest of the night is spent working out sleeping arrangements and having a good chuckle at Pop's red polka dot pyjamas. Nan and Mum are on one of the pull-out 'wings' while Pop and I are on the other. Nigel gets my usual spot by the kitchen table. There isn't room for Ken so Nan's set up her one-man bushwalking tent outside. Ken seems worried. I think it's been a while since he slept in a tent. He has to come inside to get changed.

With only the torch for light, Ken comes to life.

'Have I said, "I love youse all"?'

'No, but I'm glad to hear it now,' says Nan. 'I love you too.'

'I'm glad you said that Ken,' says Nigel.

'Well now we know,' adds Pop, dryly.

'Goodnight,' I say.

'I'll be out here if you need me.'

'Get out!' I joke, shutting the door behind him.

Nigel remains at the kitchen table, nursing a glass. He has his quiet moments too. The leaves cast shadow creatures that bob across the green annexe. Mum's tucked away in the dark next to Nan. She's been there most of the night. Mum takes her sickness camping.

'Goodnight Maudie,' says Nan.

'Goodnight' says Mum. She sounds like a little girl.

'I love you Maudie.'

Silence. I press stop on the tape.

The next day brings a bright morning, perfect for surfing, and a balmy afternoon, ideal for a barbecue tea. The only sounds around the campsite are the soft drone of the crickets and the squeak of the caravan door. I can smell rich, leafy smoke and sweet, fatty patties frying. It makes me hungry and happy. We're enclosed in our little campsite. Beyond the bush is the path and the highway and then the sea, rolling and alive. I slither my bare feet over the cool leaves and take a sip of soft pineapple juice, fresh from the tin.

Mum's in a fold out chair, nursing a glass of beer. One leg is crossed over the other and her foot is tapping away. Her eyes squint and her brow is shadowed. She came to life a bit earlier today, asking Nigel about a bloke he'd met, but now she's back to her quiet self.

'What do you think of this life Maureen?' says Nan 'Aren't we buggers? Maudie, aren't we buggers. Eh?'

'Hmm!?' nods Mum with a mouthful. It's between a question and an answer.

Nigel's overseeing the cooking on our portable 'Super Chief' barbecue. He's wearing thongs, shorts and Tina Turner T-shirt with 'TINA' written in bright red. The mozzies are attracted to it and I tried to make a joke about her being 'Ms Mozzie.'

'Hey,' said Nigel joke seriously. 'You be careful what you say about Tina.'

I feel weird because I want to play my guitar but also I don't. There's a shyness I get that makes me uncomfortable but then I feel a bit guilty because I know I should and I've already told everyone I would play. When I was seven I made up a song on one of Ken's old guitars and invited everyone to come hear me play. But I couldn't play until they all turned their backs to me. I guess if I put my chair behind where everyone is gathered it'll sort of be the same thing.

'You play us a song then darlin'. Give us the background music. It's better than the radio,' encourages Nan.

'Whatever you want,' says Nigel.

I take as long as I can to tune up and pluck away at the twelve bar blues. I'll play 'Way Out West' – it's a country song I reckon Ken will like.

'Play 'Song of Joy' Justin,' says Mum. 'I like that one.'

Joy is Mum's middle name.

Tonight is war of the worlds!

Our Jayco pop-top caravan is earth.

The aliens are small and black and communicate with a high pitched whining sound. They are foreigners who are unwelcome in our airspace. They attack our skin and pinch our blood, causing welts to appear. The welts are itchy!

Queen Edna Heazlewood stands at the caravan door with her hands on her hips and radar eyes wide.

'Look, who left that open for the mozzies to get in?'

Security has been compromised!

The metallic door slams shut.

'Sssh, you'll wake up the neighbours,' says court jester Nigel. Even his humour can't ease the drama. This is war!

'The place'll be lousy with 'squitas if you don't shut it.' This is the King Leonard Heazlewood, reclining in his sofa throne. Number 1 ace pilot Justin Heazlewood enters the caravan muttering something of no doubt great importance.

'I'll smack you,' says the Queen.

'What did I do?' Justin is shocked. He pleads in a pitch a few tones lower than the enemy creatures buzzing around the caravan.

The Queen has no time. Her detection systems have picked up two enemy cruisers at seven o'clock. It is also now seven o'clock at night.

'Look, there's the mozzies!' Queen Edna swats her heavy hand against the door. Her other hand bats the roof with an open palm.

Even Space Nurse Maudie, long scarred from the throes of battle, is moved to speech.

'The mozzies weren't here last time.'

'Get that mozzie that was floating there. Justin, you did that!'

Accused of betraying his queen and country! Ace pilot Justin stands on trial for aiding these blood-sucking bandits.

His pitch reaches new heights.

'No! But I wasn't the last one in, Ken was ...'

Justin suspects Ken may be a spy. His beard could be antennae!

'Look at that mozzie,' the Queen says gravely.

Justin laughs. 'Cool dude.' If he can't prove his innocence perhaps he can plead insanity.

'Justin, that annoys me. I've told you not to ...'

'It wasn't my fault, everybody's going in and through ...'

'But you were,' says Nan. 'You kept it open the longest ...'

At 7.10pm Queen Edna Heazlewood of Wynyard Tasmania makes a public address to the seated earthlings of the good ship Jayco at Crayfish Creek.

'Oh, there's no end of mozzies in here. This place is alive!

Oh my god, the place is full of mozzies!'

The King and Queen embrace. Their thrones toppled, their bodies huddled together, scratching. Will their final moments be spent watching these atrocious aliens invade their castle?

'Len, look at 'em around the light!'

'Yeah, get bitten like hell tonight.'

The Queen goes to her chamber and pulls out a secret weapon. A mysterious mist blasts forth, surrounding the beasts (and the occupants.)

'There's no way I'm sleeping with them,' the Queen declares.

'You may as well leave it out you'll be spraying all night,' warns Nigel.

'Youse spraying?' asks a voice from outside. It's Commander Ken, a rogue pilot who has been suspiciously absent during the invasion.

'Finished spraying, but you rush in and shut the door quick!'

Ken surveys the scene and shuts the door again.

'Can't come in.'

Again, he displays disloyalty!

'Hold me up,' Nan swats and sprays.

'Bloody sods of things! Oh Christ, they're still flying!'

The aliens are more highly evolved than anyone could have anticipated. Their bodies are designed for quick manoeuvring and they are able to evade bulky weapons such as hands. They are aware of human blind spots such as the back and shoulder. It even appears as if they have adapted to the Queen's secret spray, specifically designed for this kind of Raid.

'They weren't here like this before,' Nurse Maudie repeats.

'Let's move to Rocky Cape!' says Ace Pilot Justin. He thinks of the black box recorder and wonders if someone listening back later might appreciate some jokes.

The night brings an end to the battle but it is a restless sleep. No matter how much of the enchanted balm RID the Queen applies, her alien injuries continue to torment her, which she makes known. The next day there is excitement as news of a breakthrough in ammunition reaches the colony. Scientists have invented a device known simply as The Coil.

The Coil is a nuclear reactor device that sends out smoke, scrambling the circuits of the aliens. That night, once again under invasion, the colony are eager to deploy the invention. Commander Ken follows the instructions carefully, sitting it on the coasters box and lighting one end. A thin stream of smoke drifts skywards.

The Queen assembles her fleet. Ace Pilot Justin scans the radars, baton at the ready. By eight o'clock, there are signs The Coil is taking effect.

'This'll be interesting,' says the Queen. 'Look at that one straight up there on the roof.'

'He's a nice lookin' one that one,' laughs court jester Nigel.

There is something different about their behaviour. When Justin does a fly-by, the alien does not react.

'Look at this!' yells Justin.

'Easy meat!' says Nigel.

'Kill!'

Justin easily destroys a pair of enemy fighters, belting them with his newspaper cannon. They offer no resistance.

'I like that smoke,' says the Queen, dreamily.

'So do I,' says Justin. The rich tang reminds him of the incense his Mother used to burn.

'You old hippies you,' says Ken.

The aliens have no defences from The Coil. It's a bloodbath.

'It's smoking them silly,' laughs Justin.

'Knocking them senseless baby,' says Nigel.

'Can I have some of that?' asks Ken.

King Leonard chuckles, as rich and relaxed as the smoke that now drifts peacefully over the caravan. The Heazlewood village has been pushed to its limits, but by working as a colony, peace has prevailed.

Oh no, wait, what is that over by the light?

'Ants!'

22

It's our final full day at Crayfish Creek. Nan's been getting on my nerves and nagging me more than usual. She talks to me like a teacher when I'm just trying to have fun and be cool with my uncles.

My worst crime was getting out the cards before putting the Yahtzee set away. She sat there at the kitchen table watching me with her beady eyes as I shuffled the cards.

'Put the others away please Justin. Nan has spoken! I get annoyed, you know I do,' she says.

'Don't go crazy,' I say under my breath.

'Don't upset Nan.'

'Yeah don't upset Nan,' says Ken, half listening.

'She's always upset,' I say, heat in my cheeks. Ken's on Nan's side. Nigel keeps out of it.

'He's not learning there's a place for everything. You've got to put everything in its place.'

'I put the dice on the table instead of back in the cup!'

I have no idea why I'm in trouble. It's like she needs something to nag about.

'Yeah fair enough mate. And if everything you handled was like that it'd be a bloody mess, right?'

After tea and a few extra drinks for our last night away Nan and Pop turn in early. Mum's been asleep for ages already. Nigel and Ken and I gather around the kitchen table for a Saturday night party. I'm looking forward to recording and relaxing and having some man-time.

Ken's been telling us about how he has to 'rassle' the sheep on the new farming property he's just moved to. He lives by himself and has his own recording studio where he's just made a new tape of country songs. Right now we're making up songs about farts to the tune of other songs.

'He ain't smelly, he's my brother,' sings Nigel in a low tone.

Ken likes that one. I come up with 'I think I smell you, but what am I so afraid of ...' which is in the Top 50. This gets a laugh, which is what I'd been searching for.

Ken seems a bit drunk. He's started talking a lot slower. He sifts through the Yahtzee scoresheets.

'Amanda. When was Amanda ever here?'

'That's my neighbour, Mandy. She's a woman now.'

'Ooh,' says Ken suggestively.

'She's gonna turn eighteen soon,' I say.

'You like her?'

'She and her sister used to come and play with me. Now they've all grown up and deserted me.'

'They don't want to know ya,' says Ken.

'They've got their jobs and homes and everything,' I explain. 'But I don't need 'em. I can survive on my own. I'm a loner.'

I do voices from *Rocky & Bullwinkle*. I'm excited and nervous and want my uncles to think I'm cool.

Ken leans back. His hair and beard are dark in the moonlight. His eyes are hidden behind metal frames.

'How do your grandparents put up with you? Let alone your mum?'

'Me?' I say in my squeak-voice. 'I'm the greatest.'

'Yeah, well, we know that … but how do your grandparents put up with you? Let alone your mum?' he repeats.

My chest feels prickly.

'What? I'm really nice and friendly and easy to get along with.'

'We've heard that, but we haven't seen that on this particular holiday.'

Nigel laughs. I know they're being pretend-mean, but I still feel a bit hurt. I like people saying how great I am.

'We've heard that about you but …'

'We're seeing different visions,' adds Nigel. 'Maybe he shows a bit more decorum sometimes.'

My heart quickens. I'm not sure I like being the centre of this attention. I think Ken's stirring, but his words seem serious.

'You can shut me up after this. But my opinion is … as far as a son of a sister of mine or a grandson of a father of mine or a … an uncle's brother … and all that sort of stuff …'

'I'm no good,' I say quietly.

'You're the best in the world.'

My heart blooms.

'That's what I try to be.'

'You fuck up a lot,' mutters Ken.

My uncles are sitting across the table from me. It's strange to be spoken to like this. I'm usually the only one around. I'm an only child and the only grandchild they see. There's no-one else to compare me to. Nan and Pop and Mum know I always do my best.

'I've just got to let loose.'

Nigel laughs. 'It's good to let loose.'

'But you are the best in the world,' repeats Ken.

There's a hurry in my heart. I want them to know about my life. I want to say interesting words before they move on. I can be serious too. So far all they've seen is the kid me. I write them letters with news about school and we speak on the phone at birthdays and Christmas. I want them to know what's going on inside me. I've grown up a lot.

'I'll call you that, you're the best in the world,' repeats Ken.

'You're the best uncles in the world.'

They both laugh.

'It's pay out time then.'

23

The sea is my dad.

We've always lived near each other. From the end of my street in Montello I see its blue cap and white moustache.

Every few days we meet, especially during the summer holidays. On our way back from Crayfish Creek we head down to Boat Harbour beach. I strip down to my bathers and run full pelt into its body, leaving Nan, Pop, Mum, Ken and Nigel on the sand. I lift my foot up and out to the side to rise above the foam and the chop. I breathe in the salty air and forget about the cold and know that the sea is where I need to be.

I dive forwards while clasping my fingers together to form a spear. I pierce the surface and glide down underneath. A sheet of cold hits me but I'm already too busy to feel it. It's alright now – I'm in! I grab its sandy chest and curl my legs in to spring up off the bottom. I whizz up and shatter the surface and dive back into the day.

It's called a 'duck dive.' And I'm a strong, fit, happy duck.

I keep paddling, I keep surging forward, against the tide. I'm past the choppy stuff so now it's smoother sailing. There's waves to be caught if I just get out far enough. If I meet them too early they haven't fully formed, and if I'm too late they've already broken. They're no use to me then. They're just a loose bunch of breakwater, which you can still catch but it's nowhere near as good.

Now I'm in over my head. Once my feet can't touch the bottom I know there's work to be done. I can never stay still. I have to keep paddling and swirling my limbs like a propeller. The sea is restless and powerful and keen to drift me around and bob me along. There are rewards – you just have to show you are keen.

I scan the horizon for the next set of waves. They come in sets of seven – my favourite number. They surge in against the skyline. Big bulky heads, gliding along and up. We call them 'boomers' when they're big. 'Out the back!' A kid might scream. That's the signal. That's when you get real. That's when you need a head start. Swim settings set to 'turbo flat chat.'

This is the best feeling. Being picked up by a wave. Our energies combined, I rise up high on the sea's shoulders. It's a wild, magical beast. An awesome, steely water creature.

Then it bucks and breaks and slams me down. I skid beneath the surface into a whitewater washing machine. Froth and bubbles and spinning and tumbling. I'm a roly-poly ragdoll, underwater and everywhere and wide-eyed and closed-nosed. Then it's over. I'm spat out the end of the ride. The sea and me, playing rough and tumble. I turn around and run back into its arms. Again!

My beach legs feel good against the cool cotton sheets on my bed at Nan and Pop's. I'm pooped but not in a hurry to get to sleep. I like to lay here and reflect on the day, especially when I still have the hush of the sea in my ear.

I can hear Nigel and Pop sitting in the lounge. I feel safe with people in the house. It's still light outside and the drone of twin crickets comforts the silence. There's a faint ache around my knees. I must be getting more growing pains, or maybe its sunburn.

I think back to earlier today when I was floating in the shallows. My head was submerged except for my nose and mouth. I was a sleepy sea lion, laying still for as long as possible. I tried to forget about my body and concentrate on the sea breeze drifting in through my nose. I stretched out and floated in the atmosphere. I felt at peace.

I still have so much of the school holidays left! There are a lot of big things coming up to look forward to like Camp Clayton and surf carnivals and starting grade seven. Time goes quickly when I'm happy. Sometimes moments become memories before I'm ready. Sometimes I get sad looking backwards and worried thinking forwards. Recording things on my stereo helps me to pause time. I can replay moments as many times as I want.

I can't take my tape into the sea so I couldn't record me and Nigel playing in the water this morning. But I can see Nigel in my mind, splashing around and laughing. I didn't have my special goggles so he was blurry, but I could still make out his strong body and hear him yelling and laughing.

It'll be good to get to sleep so I can wake up early and spend some final moments with Nigel before he heads home. He's leaving tomorrow. I don't want him to go. I'd love nothing more than to go back to the start of the holidays and have all the fun again.

When I was floating and breathing in the shallows today I had the feeling I was connecting with something important. All of my memories and feelings and dreams of nature and my family gathered together with me in the centre. I felt complete. I felt like my life made sense and that my battles and struggles with Mum were being recorded by something powerful in another place. It might not be all up to me all the time, which is a comfort.

It's dark outside now. I'm more scared of the dark at Nan and Pop's than I am at home. It's a big house so there's more places for black shapes to hide. I had a nightmare about Nan and Pop's hallway once ... the lounge room lamp had come to life ... I couldn't run away properly ...

...

                         ...

                                               ...

Woah! My legs jumped! I was gonna fall! How weird. I wasn't asleep and I wasn't in my mind.

I try to feel the moment where I fall asleep but then it blanks and I wake up. Once I had grommets put in my ears. They gave me anaesthetic and asked me to count backwards from ten but I never made it to five. Sometimes if I wake up in the middle of the night I can feel my mind slipping back to sleep. Once it made the sound of water filling my ears. It's a slow sinking into a dark thick bath. Careful silence ... careful silence is holding me under ... ...

a l o n e   a r o u n d   a   t u r n i n g   t u n n e l

inside   searching   trying   hiding   s o m e t h i n g

Get Up Mum

                      low low low low
               black black! black black
                         blots boxes

                              swamp
                            a sticky
                            shadows
stuckon!

                     an egg on my ear
                          howling
                      a ghost inside

NO!

                      no face! no one
                          no name

                     ghost around me
                       tearing itself
                         open and
                             shut

                     mouth hole face
                        a dead egg

     in a shrinking head

                      i squash the lot
                   the shadow hurries
                     chasing my chest

Justin Heazlewood

                                                im backwards
                                              away away away
                                                  no no no no

                                                        i wriggle
                                                            inside
                                  away!

      i paddle paddle paddle
               up
               up
WAKE!WAKE!WAKE!WAKE!

Morning light seeps into my eyes. I'm wrapped up in my doona cocoon. The pillow is protection. There's a ring of thoughts and fever shadows. I reverse the replay. Last night's dream is a fog. There was danger and ... horror and chasing. I try to lie still and breathe. My heart can slow my mind down ... and the other way around.

    I'm okay. This is real life. The dreams can't hurt me now.

It's the goodbye day. I normally love heading to the airport. I love the extra fussing and organising, the lights on in the early morning before sunrise and the suitcases parked in the hallway. Mum manages a groggy 'good morning' from her bedroom door as I grab some breakfast and head into the lounge. I feel quiet from my bad dream. It wasn't a normal nightmare. It was something more strange. I was underneath everything. There were no actual people, only shapes and shadows. I was trapped under the surface and I wasn't alone. I was very closed off.

It was a grown-up fever dream.

I'm enjoying the emerald colours of an old episode of *Wizard of Oz* and the sweet crunch of 'Grant Kenny'. I've seen this episode before but it feels good to watch something familiar. The wizard is no longer a gigantic head but just a voice floating around the throne room. Toto wanders behind a door and drags a man out by the leg. The wizard turns out to be nothing more than a man with stage tricks.

'You can't be the Wizard of Oz!' says Dorothy.

'Sort of a let-down isn't it?'

'We'll be right,' Nigel calls from the kitchen. 'You live five minutes from the airport!'

He joins me in the sofa chair next to the couch. He nods his head in the direction of the kitchen and pulls a face. I close my mouth and snort out my nose and raise my eyebrows.

'You better keep an eye on this lot for me!'

It sucks that Nigel is leaving.

He takes out his wallet and hands me a scratchie. It's already scratched and there are three ten dollars.

'Spend it on something you really want.'

'Thanks!' I smile.

He stands up to switch the TV channel. America has a new president. He's playing the saxophone like Lisa Simpson. The Australian Open is on. Nigel and I agree that Steffi Graf has great legs.

I have my shower and sit on the toilet and tie my shoe laces in record time.

'Have you cleaned your teeth?' asks Nan.

'Yeah you don't want 'em lookin' like mine,' says Nigel.

'Uncle Nigel'll tell ya if you don't look after 'em you're gonna lose 'em.'

'You'll lose that tooth on the left hand side in no time. It's the Heazlewood curse, because I didn't clean my teeth one time.'

'Oh yeah,' I reply dryly. I'm a bit old for tall tales.

We're out the door and in the car and arguing about parking at the Wynyard terminal. I love the airport and anything to do with planes. Space shuttles are my favourite thing to draw. I breathe in the busy, important smells.

The quiet terminal turns to a throbbing drone as a plane touches down. The mighty roar of the engine coats the room along with the rich waft of fuel. The Kendell jet has a long narrow nose with black and red racing stripes and twin propellers. It rolls towards the airport and I imagine what would happen if it kept going and smashed through the windows. It parks side on and powers down its engines with a satisfying shudder. Passengers trickle down the stairs. I watch their faces light up as loved ones laugh and greet them. It's a private thing to witness – other people's happiness. I wish Nigel was arriving rather than leaving. We could have more barbecues and go for bushwalks and swims and play games of Yahtzee. I won't let him notice I'm sad. I want him to remember me as his cool nephew.

'Kendell Airlines wishes to call all passengers due to fly to Melbourne please board through the gate.'

I wonder if it's okay to hug Nigel even though he's a man? We just shook hands on New Year's Eve.

'Alright Sucram, you keep kicking butt and good luck with high school.'

My middle name backwards is 'Sucram' so I've decided it is my new computer name because RAM is a computer term.

'I know you'll do well because you're a champion. Just watch out for them grade nine girls!'

Get Up Mum

Nigel holds out his hand. I open my arms and rest my cheek against his hard chest. He makes an 'ah' of surprise and I feel his hands on my back. I like the cool touch and friendly scent of his windcheater. Pop laughs and Nan makes a noise.

Nigel closes his mouth and breathes quickly in and out through his nose. I pull back and see his creased brow – it looks like he's frowning even though he's smiling. His eyes twinkle with softness. There's a sinking in my stomach as I think about all the things I want to say, but thickness sticks in my throat. Nigel walks away and stands in the line of strangers. I watch the line of his jeans and belt. The shape of his shoes. His red top and backpack. His quivering dimple and wavy brown hair.

The plane is glary in the light. Mum tries to point out where Nigel is and says he's waving from the tiny round windows. I can't tell. I'd rather watch the propellers as they start to spin. I lock my eyes onto a blade and follow it round and round.

Round and round and round and round.

Round and round and … roundroundandroundandrou rourourourrrrrrrrrrrrrrrrrrrrrrrrrrrrrrr …

There, I lost it. The blade has joined the blur. The buzz increases its pitch as the plane rolls forward and steers away. The toy that weighs a ton is going to speed up and soar into the air. Nigel gets smaller against the runway of green. The plane speeds from right to left. I follow it along and finally, up.

The airborne moment.

Nigel and I are apart.

I track the plane until it's impossible to see.

Now I'm standing at the window with my family.

'We'll miss him won't we!' says Mum, her eyes sideways.

24

The next day Nan leaves for her massive ten day bushwalk down the South-West Coast. She's been training for ages but we're still a bit worried about how she'll go. With her and Nigel gone it's suddenly very quiet. It feels like there's a space that needs filling but none of us are the right personalities.

It's good timing that I'm heading off to a summer camp in Ulverstone with Nick. Nick's mum signed us up a couple of months ago. Camp Clayton is supposed to be three days of fun activities and cool stuff for grade sevens and eights. I don't know anyone else going except Nick. The campsite is a sprawling parkland with a giant rope swing and two huge trampolines dug into the ground. Apparently the camp might have some religious stuff but I'll worry about that later.

When Nick and I arrive we see the camp leaders dressed as doctors and nurses because there's a hospital theme. Our cabin is 'Ward 1F' and our 'orderly' is a friendly bloke called Matt. We're welcomed by the 'Chief Surgeons,' an older couple called Diane and 'Lizard'.

We divide up into groups and play a few 'icebreaker' games.

Afterwards we watch a video of a stand-up comedian and then have dinner in the big dining hall where we click our fingers and sing grace to the tune of the Adam's Family.

'Do do do do'
(Click Click)
'We thank you for the food
The food is really good
the cook is a real dude
Camp Clayton family
Amen (Click Click).'

Camp Clayton is turning out to be more Christian than I imagined. Most of the kids seem to come from Leighland Christian School. They're way more knowledgeable of the songs and some of them make the sign of the cross on their chests. The Christian songs that Amy Grant sings on TV are very daggy. We sing one called 'Shine Jesus Shine' that reminds me of 'The NeverEnding Story.' It's a powerful song with minor chords so I feel both happy and sad.

'Shine, Jesus, shine
Fill this land with the Father's glory
Blaze, Spirit, blaze
Set our hearts on fire.'

There are pretty girls with blonde hair and glasses singing with their mouths open wide. They seem very comfortable with the songs and don't even have to look at the lyrics. It's like they're all part of a club that we don't know about. I'm glad I have Nick next to me. He's mouthing the words but not really singing. Neither of us are religious. At Montello they sang grace over the PA at lunch and we had scripture with Mrs Brown, but no-one took it seriously.

The next morning is a bright sunny day. Nick and I laugh through our showers because they're so temperamental. Camps are fun because you do everything you normally do but in a different way. The kitchen offers a buffet of cereals so Nick and I make a 'breakfast cocktail.' The toast has 'Joy' stamped into it and comes with little spreads of vegemite and jam. We gather in the assembly room. I notice a pretty girl, but she doesn't see me.

Suddenly a wide-eyed man rushes into the room.

'Guys! Quick. It's an emergency. There's a group of terrorists outside and they're armed with machine guns! They're holding us hostages! They said if their demands are not met they're going to come in here and start shooting hostages one by one.'

He has a white baggy T-shirt tucked into jeans. The shirt has a drawing of a cross on top of a hill with a lightning bolt and says 'DYING TO KNOW YOU'. He has one arm pointing to the doorway. The other hand is cupped around his mouth, as if telling us a secret.

'What are you gonna do?'

My heart is beating faster. I know it can't be real, but he's good at pretending. The crowd of kids stares up at him. Are we supposed to answer something?

Nick sneezes. I laugh.

The man claps his hands together.

'Okay, I'm gonna let you in on a secret … there aren't terrorists outside. You can all relax. That was just a demonstration. I'm sorry if I worried anyone, but there is an important lesson in there. Let's say there really were terrorists outside, and they came in here and started killing people. If you didn't believe in Jesus at the time that you died, it means you could end up going to hell.

Now trust me guys, you don't want to end up in hell. It is NOT a nice place. Imagine the most excruciating pain, and then imagine it lasting for eternity. Obviously when you're a baby you haven't committed any sin and you're not old enough to make a decision about Jesus. So God automatically sends them to heaven.'

The man asks us if there are any questions. One kid wants to know if there really are terrorists outside. It's a relief when he winds up and hands over to our main leader Joppo. Joppo's friendly and way more on our level. He has a goatee and bandana and calls us 'dudes' and 'legends'. He's in a wheelchair.

Joppo tells his story and answers the two questions everyone's been itching to know.

'Why are you in a wheelchair?' (A car accident involving a drunk driver.)

'Why are you called Joppo?' (It's short for his last name).

After his accident Joppo was angry at the world. Through the Bible and the teachings of Jesus, he was able to see life in a new light. I stare at his jeans. His legs just sit there, at a diagonal angle.

I wonder why he still wears shoes?

Behind us a girl – I think her name is Rita – starts crying.

'My Pop's going to hell,' she blurts, before standing up and running off.

Lizard goes after her.

After lunch Nick and I get dressed in helmets and gloves and goggles and overalls. We sit on a piece of blue foam tied to the back of a ute. My legs are straddled around Nick as I grip onto his waist and he holds onto the rope handle. This is how we go down waterslides because you get more speed up. Right now I'm worried about flying off and taking a massive tumble.

Rob, the driver, takes off and we're soon hooning around the oval. I can feel all the grass and bumps whipping under my bum as Nick sticks up his thumb, which is our signal for 'Faster!' Rob fangs the engine and guns left. The G-force has our sled skidding sideways at an impossible angle. I squint my eyes and yell and lean into the corner, as instructed.

My stomach is still buzzing later as we sit down for a 'reverse course' dinner (dessert first!). After tea we get into our hospital costumes. I have a T-shirt with bite marks and blood stains that says 'Shark Attack!' Our cabin works on an act for the entertainment night. We do a comedy news report – I write most of it. I pretend to be the Queen while Nick is Paul Keating, chasing me around the stage trying to grope me.

We break for supper, which is a fancy way of saying 'Milo and biscuits'. I ask Nick what he thinks of all the God stuff. He says he's sceptical, which is a word I'm not sure of. Nick's into science and electronics and says he'd need to see some proof first. I think I'm more open to it because I was baptised Catholic and Mum reads the Bible sometimes.

'Hell'd be scary eh?' says Nick, dunking a biscuit into his Milo.

In *The Simpsons* they make fun of Hell. For the video of 'Deep Deep Trouble' Bart gets the electric chair and goes to Hell. The devil spins a 'Wheel of Misfortune' and Bart is reincarnated as a snail.

'I'm glad they don't send babies to Hell,' I say.

'Yeah how unfair would that be,' Nick laughs. 'You're this little baby with Satan stabbing you over and over with his hot poker.'

I frown and bite a butternut snap. Nick often goes into too much detail. Hell doesn't seem fair for adults either. What if you'd learned your lesson but were stuck there forever no matter what?

It takes ages for everyone to get settled into bed. Our cabin is the most sensible because we end up in our bunks talking while the other cabins are still going nuts. Apart from me and Nick there are two other boys in the cabin, Adam and Stuart. Our 'orderly' Matt comes to check we're ready for lights out. Nick asks Matt when he first became Christian. He says he grew up going to church but it wasn't until he was our age that he formed his own connection with Jesus.

I say I'm not certain there's a God but it feels like life is too important to be caused by a random series of chemicals. I like the idea of something watching over me (but I don't say this to Nick and Matt).

Matt asks if he can say a prayer on our behalf, inviting Jesus to reveal himself to us.

A calm comes over the room. Even the kids in the cabin next door have settled down.

'Lord Jesus, I'd like to thank you for this wonderful camp and the opportunity to meet Nick and Justin and Adam and Stuart and all these great guys. I'd like to ask that you come to Camp Clayton and make your presence felt. I know that everyone here is really curious about you and keen to meet you, so I pray Jesus that you enter the hearts of everyone here and fill them with warmth and love in the hope they might be able to begin a relationship with you.'

I'm lying on my back on the top bunk, inside my sleeping bag. I stare up at the roof. There are patterns floating around my eyes. Matt's voice is gentle, like rain.

'Lord shine your light and your love and fill their hearts so that they may know you and feel you.'

It starts with a warmth in my chest.

'Lord I pray that this is the beginning of a new bond. Help these boys to understand your message and guide them on their journey. May they discover a peace through you. And a sense that they're not alone and they no longer have to carry the burden of original sin by themselves.'

There's a warmth and the warmth is spreading! A slow, glowing pool. It's melting over my ribs and lungs and down into my tummy.

Holy crap!

'Lord we pray that this is the start of a great adventure. May you enrich and enlighten everyone who may not have had the chance to experience your light and are still uncertain. Allow them to feel your love and your power in a way that's real.'

I feel a spirit! A presence. A comforting force. It's something other than me and it's inside me but I don't feel scared. I'm alone on the top bunk at the top of a safe cloud.

Matt's words float and glow around me.

'May the power of the holy spirit reside within you ... In Jesus' name ... Amen.'

'Amen.'

I barely move my mouth. My eyes are soft and full of love.

I can't even feel my heart it's so cosy.

Something has changed. In a way I've always wanted.

Someone special has arrived.

I knew there was more.

God is real!

And I have proof.

I am proof!

I bathe in the gold shimmering inside.

I'm not alone.

25

There's a rainbow over Montello when I get home from camp. Slow drifting clouds have coated the streets in rain. The clouds are going white at the edges but there's still a layer of bruisy black storm behind them. Patches of blue are breaking through making it look like two different weathers at once. The glowing colour arch is projected onto the clouds, fading out at each end. A soft curvy stream of all the colours. It feels like a good sign.

I climb the steps and face the screen door. I'm nervous about what's on the other side. I think something in me has changed. I have a new confidence. Whatever happens with Mum or with the future, I'm not alone now – I'm a Christian, which means I'm part of God's team. Joppo gave us a Bible to work from. I'll be able to read it and pray and ask for help. Jesus can guide me and back me up.

Mum peers out cautiously from behind the screen door. She's still in her dressing gown, even though it's the afternoon. She says she was about to have a shower. As I step inside our unit I glance around the lounge, looking for clues for what Mum got up to while I was away. The silver ashtray is on the couch. There are takeaway containers on the sink. Mum got all kinds of fun food. I can still smell the hamburger. I stack the containers and scrunch up the empty wrappers and take them to the bin. She's going to put on weight.

'Oh just leave that, I was going to do it,' she yawns. 'How was camp?'

'Yeah it was really fun and we learned a lot about Jesus. I'll definitely go to the next one.'

'Oh, good.'

I stare at my blue certificate from camp. I won the 'shonky torch award (and generally a good bloke).' Hopefully I can make more of an impression next camp.

Mum lights a cigarette.

I'm excited to tell her about the prayer and the warm feeling, but I won't yet. I imagine myself back in the camp bunkroom in the dark. Did it really happen?

'How have you been?'

'Oh, just keeping busy,' Mum's eyes are wide. I can tell when she's pretending.

Already the house feels hollow. It's still school holidays so the street is quiet. It's Friday but it feels like a Sunday. There's a nagging feeling of not having anything to do. I go outside to find Blossom. My trampoline looks cold in the shade.

I crouch down and waddle through the gate to under the house. Sure enough, Blossom is in his basket. He was curled up asleep but is happy to see me. There are cobwebs and cold powdery dirt and white snail shells under the house. I used to play under here and once found an old newspaper from the 1950s. I sometimes think of Blossom under here in his basket. It seems like the right kind of stakeout for a deep, thoughtful cat.

I go inside and grab a lickety-sip and take my bag to my room. Mum's back on the bed.

Get Up Mum

'Hey Mum, you better get up now. It's afternoon.'

'In five minutes dear, I'll have a shower.'

I go back in the lounge and turn on the TV to watch the fourth test. West Indies are 5/134 but Lara's in. I wish Australia was batting. I wish Nigel was here. It feels so quiet now, after camp. I don't really feel like doing anything but I don't want to do nothing. I don't want to worry again. Mum needs to go shopping. I'm sure the floor needs a vacuum. The afternoon is on pause and it's heavy in my stomach. I can't start anything knowing Mum's just lying there. I clomp back to her bedroom.

'Mum, it's been more than five minutes!'

'Alright dear, I really will get up, I promise.'

I breathe out a heavy sigh. Why does Mum say she'll get up when she doesn't mean it? Does she care that it's annoying for me? I'm wasting my time when she should be spending it with me.

I'm getting pissed off now.

I grab the hall door and swing it as hard as I can. It doesn't even slam properly. It shuts with a soft bang. There's too much carpet underneath. I stand and listen to see if Mum says anything. Does she even care? I poke around the laundry. My cricket bat and ball are there but they're useless on their own. A line of ants have gone into the laundry sink. They form perfect circles around the three soggy cat biscuits. A beach towel hangs on a nail. It's nice outside now – why aren't we at the beach? There's waves going to waste.

I shove the hall door and squeeze the frames of Mum's doorway.

There's a lump in my throat.

There's a lump on the bed.

'Get up Mum!'

'Okay dear, in a minute,' Mum replies in a gurgle. She's lying on her side with her eyes open. What Mum is doing is worse than sleeping in. It's worse than being lazy. It's nothing! Mum is doing nothing and she doesn't even seem that happy about it. She's just an empty space in a lifeless room on a nothing day. The fire inside me spreads. I'm sick of this game. Angry at this game. I'm not going away.

I raise my voice in a whine.

'Get up!'

I don't think.

'NOW!'

I rip the rage from my gut. Ripples burn my throat.

My voice echoes against the bare white walls.

Mum sits up, slowly. I don't know whether to say sorry or scream again. Her eyes are bleary and pleading. Her voice is quiet.

'Don't shout please dear.'

That night the dark clouds roll in across the sea. This morning's rainbow is torn apart by an awesome storm. Heavy rain pelts down as distant grumbles are matched by flashes of lightning. God's crying while taking photos. I open the curtains wide and enjoy the scary show. I pat Blossum on the couch to let him know everything's okay. The downpour pummels away the silence. A rumble of thunder cracks across the sky. I feel a boom in my chest. Heavy weather surrounds the house. Wild seas and restless trees. As the rain dies down I set myself up in bed to listen to my favourite tape with earphones.

The Synthesiser Album is a tape I got Mum for Christmas but I've been borrowing ever since. It's an album of instrumentals so it's perfect for drifting off and daydreaming. The music has a special, separate atmosphere. I jump my powers of concentration from one layer to the next. The string melody, the keyboard sighs, the drumbeat and twinkly swirly bits hiding in the background. Each song is different from up-tempo to sad ones to action-adventure themes.

It brightens my mind as my feelings match the moods. Thinking is more fun when you're inside music. With the earbuds that Nigel got me for Christmas it sounds like the songs are connected to my brain. Each time I play the tape I'm in a different space and notice different details. Last year I played the tape during our trip to Lake Mackenzie. I couldn't believe how well it matched the drifting scenery.

A chorus of flutes swell as I float with angels. The drumbeat is dramatic and now I'm watching a battle in distant space. The chords become mysterious like magicians' music – it's a race against time to solve a riddle and save a kingdom. Then I come to rest in the peaceful chords and gentle beat.

The last song is 'Telstar', which is a bit of a silly one. It has the sound effects of a UFO landing at the start and sounds like an old sixties song except it's also futuristic. I imagine a beautiful alien princess kissing me. The tape ends in silence. Now I have the memory of all ten songs floating around my brain. I put my hand under my shirt and run my fingers over my ribs. I wonder where Jesus lives now.

The next day Mum and I head up to Parklands High to pick up my uniform and books. They come in two big brown paper bags. There's a compass and protractor, graph book, different pencils (6B, 2B, HB) and a scientific calculator with about fifty confusing buttons – suddenly I feel nervous. But I'm looking forward to school. I'll get to see my friends again. The holidays can get a bit lonely and I'm ready for a new challenge.

I watch cricket for the rest of the day. David Boon is batting. I cheer him on because he's Tasmanian and my favourite cricketer. Australia end up all out for 213 with Boon not out on 39. What a champion! Big Curtly Ambrose takes six wickets.

At least Mum was good while we were up at the school. She concentrated and seemed to fit in. I spread the exercise books over the floor and make a start on covering them. I cut out pictures of my favourite bands and girls and surfers and cars. I try to cover one book in contact but it comes out all crooked, full of wrinkles and bubbles.

'Mum! Can you come and help me!' I yell.

'What?' she calls in the distance.

'Just come and have a look.'

Mum emerges from the hallway and kneels down next to me.

'I can't do the contact. It goes all crinkly and crap.'

Mum's good at this kind of thing. She has fingernails and steady hands.

'Show us your ruler.'

I scrounge around the bag and pull out a white plastic one – Rulex. I watch Mum use it to smooth down the air bubbles. She takes a fresh book and shows me how to lay it out and cut squares out of the corners.

'Sorry I yelled yesterday.'

'No, that's alright dear. It's okay to get upset sometimes. Perhaps tomorrow we could go for a drive and have a barbecue at the park?'

We get chicken and chips for tea. I don't mind because at least it's a Saturday and it's normal to get takeaways on the weekend. Afterwards I set up a game of Monopoly. Mum is the thimble and I'm the racing car.

'If only it were real money Mum,' I say cheerily.

It's something she normally says.

She stares blankly at the dice.

'Yes.'

She plays along but I can tell she's not concentrating. She starts mashing her mouth and her eyes gather shadows.

I roll seven and land on Community Chest. 'Second prize in a beauty contest.' I always laugh at this one.

'Did you ever want to be a model, Mum?'

'No, I was too shy,' Mum says vaguely.

Her eyes twinkle as she sniffs at tears.

'Sorry, something's made me upset. I'll finish playing later.'

She makes a little moan as she wanders off. I sit at the table, flipping through the cards. I take the front door key off the hook and head outside. I walk to the Mace Street shop and buy a Golden Gaytime. I eat it on the park bench next to the phone box. When I'm finished I walk back home as slowly as I can, taking the long way round.

It's quiet when I return.

'Justin, can you bring me some Panamax?' Mum sniffs from her bedroom. I go to the cupboard and get a glass of water. I trudge into her room as she sits up. She takes the Panamax from my hand. The tips of her fingers are warm against my palm.

'Thank you dear.'

'Have you had your other tablets?'

'Yes, I took them before.'

I think back. Did I see her take them? Mum gulps the water with a squelch in her neck.

'Could you bring me some toilet paper?'

I go the bathroom and tear off a few sheets. I hand Mum the paper. She does a big blow.

'Oh.'

She gives a murmur and a sniff.
'I'll be right now.'
'What's upsetting you?'
'A thought from my past.'
'What?'
'Oh, just people Justin. Bad people who tried to hurt me.'
I sit, staring at the carpet, waiting.
'Can you stroke the top of my head?'
Mum lays her head on the pillow. Heat shines on her cheeks. I run my fingers over her scalp. The hair feels thin. The skin is hot.
Mum has hell in her head.

PART THREE
1993: Grade 7

26

It's my first day at Parklands! I'm standing in the quadrangle on my tippy toes scanning the crowd. Classroom windows loom overhead in every direction. We're all clustered in together, fresh and jiggly in our navy blue uniforms. I peer over the rough boys from Ridgley, the tall skinny girls and the cool kids with undercuts. There are mouths open wide to yawn and whispering away in a giggle. Backpacks are nursed between legs like penguin eggs. Everyone seems nervous.

The morning shade nips at my knees as I jiggle them back and forth. I dunno where Nick is. He's gonna be late for the first day of school! I can see Tennille in the corner. She has black stockings with white socks over the top and her arms crossed. She looks grumpy. I don't think she's as good looking anymore.

An older man with wavy silver hair and a smart grey suit stands at the front of the crowd of new students. He turns to a female teacher and then looks over her shoulder and down to his folder.

'Good morning everyone. My name is Mr Allardice. I'm the principal at Parklands High and it's my great pleasure to welcome you all here to your new school.'

My new school! I caught the bus this morning along with the other excited Montello kids. It felt like we were going to camp.

'I won't keep you standing too long, as you can tell the school does get quite cool of a morning. I can already see some familiar faces from your orientation day last year and I'm looking forward to getting to know the rest of you over the coming year.'

Mr Allardice speaks in a formal accent. He seems like a prim and proper man. I've heard that they give out the cane at Parklands. High school is where you can get into serious trouble.

'Soon enough you'll be going off and forming into your homeroom groups. I'm sure you're all full of beans and full of questions, and I know this is an overwhelming occasion so just take your time and remember that if you need help it is okay to ask any of the teachers on duty to help you. That's what we're here for. I hope you had a big bowl of corn flakes this morning because you'll be taking in a lot of information.'

Is Weet-Bix okay? Will I know where to go? What if I forget my locker combo? I'm wound up tight with everything I have to remember. I'm wriggling my fingers in my pockets. The first week back at school is usually pretty slow and foggy as you get back into school mode. I feel worried and then suddenly lonely. I think of Uncle Nigel and wonder what he's up to.

I'm in Nairana house so my homeroom is on the very top corridor known as 'Top C'. The corridors stretch up for yonks with several sets of stairs and across ways with ten classrooms on either side. Instead of drawings on the walls there are wooden bag racks and blocks of metal lockers so the whole place reminds me of Summer Bay High. This is where the grown-up kids go! Even the toilets seem more mature with a urinal.

I find the right class and take a seat. A cool blond haired boy wanders in and sits next to me. I can tell he's staring.

'My god! They're the thickest glasses I've ever seen.'

'Yeah, I'm short-sighted.'

'Hi Short-Sighted, I'm Billy.'

'Yeah,' I fumble and mumble, 'I'm Justin.'

'Okay Justin, I think I'm gonna call you Geek!'

'Hey Geek, I'm Hayden,' grins the boy next to us. He has bright eyes and a floppy undercut parted in the middle.

It'd normally be an insult but I'm so excited to be entertaining that I don't mind. In primary the kids would yell 'four eyes' and I'd have to say 'points for originality.'

'What footy team do you go for?' Billy asks.

'Carlton.'

We all go for Carlton. This seems like a good sign. I relax a little inside.

The first thing we have to do in homeroom is fill out a questionnaire. The one I find the hardest to answer is 'favourite song.'

9. I think most adults see me as a _thoughtful, reliable_ type of person.

10. I feel my friends see me as an _interesting, funny_ type of person.

11. The part of my personality I would like to improve is _my self-confidence_

12. The kind of person I get on best with is _someone with my same interests_

13. The kind of person I find it hard to get on with is _an arrogant person_.

14. The thing I find most enjoyable about life is _my success in things I try._

15. The thing I find most difficult about life is _the pressures of doing well_

16. If I ever had a difficult personal problem the person I would probably turn to for help would be _mum._

We drift out of home room on our first mini-adventure: finding Social Science in a room called B1. At high school you have six different periods and the classes are mixed up across each day. My timetable is a cryptic set of codes: H/E C6, MDT R6, S/S B1.

At Montello we kept all our books in our tubs or under our desks. At Parklands you have a locker and take whatever books you need for each class. The fun bit is our locks, which have a combination like a bank vault. You have to dial it twice right and once left and then right again. We've been told to keep them top secret. Mine is 26-20-8. Luckily I have a good memory for phone and rego numbers.

Billy already has his timetable folded down into a tiny square. He knows a bit more than me because his older brother used to go to Parklands. It turns out we have all the same classes. We wander down the stairs and turn into the first noisy, crowded corridor. 'Whatever you do, stick to the left,' Billy tells me, as we watch Hayden get cleaned up by a pair of grade tens. I can't believe how busy it is. There are two lanes of bustling arms and legs, clutching books and slamming lockers. I stick close to Billy as we dash into the first class of Social Science with light blue chairs, a clean blackboard and a cranky looking Mr Jordan.

'Jelly Belly' Jordan is an old Pommy with a comb over, magnified lenses and a big gut inside a tight red jumper. He hands out pieces of paper while threatening to fail us and recounting a wonderful trip he had to Geneva where he had a particularly enjoyable pork pie. I can see already that Billy and I will have plenty to work with.

Maths is in a small room in A block with red plastic chairs. Mr Dickenson is the teacher. He has a deep voice and a moustache that makes him seem very sensible. He hisses the s's in 'Axis' enough times for Billy and I to make it into a catchphrase.

At recess I finally find Nick, looking dazed and excited by the basketball courts. He's in Breone, which means we won't be in any of the same classes. We huddle by the basketball courts and swap stories with the other Montello boys. Elvis is already talking about the running spikes he's bought for the grade seven gift at the grade seven sports day. I chew on my rollup and watch the older kids strolling around in their gangs. They all seem so confident and relaxed and organised. It still feels like orientation day and we're just visiting Parklands.

Last year we were the kings of Montello. The tough kids had moved on and we could finally stop worrying and roam where we wanted. Dion points out how there aren't any four square lines drawn up because everyone plays basketball at high school. Four square has simple boundaries where you can hit the ball, like table tennis. You work your way up to 'king' until you get out and go back to 'one.' Basketball is too complicated. You have to know what you're doing.

The bell goes and Nick and I walk back to our lockers. His hair has grown in the holidays, giving him even more to shake out of his eyes.

'Are you still thinking of becoming Christian?' he asks.

'I'm not sure.'

'I wish I'd felt something.'

Speech and Drama is held downstairs in the 'dungeon' and seems like the first subject that might actually be fun. Miss Mcfadzean is a young woman with red hair and pale skin who shows us an improvisation game called 'Space jump.' Billy starts by digging a hole and then I come in and ask him why he's holding an elephant. The weirdest teacher is Mr Verze who takes us for Science. Billy and I are perched on stools up the back quietly cracking up at his nasally voice and wispy hair and the way he leans suspiciously on the corner of the desk. I'm so glad Billy's as silly as me.

At lunchtime he hangs out with kids he knows from Havenview and Brooklyn. Nick's nowhere to be found so Dion and Elvis and I join a game of 'Starlight' on the grass. Parklands doesn't have much bushland like Montello. It's mostly cement or lawn with a few big bushy trees. A long hill slopes down to the oval but that's out of bounds. The whole school is perched high up on a hill, so I can still make out the dark blue sea below.

In 'Starlight' a kid kicks the footy to the pack and whoever marks it is up. The ball gets drop punted high. Crap, it's coming right for me! I feel hard, sharp pressure on each shoulder as I'm forced forwards. The ball sails overhead as the weight pushes down painfully and lifts. The force bends me over as I totter forward and collapse onto the grass. A shock runs through me as I work out if I'm hurt.

'Capper!' Elvis yells. A chorus of boys are laughing.

I gaze up. A tall boy with a goatee grins down at me. His head blocks the overhead sun. He could be about twenty.

'Thanks Bottles!'

Dion and Elvis are in fits.

'The Coke bottle kid got Cappered!

It's my first day of high school and I've just been used as a stool.

And now I'm being called 'Bottles.'

I feel small.

27

First day, outta the way!

It's good to come home and throw my bag on the floor. My mind is buzzing from so many thoughts.

Mum's up, which is a good sign. She's had a shower and there are groceries on the bench. She made a real effort to be up earlier this morning for my first day of high school. Now she's on the couch with one leg tucked under, smoking quietly. A silver ashtray rests on her leg. She draws in gentle puffs, narrowing her eyes like she's questioning something.

'I know I shouldn't but it does relax me,' she says. I usually hate smokers but with Mum's Benson and Hedges I don't mind the smell. It's like the petrol fumes at the servo – there's something sweet and relaxing about it.

I tell Mum all about my first day. The different classes and teachers and canteen procedure.

'What's MDT?'

'Materials, design and technology. We're doing woodwork and learning how to engrave with a soldering iron.'

'What's a soldiering iron?

'No, soldering,' I laugh. 'It's like an electric pen with a hot tip.'

'Oh, you be careful won't you.'

Mum's smoke drifts towards me as her foot taps away on the carpet. I want to tell her something that's been on my mind for a while.

'Mum, at Camp Clayton on the last night our cabin leader said a prayer for us asking Jesus into our hearts. As he was saying it I felt a warm feeling inside, like a presence.'

Mum's eyes widen.

'Oh Justin you might have had divine intervention.'

'What's that?'

'It just means that God might have touched your spirit, that sort of thing.'

I fiddle with the elastic rim of the tablecloth, underneath the table. If I pull it a bit it snaps back.

'So I believe that God's real now and I've started praying at night and am thinking of becoming Christian.'

It's feels funny saying it out loud. Mum smiles and taps her cigarette.

'Oh, isn't that lovely that they'd do that for you. Yes, religion can be a great comfort. I know God has helped me a lot over the years.'

We've never been to church but Mum does have a Holy Bible next to her bed. The Jehovah's Witness lady brings her *Watchtower* magazine, which is about the only thing Mum reads.

She snubs the cigarette out neatly on the ashtray.

'When I was seventeen I lived in Hobart with my friend Isabelle who we called Izzy. She went to art school and I was staying with her in a boarding house. One night I woke up and I was looking at my feet and the next thing I know this outline of a spirit went like that on my foot.'

Mum swipes her hand across in mid-air.

'He just tapped me on the feet. It was an outline of a man, flittin' around like a fairy and then disappeared.'

'Far out,' I say, shifting positions. I feel a tingle down my spine.

'And then when I was in Norway I left Grong and went down to Oslo and stayed one night in an old folks home. I woke up and thought "Gee, there's something behind that curtain." I could feel it. Then this gold outline of hands went like this in front of me.'

Mum holds her hands up in the prayer position.

I feel another tingle.

'How long were they there for?'

'Not long, these gold shimmering hands.'

'And that really happened. You weren't dreaming?'

'No, I was wide awake.'

I picture the hands in my head. I'd die if anything appeared to me in the dark.

'Were you scared? Was it a ghost?'

'No I wasn't. They had a calming effect. I knew they were there to protect me. They knew I was sometimes on my own.'

'Has anything like that happened since?'

'No, not after the hands appeared. It must have been my guardian angel.'

Mum stares off to the side with a worried smile. She takes a deep breath and sighs and springs herself up. She empties her ashtray into the little brown bin. I stare out onto the street picturing the scene. Mum stays at the sink behind me, whispering to herself.

I open the letterbox to find an envelope addressed to me! It's from Joppo at Camp Clayton. I wrote to him not long after camp with some questions about God. He's written back on fluoro orange and green paper decorated with funny stickers. I wanted to know whether he forgives killers and people who commit adultery and still lets them into heaven. Joppo says the short answer is 'Yep.'

'That doesn't mean we can treat God like some sort of Santa Claus or tooth fairy though. We can't keep sinning 'cause we know we can just waltz up to god and say sorry knowing that he'll forgive us. That's not how the deal works.'

That seems fair enough. I wonder how you're supposed to know whether God has forgiven you then, if there's no sign.

My second question was 'If you are Christian, how do you know you are onto the real thing with so many religions around?' Joppo gives a long answer for this one, four pages!

He says that there's heaps of evidence to prove Jesus was on earth and one of them is our calendar is separated into B.C. and A.D.

'Now, do you think that when they started the calendar they sat around in a circle and had different people like Mickey Mouse, Superman, Buddha and when they span the bottle it just happened to land on the name Jesus? Christianity is the only religion where you can have a personal relationship with God. With other religions their so-called Gods are out of reach.'

'I suppose for me, Justin, the bottom line is that I've looked at all the evidence and I've experienced God change my life and I know it's the only real thing. I could give all the proof to someone else but unless they believed, they would find some excuse for the proof. I'd really encourage you to check it out for yourself, Justin, and if you come across anything that boggles you, just holla for me.'

Being Christian is a bit like being in a secret club with an imaginary friend who's actually real, but you can't be totally sure. It's seems quite complicated at times, especially with the difference between God and Jesus and the Holy Spirit. I don't quite get the difference between being Catholic and Christian either. It was good of Joppo to write. He's included a study book but the last thing I want is more homework.

That night I follow the reading plan in my 'Good News Australia' Bible. The pages are as thin as tracing paper and it's written in an old style that gets a bit repetitive. Each chapter is quite short and doesn't go into much detail. When Jesus is tempted by Satan it just says: 'Wild animals were there also, but angels came and helped him.'

I kneel down beside my bed and press my hands together. I close my eyes and form a prayer in my mind. I let the words flow out and whisper them into my hands. These are my most personal thoughts, my most important wishes. I picture each family member and ask God to watch over them. I concentrate on Mum the longest. There are different sides to her.

After praying there's a peace in my head. I feel whole and full in my heart. Amen can be like saying 'The End' to the day. I can imagine my prayer as a letter getting sent up to Jesus's or God's letterbox or whoever is up there now, I don't mind. As long as someone knows how much I care and can see that Mum and I are kind-hearted people who need a guardian angel.

There's a lot happening at school each day so I've bought a Countdown Diary. It has all the celebrity birthdays and quotes and photos. Pop keeps a diary and has a collection dating back to when I was a baby. It's nothing too exciting, just the weather and what they did that day. I like sitting next to him in the lounge while he writes away quietly. He uses school notebooks but still fills out the details on the front. (For subject he puts 'diary' and for school he puts 'home.'

I haven't kept one since grade two.

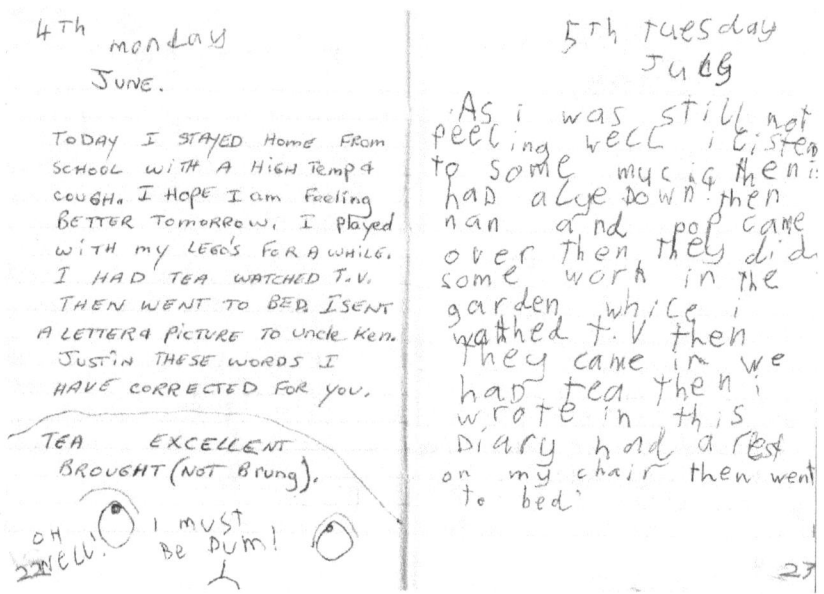

It's weird to look back at the days I once had. Sometimes Mum would write in it for me and help me with my spelling. I remember it being a good thing to do at the end of the day. Now high school feels like an important time in my life so I want to keep track.

I've been flat out with sport lately. I'm playing table tennis and cricket each week and we just had our state championships for surf club. I won gold in the beach flags! The next day I won the fifty and hundred metre freestyle at the school swimming carnival but missed out on age group champion. The grade seven gift was run like the Burnie Gift and we were given handicaps to run off. I was almost fastest with a handicap of five and even ran in running spikes but only managed third. Justabout!

The good news is Mum is definitely getting better! Each day more of her personality shines through. Her cooking's improved and the house is looking nicer. When I got home today she was over having a coffee with Barbara. Yesterday I caught her screwing up her lips but instead of yelling I just told her about Home Economics and how we're making a casserole carrier.

'We have to bring our own quilted fabric.'

Mum soon snapped out of it.

'Right, how much?'

The weather is fine on the weekend so I head outside to have a bounce on the trampoline. I can feel my hair flopping from the undercut I just got. I love sliding my hand up and feeling the spiky bristles on my palm. Mine's only a number four but at least it's something.

Mum's having a cigarette on the swing seat after doing some watering. She's wearing a colourful top I haven't seen in a while – a black windcheater with clusters of white and blue and mauve leaves.

'I like your top.'

'Oh thanks dear, yes it fits well when I'm not carrying too much weight.'

I tell her how the grade ten boys keep asking to try my glasses on. One puts them on and staggers around like he's drunk while the rest laugh. Billy reckons I'm becoming a celebrity.

'Some kids are just pillocks,' says Mum. 'They aren't that bad Justin. Nigel's were thicker than yours.'

'I don't mind because they're not really teasing me. They seem impressed that I can wear them.'

Mum says kids used to call her Goofy because of her shoes.

Mum pronounces it funny, so it rhymes with 'Sooty.'

'Just because Nan would get our shoes a size too big so we could grow into them. I dunno Justin, some kids are so strange at that age.'

'I remember in grade four I had a friend called Desley. She was a lovely little girl. Each morning we used to tell the teacher if we had any news. Desley said "My budgie died" and the other kids all laughed in chorus. I thought "How awful kids can be." I wouldn't have laughed. Not at a budgie.'

Blossum's a curved black outline on the back fence. He looks handsome against the pale blue.

'It's a shame I couldn't be myself when Nigel was here.'

'You're taking your tablets aren't you?'

'Yes and thank heavens I'm sleeping better. I don't know Justin, what comes over me sometimes. I wish I could be as strong as Nan. She doesn't let anything get to her.'

Mum's white smoke drifts and curls in the afternoon light. It's soothing to watch. I'd like to ask Mum why she keeps getting sick, but I'm a bit shy so I just keep bouncing, watching Mum and the world slide up and down.

28

Today I started hanging out with Billy and his group by the gym. They've all got cool basketball shoes with ankle socks and surf brand shorts and floppy hair with number one undercuts that are shaved to the top of their heads. I haven't been seeing Nick as much lately. He's started hanging out in the music room. Some mornings he comes to school looking pale and spaced out. His Mum is different to mine and doesn't care about when he goes to bed. He drinks coffee and stays up past twelve watching Steve Vizard and *Unsolved Mysteries*.

One the bus home I sit with Elvis who's too busy coughing to chat much. I press the red button and the bus bell clanks. I've figured out the best bus stop is the one past the brown diamond mural so I only have a short walk avoiding the German Shepard. I've got 'Heal the World' in my head – the girls were singing it on the bus.

'Heal the world, make it a better place … for you and for me and the anti-human race …'

Why is it the anti-human race?

Freezing breeze messes my hair as I scurry home. I knock

on the door and then remember it's Tuesday so Mum's at her housekeeping job. I grab the spare key from the white meter box. Inside are wild dials and humming metal discs that used to frighten me as a kid. I hurry inside, plonking my bag down and heading straight to the cupboard where I take out a bag of Violet Crumbles. I turn the heater on. It hasn't been used in yonks so I switch it to 'Auxiliary' – the bars glow red as the smell of burnt dust reaches my nose.

I slide in a video of my *Simpsons* compilation and press rewind. I take a chocolate square out of the bag and hold it in front of the heater bars. I press play with my little finger and lean back as the warm air swirls around my bare legs. Once the Violet Crumble is warm and melty enough I clamp my teeth around it and carefully nibble each side off. The top is the thickest layer and comes off the easiest.

Now the square is stripped gold. I start in on the honeycomb. The spit on my tongue brushes the honeycomb and it melts electric. It shoots sparkles down my tongue and makes my tummy sing. I chomp and munch away and watch my favourite cartoon.

Lisa tells Ralph that she only gave him a Valentine's Day card because she felt sorry for him. Bart is showing her slow-mo footage on video. He clicks the remote frame by frame, which I used to do sometimes so I could read the fast writing in the opening credits of *Fast Forward*.

'Watch this, Lise. You can actually pinpoint the second when his heart rips in half ... and now.' Ralph's head shrinks into his body as he closes his eyes and bears his teeth. You can hear his groan even though the video's in pause mode.

The episode wraps up and I go into the kitchen to put away the bag. There's a fresh packet of photos sitting on the table. I flick through the dull ones of Nan's garden and bushwalks. There's the lounge room covered in Christmas wrapping, my traditional photo of the 'Christmas mess.' Nan carrying a big bowl of punch down to the barbecue on New Year's Eve. There are a couple of Nigel and I playing on my backyard waterslide for the first time. I feel a slight ache as I remember the sun and the spray.

I drum my fingers on the table.

Righto. Now what should I do?

Mum's still not back so I'll have a quick poke around her room. It's looking neat and tidy today. Her bed is made and a light pink bedspread over the top. The air smells fragrant from the potpourri and perfume she wears when she's well.

I open her wardrobe and brush my fingers over the racks of dresses. The material is cool and soft with the occasional scratchy, fuzzy jumper. There's a black satin shirt with green flowers on it that Nan made for her to wear to a disco and a brown jumper with a koala on it, which I've never seen her wear. On the top shelf is an old jigsaw puzzle box chockablock with greeting cards. Mum must have kept every one she's ever gotten (and in some cases, given)!

Some of the cards haven't even been written in. There's orange butterflies against golden sunsets, close-ups of dandelions and bouquet candles with fancy gold writing and 'Thinking of You.' That's what Mum's best at – being thoughtful. Sometimes she has too many thoughts.

She often writes to Nigel and Ken with copies of my cartoons and schoolwork.

'I always make an effort to keep in touch,' she says, 'because not everyone has time.'

Mum makes time.

I pick out a big blue one with a little boy in a basket being carried by a stalk.

Hang on – this card is for me!

'Happy Birthday baby Justin. First birthday. 1981.'

This is the first I've seen it. It's funny to think of myself being alive but having no memory of it. All that playing and sleeping and crying and eating while I was stuck in a big baby dream. I love how Mum bought me a card even though I couldn't have any idea. I feel special. My chest shimmers with love. I'm lucky to have the Mum I do.

Mum's room has the same inbuilt dresser as mine – a small alcove next to the wardrobe with a mirror. She uses her space to put all the old history books she collects from the library sales. At the moment she's mostly interested in Egypt and stories about the old pharaohs. But I've never really seen her reading them.

The last time I remember Mum reading a book was maybe when I was in Grade Three. It was one about Mozart. I remember hearing her in bed giggling out of her mind. I might have been worried that she was getting sick because she was dabbing at tears. I asked her what was so funny and she read the part to me. It was describing how Mozart used to walk quickly and he referred to himself as 'old scissor legs.'

Mum started laughing all over again, imagining his legs going like scissors.

I cracked up too – I could see how silly it was.

Close to the bedroom door is a wooden set of drawers. On top sits Mum's jewellery box and knick-knack collection. There's a diamond necklace and pins and pendants and an old style fob watch and nametag from when Mum was a mothercraft nurse. This is where she looked after other people's babies that had just been born.

Mum did a training course at Calvary Hospital in Hobart sometime before she went to Norway. In the photo album there's a black and white picture of Mum being presented her certificate by an archbishop in robes. Mum is young and pretty with her shiny cheeks and shy smile. She's wearing her uniform of white gloves and cap and a cape. She looked like little red riding hood.

After she returned from Norway she went back to Calvary to work as a mothercraft nurse. She said it wasn't as good then because there were different nurses to the ones she trained with. Then she had to move back to Burnie and worked at the Burnie hospital for a while. That was a couple of years before she had me. Sometimes I wish Mum was still a nurse.

I check the drawers in the lounge. The one on the left is mostly games and colouring stuff while the right side is Mum's greeting cards and old sunglasses. I like the lolly tins Mum brought back from Holland. One has a black and white photo of a young girl wearing a nurse uniform.

In one of the drawers buried under papers is 'The Sesame Street Library' volume with Big Bird on the cover. *Sesame Street* was always my favourite show when I was little. I'd watch it in the morning and then again in the afternoon. Mum wanted to watch *The Sullivans* in the afternoon but I'd demand to watch *Sesame Street* again.

'But you've already seen it this morning!'

I'd grizzle and get my own way. I was so young. I should have shared.

I flick through Big Bird. In the white borders it has my red texta scribbles. This was from when I was in bed trying to read and Mum was crying in her bedroom. I started drawing spirals to keep track of the volume levels. When Mum was quieter I'd draw small spirals. When the howling got louder the spirals would stretch. That's my first memory of Mum's symptoms. I didn't know what it was but I knew it wasn't right.

29

Today we have double PE with Mr St John. Normally this would be something to look forward to but today we're doing dancing! They're daggy barn-room dances like 'Pride of Erin' and 'Heel and Toe Polka' that involve choosing partners and holding hands so Billy and I are nervous.

Parklands has a huge indoor gymnasium and basketball court where the assemblies are held. It's pretty cold this time of morning but there's already heat building under my arms. I'm wearing my new Kuta Lines top that Mum got off layby. It's a fawn mottled T-shirt with long black sleeves and a hood. It's my first proper surf brand clothing and so I hope I look cool.

The girls are sitting quietly in a group on the ground while the boys are standing around opposite them. The boys have to choose first. I locate Bianca.

Bianca is pale and mousy with a brown ponytail, bright blue eyes and pale skin that gets so cold she has to pull her jumper sleeves over her hands. She's shy and quiet whereas her best friend Sarah (who is also pretty) is a tall tomboy. They're both squares who sit up the front but they're also sporty and friendly so they're okay.

Each day I add to the clues about whether Bianca might like me or not. Part of me would like her to know I like her but then I think I don't want anyone to know. Sometimes I look at Bianca until our eyes meet. I feel a zap and quickly look away. When I look again she's usually not looking, which is a relief and a disappointment.

Boys are walking up to the girls so now it's a race. I scurry over to Bianca.

'Ah, Bianca?'

She looks to the side and smiles with her mouth closed. I can see her braid and green band up close. She's wearing a long-sleeved white T-shirt tucked into black shorts. Her knees are patched with pink and white.

'Okay take your partner's hand. Don't be shy – they're not going to bite!'

Bianca and I take each other's hand. We look at Mr St John. Bianca's fingers are smooth and delicate. I hope my hands don't shake.

'Now put your hand around their waist!'

My palm rests gently on Bianca's curve. I've never touched a girl there. It feels nice. We're looking anywhere but at each other when suddenly the music starts.

Now we're skipping and we're slapping and we're twirling and now Bianca's gone. Now I'm dancing with Melanie who has her windcheater pulled over her hands. She doesn't want to get boy germs. I watch Bianca skip away around the circle, hoping to catch her eye and feel a zap again.

After PE we have to shower. This is one of the big differences between primary school and high school. The showers are all together in one big block. At surf club you get your own cubicles. I don't stay under for very long – just long enough to get wet. A fat kid called Michael is already being teased because of his funny-looking doodle. I don't look. Sometimes it's good not being able to see much without my glasses. The air is thick and sweet with Lynx Java deodorant.

'You and Bianca looked pretty comfortable together!' says Billy.

QUOTE OF THE WEEK
"Prince is half-gorgeous and half-repulsive and that's probably why I like him. Sometimes he's just so gross but that kind of excites me."
Kylie Minogue

5 Monday yep, I love bianca. A lot. She is gorgeous. Went to Paul's. Mucked around. BYE

BETTE DAVIS 1908

6 Tuesday School was good I ♡ B.S. Not going to ask her out yet. Table tennis was average. SEE YA

CANDACE CAMERON 1976

7 Wednesday School was cool. Ryan busted up sarah in Manual Arts! Boy it was funny. went to TT we won 10-1. LATER MAN

I'm writing in my diary in the lounge when Mum appears, fresh from the bathroom. She has a towel wrapped around her hair like a beefeater's hat. Sweet steam drifts into the room. Her face is covered in white

'Is that your "night magic"?' I ask from my beanbag.

'Look out, it's a ghost!' says Mum.

I love Mum's face.

The midweek lotto draw comes on the TV and that means *Melrose Place* is nearly on.

I call out to Mum who is tottering around the kitchen waiting for the kettle to boil, the towel still wobbling on her head.

'Coming.'

I draw the curtains and switch on the lamp above the TV. Mum switches off the lights in the kitchen and lounge room. We like to create the right atmosphere for *Melrose*. Mum carries over her drink and gets in position. I can smell blackcurrant.

'I've got my hot toddy!' she says.

I've got my rainbow popcorn. We're set.

The electric guitar theme plays.

'What are they up to this week?'

'Michael's having an affair with that other doctor Kimberley.'

'Oh dear,' Mum says with a sigh

Melrose Place is about a group of twenty-somethings who live in an apartment block in LA. Everyone is cool and sexy and always finding excuses to take their clothes off. It's about as far from our block of flats as you can get. They even have a pool and each scene starts with a shot of a guy cleaning it. Billy and Jake have muscly chests while Alison and Jane have tanned, shapely legs.

Mum thinks it's funny how they always have perfectly manicured hair, even when they've just got out of bed.

'I wish I looked that good first thing in the morning. Instead of like a bomb's gone off!'

I laugh.

Michael and Kimberley are in an elevator at the hospital. Michael whacks the 'stop' button and they start going to town. The love scenes get a bit uncomfortable so it's good to joke.

'They look like they're trying to eat each other.'

'Everyone's tearing each other's clothes off. Going at it like there's no tomorrow,' says Mum.

'As if that would happen at a hospital,' I say.

The scene fades as they're unbuttoning their clothes. I often wonder what happens after.

In the next scene Michael comes home and asks for Jane to open a bottle of Chardonnay.

'Chardonnay,' Mum says in her 'Cambridge' voice. 'Go and open a bottle of Chardonnay for me Justin!'

Mum's back to her funny self.

Billy and Allison live together but aren't going out. Mum and I want them to get together but Amanda from D&D Advertising used to go out with Billy and keeps sticking her nose in.

Billy's at home on his computer with no shirt on. Mum and I laugh.

'He must get hot doing all that typing Justin.'

Mum isn't happy with Michael having an affair.

'Ya randy old thing!'

Mum always goes on about people having affairs and divorcing. She's very traditional about marriage and seems to take it personally. She's very disappointed in Charles and Diana having an affair.

'After that big lavish wedding and standing in front of everyone saying the sacred vows … I don't know Justin, some people need to be clocked on the head!'

I'm not sure why she cares so much. Perhaps she thinks it's unfair because she never got to marry.

Alison's confronting Michael in the laundry about him

kissing Kimberley in the hospital parking lot. Alison is shy and good-hearted while Michael is smarmy and selfish. Michael throws a towel over his shoulder and leans in menacingly.

'Guys are like that Alison. You know sometimes we need variety. Sometimes we need to feel good about ourselves. Sometimes we can't say no to temptation!'

It fades to black and my favourite ad comes on. It's for Uncle Toby's porridge and features the goofiest, dorkiest kid I've ever seen.

'That's NO how you make porridge!'

His hair is flat and his buck teeth stick out as he peers into the camera. It's funny in an embarrassing way.

'Everyone needs softness, needs a little care ...'

A little kid is in the bath. Her rubber duck turns into a duckling. The mum dries the girl in a white towel. The little girl dries the duckling with a tissue.

'Put some Kleenex tissue softness in your life.'

My chest aches. The screen goes to black.

Jane has found out about Michael and Kimberly's affair because he was supposed to be at work but instead he has sand in his shoes. Mum says he's got half the beach in there and I laugh. It's looking like this is the episode where Billy and Allison will finally get together.

Crack!

My heart jolts.

I whip round.

It's Mum! She's cracking nuts.

'Sorry dear,' she smiles. 'Do you want an almond?'

QUOTE OF THE WEEK
"I got a takeaway burger in LA the other day and inside the box was a pair of panties and a phone number. I guess you gotta expect that when you ask for the lot."
— Luke Perry

10 Monday Bianca knows I like her. That's something. raining today didn't do much. had nice fish for tea. SUMPAI JUMPAH!

BONO (U2) 1960; YOUNG MC 1967

11 Tuesday Pretty quiet day considering. School was good. Mr Jordan is funny. Did some practise for cross country. BYE.

12 Wednesday School was cool. went to table T. Elvis was banned so we only won 6 games. had tea with mum and pop. SEE YOU.

BILLY DUFFY (THE CULT) 1961; EMILIO ESTEVEZ 1962

13 Thursday I've given up on Bianca. she likes Billy so he can have her. I've decided she's too dull. had swimming training. that was hard. I must win cross country. BYE MAN

1993

14 Friday Bianca is only shy. I still like her. Dilly is a good mate. Came home. Went over to ~~nan and p's~~. ~~watched T.v.~~ Nich S. to sleep. Played 113M watched T.V. ~~Seega~~

DANNY WOOD (NEW KIDS ON THE BLOCK) 1970; C.C. DEVILLE (POISON) 1959; DAVID REYNE 1962

15 Saturday stayed up till 5am. went to showcell came home at 3.30 went over to nan and p's. I was pretty tired so I went to bed early Good Night!

16 Sunday went with field nats to a place near devonport. was a good walk. Came home watched T.V. Trained for F.V. cross country Carlton lost to Footscray. ~~see yerier~~

TRACEY GOLD (GROWING PAINS) 1969; JANET JACKSON 1966

Notes

BIG LENNY NO:2. Dan 4!

30

It's a cold overcast day when we set off for Greens Beach. Mum and I went over to Nan and Pop's early in the morning to load up the car and hook up the caravan – we're even taking Sparky along for the trip. There was the usual buzz of last minute packing and checking and hypertension. But I've got my bat and ball and Coke and chocolate so I'm happy. The all-important stereo is nestled away beneath the doonas in the boot. It's school holidays and my birthday soon! And Mum's well so we can all have a breather.

Nan starts her backseat driving, from the front seat.

'You take it slow around those corners Len – you're carrying a big load!'

'I know what I'm doing!' he grumbles. Pop's a good driver.

I slip on my Walkman headphones and press play on the *Synthesiser Album*. I like listening to music on car trips – it's a way to escape that isn't considered rude. I don't feel like I'm missing out either because I can still hear my family, I just don't have to take it all in. I've got thinking to do. I've got places to go inside the sounds. I'm rolling along a runway of oceans and fields and hills.

Get Up Mum

Mum's tucked up quietly in the backseat next to me. She nurses her head on her hand and stares out the window too.

We arrive at a completely empty Greens Beach Caravan Park. It lives up to its name with a golf course next to a grassy oval. The sea is misty and choppy in the distance. It's too cold for swimming but there's plenty of beach for rock hopping and fishing. I'm looking forward to a nighttime walk or two.

Setting up the caravan is wicked fun. There's latches to unlatch and canvas to secure and legs to unwind. The first mission is to wind the pop top. As chief winder I unclip the flap and insert the square handle in the hole and start winching like crazy. The clacking motion causes the roof to rise and slowly a house appears.

I'm stretched out on my stomach with my head inside the fridge. The tricky bit with the caravan is getting it level. Once we unwind the four legs and adjust the jack at the back my job is to monitor the little bubble inside the fridge. I like being first inside the caravan, which smells all sweet and musty. I use the opportunity to slide my stereo into position and press record. I want to capture all the different stages of our holiday with interviews and commentary along the way.

Without Nigel and Ken we're back to our usual routine. Nan's on the warpath, Pop's in trouble and Mum's staying out of it.

'Aww what have you done? All you had to do Len was move those two bottoms ones 'cos all these other ones were correct!'

'I know it's them two.'

'Well go back and do it and leave these top ones alone.'

She stomps past me.

'Look out Justin! He's so stupid!'

I don't like Nan calling Pop names.

While her and Pop have it out, I narrate to the tape.

'Well here we are at Greens Beach on the west side of the Tamar River, up towards the North. We haven't been able to find the manager. He's probably out to golf. We're just setting up. This is normal caravan procedure. If you're wondering why there's so much arguing. Well, we can't get this level right. And we've been struggling a bit.'

Clomp. Clomp. Clomp.

Nan storms back in, eyes a-scowl, mouth downturned. She looms, hands on hips, blocking the light in the doorway.

'You're not even doing anything, thank you very much!'

I am doing something!

I'm documenting.

It's just turned winter so it's pretty cold in the caravan. It's good for our drinks but not for Pop, who feels the draft coming in through the door. With a beer in her hand Work Nan cheers into Relaxed Nan. Her beady eyes pick out my red light.

'You rotten little cow!'

After tea I'm eager for a night walk adventure along the beach. To my surprise Nan takes a bit of convincing.

'I'll get home before he gets me too cold. I'll kick his bum if he doesn't.'

Mum starts the washing up. Nan reminds her about boiling the kettle for hot water.

'I know!' says Mum in a high pitch.

Nan and I step out along the grass. The cold slaps my face awake as I gulp in the crisp, salty air. The best part of camping by the sea is lying in bed listening to the hush of the waves. Nan does a big sniff and cranes her neck to the sky.

'It's a beautiful clear night. I can make out the pot.'

'Paddy's Lantern is big and bright,' I say.

Tomorrow there's a lunar eclipse. The moon will pass through the centre of the earth's shadow. I'm not sure what it means, but it sounds cool.

'Oh, feel that air fresh in your lungs! Isn't it good to be alive?'

I'm glad to have Walking Nan to myself. I like Nan's dramatic language. It makes every conversation a memorable one. Her action words are always original. Nan says 'I had to peel my jumper off twice today' instead of 'take it off.' Instead of 'I got scratched in the garden' she says 'My roses attacked me.'

We head down to the empty beach. The sea at night is secretive. A band of white foam blending in with a runway of grey. It laps over the sand as it swells towards high tide. Dad has to do the washing up too.

We scrunch over the softer sand and head towards the water where it's firmer. Distant house lights bookend the bay. Out on the horizon I see a dot of red light blinking to greet me.

'We'll get out to the jetty early tomorrow and get a good possie for high tide. Let's see if you can't catch two fish on one line like you did at Bridport!'

Nan's enthusiastic. 'Can't' isn't in her vocabulary. She gets jobs done and makes things happen. She wants to get to the top of the mountain and the bottom of a problem.

'Where to now lad? I'm following you this time.'

I survey the scene. I'm nervous about leading us astray. Nan's bushwalking head torch is strapped snugly to my head. Whichever way I look, the light beams ahead.

I suggest we follow the beach around and see where it ends up.

Nan's hand grips my shoulder as she points upwards.

'Can you see the brightest star up there Justin? I think that one's Jupiter!'

I squint up. The light from the head torch can't reach that high. Strong bright points stand out against the black dome. A misty cluster marks the Milky Way.

'One day in the future Justin, when I'm gone, you'll be able to look up and say "There's Nan". I'll be Jupiter in the sky. You'll be able to say, "There's Nan, looking down on me."'

I feel suddenly worried as I memorise Nan's words and block out the idea.

I can't think about a future without Nan.

I'll never forget Nan or her words.

I'm the recorder now.

The next day we head down to the jetty at Garden Island to fish. It's a small path that juts out overlooking the Tamar River. I get a possie on the rocks between Nan and Mum. Nan wants me to watch her set up my rod so I can learn how to do it myself. I'm on holidays! I don't need to be learning anything.

Nan baits my hook nice and secure with a piece of frozen whitebait. There's nothing worse than your bum going numb only to find you've got a bare hook. Nan pierces the beady, unblinking eye and bends the tail around. I wish fish would close their eyes.

I'm not sure how I feel about the killing of fish. I guess Jesus caught five thousand to feed all those men. Apparently it's not counted as murder if it's hunting, just like it's not a criminal offence if you kill someone during a war.

We manage to catch a couple of fish. Nan does the gutting and Mum fries them up for lunch. Delicious!

Australia are in England right now playing for the Ashes. I've been listening to the coverage on my Walkman.

'Who's winning?' Mum asks.

Test cricket doesn't really work like that. I drum my fingers on the kitchen table to the horse racing song.

'D-rum d-rum d-rum rum-rum!'

Mum's eyes the stereo beside me.

'What station are you putting it on?'

'What do you mean? I'm taping it.'

'Oh, are you?'

She sounds unsure.

Nan comes back from the toilet block. She's lost her comb. Well, actually, she's trying to work out which one of us lost her comb. I point out that she was probably the last one to use it.

'Not me. I'm too responsible.'

'Yeah, but you did your hair over there. You came over here with your hair done.'

She claims I used it last, so I'm a suspect too.

'You blame everyone except yourself,' I say quickly. 'What about you? You could have lost it.'

'I know I could've.'

'Well?'

'I'm checking you out.'

'Well I didn't.'

Nan's latest nickname for me is 'Absent Minded Professor'. Apparently I'm clever but forgetful – I lose things and don't put the toilet seat down. I don't think I'm any worse than other kids my age. I probably left my goggles behind at Surf Club once when I was eight and Nan's never forgotten.

'Do you know what you're going to get me for my birthday?'

'I have no idea,' says Nan flatly, tidying away dishes. She's back to Work Nan.

'What you're hinting at is dollars and dollars and dollars.'

I've been hinting at an IBM computer. It would be

educational as well as improving my hand eye coordination. I do an impersonation of Nan.

'A cake of soap and a washer will do me.'

'That'll do,' she says briskly.

Mum laughs.

That night we go for out for a counter meal at the Golf Club. I love how the cutlery comes in packets and there's always a slice of orange on the side of the plate. I order a raspberry and lemonade drink and ask for twenty cent pieces so I can play the *Galaga* game in the corner.

I swap Mum some chips for a baked potato with dinner. Nan finishes up on a Drambuie liqueur. By the time we get home Nan's tiddly and hilarious. She props herself up in bed and takes her shoes off.

'Peeew!' says Pop, sitting at the kitchen table.

'Pop you're supposed to kiss their feet not sniff at them!' jokes Mum.

'He wouldn't know,' says Nan.

'Nan you're supposed to pose in the nude and Dad's supposed to kiss your feet,' Mum laughs as she talks. 'And then they put you in the *Woman's Day* for the whole of Australia to look at.'

She's referring to Fergie and the toe sucking scandal. I like Mum's joke.

'Where's me thing-er-mi-ricks,' Nan slurs.

She can't find her hormone patches or her pyjamas or the opening of her sleeping bag.

'God woman,' Mum says under her breath. 'You're disorganised aren't ya?'

The way she says it reminds me of Uncle Nigel.

I want to go for another nightwalk.

'C'mon Nan,' I say meekly.

'No way, look at me stripped off!'

'You still want to go?' Mum asks.

'Yes, take Mum for a walk like you took Nan last night. It was lovely. If Mum wants to go please do it.'

'We won't go for a very long one.'

I want to go but also stay to catch Nan being funny.

'Shit, I can't get me leg in.'

I cackle and cough. At least I've got the tape running. I tell Mum we should go along the beach.

'We might go along the road perhaps.'

Far out, it won't be as fun without Nan. Mum's got a sense of humour but not a sense of adventure.

31

It's a groggy, foggy morning in the caravan. I'm trying to sleep in but it's not really possible in a space this size. The best I can do is hide inside my bag. I've just heard the devastating news that I've been nominated to go to the shops to get stuff for breakfast. Rumour has it that if the sugar situation gets any worse, Pop may have to resort to using honey in his tea! This kind of rationing hasn't been seen since wartime.

My legs are smooth and warm inside my inner sheet. I'm a baby emu, gangly and folded inside a cocoon. My hands are in prayer and pressed between my thighs. I'm not ready for outside. I ferret my nose under the covers.

I reach for the recorder on the end of the couch, covered with cushions. I'm trying to collect all the different time periods in caravan life. I haven't recorded the bustle of breakfast yet.

'Morning on the fifth day,' I say just loud enough for the tape to hear.

'Awwwwwwwwwwn.'

I let out a power yawn. It's going to take a lot of air to light a fire under this bum.

Nan's spills something near the stove. She stifles a swear word.
'Sssssssssssssh.'

It's my least favourite sound. For a second I shiver.

'I don't wanna get dressed.'

'It's so we can have sugar on our breakfast,' says Nan.

'Oh look Pop's up. What a coincidence.'

I think Pop should go. It'll be good exercise for him.

'Yaaaaaaawn!' Woah. Big yawns are fun. I stretch out like a horse on its back in the sun.

I watch Nan use the clicker to ignite the gas. In the mornings she doesn't do her hair. It juts out in a long clump and hangs there. Streaks of grey waft through her wispy mane. It makes her look older but a bit friendlier. I tell her it's a mess.

'My hair's a mess?' she says, sounding defensive. 'I like my hair. It makes me look more like an old witch than I really am an old witch.'

'That's your opinion,' I say. I won't be tricked into offending Nan.

Sparky's going berserk in his cage with a steady stream of laser chirps and static chatter.

'Good morning,' he says in his birdie voice. It sounds like a robot through a walkie-talkie.

'Good morning, eh, how are you?' Pop replies jollily from the table.

'Good morning!' beams Nan. 'Lovely day!'

I shed my goose down cocoon as slowly as I can and try and find my last clean T-shirt.

'You going down are you Justin?' says Pop. He's the last one to know.

'Mum told me to.'

Nan hands me a ten and a five.

'Justin don't lose any of that please.'

Nan has a sour tone. She's grouchy this morning.

Lucky she said that. I was planning to let the money blow out of my hand!

I repeat the shopping list.

'Orange juice, sugar, margarine, milk.'

As soon as I step out of the caravan, I hear Nan and Pop start to argue.

'I wonder if we needed all those things.'

'You're confusing the boy. You'll squark if you haven't got your sugar.'

'Just thinking about him carrying it all,' says Pop gently.

'God! He's not a baby anymore! Just hold your tongue.'

'Might be a bit much.'

'He's a man,' she says briskly. 'He's doing a man's job.'

'What are you doing?' says Sparky, doing a bird's job.

It's my first grocery shop! Well, not counting buying cat food and milk at home, but never a whole shop. The bell jingles as I push open the door of the corner store. I scan past the breakfast cereals to where the sugar is. I recognise the CSR one Nan uses for the home-brew. There are a few different margarines, but only Mrs McGregor's has the 'INSTANT WIN!' Nan and Pop usually get orange and mango fruit drink but I'm excited to try the fancy 'Valencio' orange juice. We can treat ourselves because we're on holiday.

I feel shy and self-conscious putting the items on the counter. The bloke looks at the price tag on each item and stabs the buttons on his register. I wonder if he thinks I've run away from home or live in a caravan by myself.

The wind smacks my jacket as I walk back on a path across from the beach. I feel quite mature with my plastic bag of groceries. I didn't even spend any of Nan's money on lollies. The caravan is warm with the smell of toast. Pop's happy to see me.

'My boy! I just put honey in me tea.'

Ye gods! I was too late.

'Told you he could handle it,' says Nan flatly.

'I bought some different things,' I mumble, 'I was trying for a change.'

Nan turns and scans the items with her beady eyes.

'You bought the dearest one. You didn't look for the cheapest!'

My heart flutters. Did I do it wrong? I bought everything she said we needed.

'What sort of sugar did you want?'

I was in a fun little trance at the shops. Now I have a bad feeling in the bottom of my tummy.

'You know, I hope you didn't get white, because we don't use it,' says Nan.

'Why not, it's the same as brown … sweetens it the same,' I say quickly.

'I really don't like white sugar.'

There's pressure in my throat. My voice sails high.

'What's the difference between white and brown? Absolutely none!'

'There is,' says Nan.

'The taste dear,' says Mum gently. 'Don't worry,' she adds with a laugh.

I feel a prickly heat in my chest. This tiny room. Some kind of regret. I'm panicking.

'I knew I should not have sent you,' says Nan.

'You only wanted a small one Justin,' says Pop, holding the big tub of margarine.

'I only got this margarine because you can win money on it.'

I give a little laugh. I'm trying to lighten the mood. There's no Nigel to back me up.

'He might've looked at all these items before he bought them Maureen.'

Heat rises as I clench inside. Now I'm fed up. Nan's talking about me like I'm not here!

'What's wrong?'

My pitch is high.

'Jeez. Aren't you happy with anything I do?'

It's suddenly very quiet. A cavern of space. I stare at the brown carpet, underneath the table, next to Pop's socks.

'Yes, thank you dear,' says Mum.

'I didn't say I wasn't happy,' says Nan grimly.

Dark ripples spread on my skin. A buzzing crawl.

'I didn't say I was unhappy Justin. If that's the way you took it. That's your fault!'

I keep my eyes on the floor. I can't bear the thought of Nan's eyes.

She's behind me, at the grill. Her back is turned.

I can't look. I can't have Nan mad at me.

'Yeah, you said I should've seen the price on everything ...' I mumble. I don't want a fight. I don't know what to do so I open the margarine to see if we've won. Nan scrapes away at toast. I can feel something's totally wrong. There a planet of silence and I'm spinning around it.

My throat tightens – the worry explodes.

'No it'll be right!' Mum sounds impatient.

'It doesn't matter what sugar we have!'

I watch Mum's mouth. There's a quiver in her lip.

This feeling is awful. I'm cross at being in trouble. I'm in trouble for being cross.

'I'll have a bit of orange juice Maureen,' says Nan.

I stay frozen. I don't want to know if she's ignoring me.

Does she not like me anymore? Did I let her down? I'm so confused. I peel the protective layer off the margarine. My hands are shaking. I have to know what's happening. I have to know!

Nan clinks and clanks, carrying on as normal.

Where am I? Am I in a fight? Am I in my family?

Was I too silly? Can I take it back? Will everything be alright?

I'm with my family but I'm alone and my voice has shrunk. The cold spreads across my chest. I'm numb and dumb.

Nan's on my side. I'm her Justin.

The margarine lid says 'second chance draw.'

'Oh no, we didn't win anything,' I joke.

'You didn't believe you would, did you?' says Nan.

SHE TALKED TO ME! The space is coloured in. Everything is okay.

I ask Pop not to shake the orange juice up. I don't like the bits.

'That's what you're supposed to have!'

Nan's voice rises in a pitch of disbelief.

Whoops. Wrong again. What to say.

Shut up Nan.

32

I wake up cosy in my bedroom in Burnie. We're all back from camping and it's still school holidays.

I look at my watch.

7.29.

Excellent!

The two famous people born on June 12 are the Australian fast bowler Terry Alderman and the bloke from Roxette, Per Gessle.

I was born at 7.33am.

'Like the records that you play at thirty three and a third speed,' as Mum says.

My tradition is to count down the final moments.

There's four more minutes of being twelve.

Four more minutes of being a kid.

This is big. Soon I'll be a teenager.

7.30.

Each year it's a chance to do nothing but watch time for a whole minute. My watch is on the exact time because yesterday I rang up 1194 and the man said 'On the third stroke it will be …' This is my way of celebrating – a quiet time to reflect, just for me – before I open the door and Mum greets me and the celebration begins.

I think about my childhood and the past. I used to go to the phone box around the corner on Mace Street and press any buttons and pretend I was talking to Mickey Mouse and Donald Duck. Once I dialled the operator by accident and a woman's voice answered and I dropped the phone and ran home, thinking I was in trouble.

7.31.

Orange, green and blue. Those are the colours I remember from when I used to help Pop work in Cosi Cartie's garden. The orange of carrots he'd pull from the ground. The green of the lawn. The blue of the sky. Pop and I exploring someone else's garden. White moths and rainbow mist, grabbing handfuls of freshly cut grass.

Seeing the tall ships with Mum in Hobart. Some teenagers had a skill tester where you had to move a small metal ring around coils of wire. If the ring touched the wire it buzzed. I had three goes. My hand wobbled and I buzzed. I tried going faster, which made it shake less, but I wasn't good enough. I remember how the boy and girl smiled and were kind to me.

7.32.

At the Civic Centre in Burnie we saw a play of Snow White. The characters were gathered down at Kmart. One of the dwarves took a step backwards and trod on my foot. His heel was so hard. It surprised me so I cried. He turned around and apologised.

I feel a tingling. A force field.

I will remember these moments.

The events of my life.

The blue of the sky and the grey of the footpath as Mum pushed me to Burnie Park in my pram. My first ever memory.

I'll be wide awake and ready the second I turn …

My eyes go fuzzy. I'm ready.

The dots blink on and off.

On   off

On   off

On   off

Change

7.33.

I'm thirteen!

The hairs on my neck prickle.

Twelve is over.

I'm no longer a little kid. I might miss the days of Play Doh and fairy bread and 'Duck Duck Goose'. Rubber spiders and pink scented note paper that smelled like girls.

That's okay. I'll make more memories and have new adventures inside the grown-up world.

Mum always gives me great gifts. This year she gave me glow-in-the-dark planet and star stickers! I'm standing on a chair peeling them off and sticking them to my ceiling. It's freezing so I'm wearing my new sheepskin foot warmers with explorer socks. I've got the heater going in the lounge so the warmth can drift around my legs.

Saturn's in the corner. Jupiter's on the other side of the light. The space station can float by the door. Where to put the moon?

Mum stands by the doorway.

'The moon! The moon!' Mum laughs. 'You used to stand at the window and your eyes would be wide and you'd point up and say "The moon Mummy! Look, it's the moon!"'

I do have a memory of that. It was a big glowing circle against the black. It could have been an alien or a magic gateway.

Mum goes back to the kitchen. She's cooking rainbow trout for tea – my favourite!

I press the moon close to my light. That way it'll get the most charge and glow the brightest. I make the Southern Cross and 'Pot' constellations and stick heaps of remaining stars close together to resemble the Milky Way.

It's been a good end to the holidays. On Friday I stayed up until 2.30am to watch Boony get a century in the second Ashes test. He ended up with 164 not out! (It was his first hundred in nine tests, so a return to form). The next day I slept in till noon which is a record for me. I got away with it because Nan was off bushwalking. Carlton walloped Adelaide by seventy-nine points so we're fifth now. *Dances with Wolves* was on over two nights and is one of my favourite movies. I looked in the credits and the name of the horse was Justin!

The only bad part of the holidays was when I had to have a mole cut out of my back. It required a local anaesthetic (which is impossible to spell) but I could still feel the sensation of the scalpel moving around! I have stitches and a patch now so I'll have to miss out on Surf Club training.

After tea I leave my bedroom light on for an hour as it says on the sticker packet. Mum and I do a countdown and switch off the light. Our eyes adjust as a soft green glowing galaxy hovers above us.

'Ooh, aren't they pretty!' says Mum.

'Yeah, they're cool!'

Mum heads back out to the lounge to watch TV but I don't feel like watching anything. It feels like the right occasion to go to bed early and enjoy my room and do some thinking. I go to say goodnight to Mum. She's standing in the kitchen now, waggling her fingers at the stove. I haven't seen her do that in a while.

'Goodnight Mum.'

I give her a hug.

She goes back to counting.

'Yes, goodnight dear, I'm just making sure the stove's off. You know how I am.'

That night in bed I keep my glasses on for a while and stare up at the roof. The moon even has the craters. One of my best memories is being in Mum's bedroom with the lights out and Mum singing 'Memory' from *Cats* to me.

It's such a sad song, but a lovely tune. I thought my mum was magical.

I take my glasses off and fold up the arms and sit them off to the side. Now it's a fuzzy halo of twinkles. I rest my eyes and picture everything I want and all I have to look forward to. Rain starts pattering down on the roof, slow at first and unsure, like Blossom's paws when he first hops up on my bed. Then the rain gets the go-ahead and streams down in lovely, heavy sheets. Blossum curls up by my feet. He gets comfortable and starts rumbling himself to sleep.

I can't believe how cosy I feel with the warmth of my electric blanket underneath my pyjamas, the glow of the universe on my ceiling, and the weather drumming away outside. I rub my palms over my bare arms. I cup the muscle of my bicep. It's definitely getting bigger. I'll be ready to take on everything at school tomorrow. We'll probably have an assembly and I might win a subject award.

I hear the toilet flush.

I hear Mum turn out the light.

I hear the bed frame creak as she tosses and turns.

To Justin.

"Happy. Birthday."

33

'Mum, do you know where my apron is?'

Mum doesn't respond.

'Mum! My apron for cooking?'

'Wait on please dear, I can only do one thing at a time!'

Mum has to heat the milk for my Weet-Bix. She carries the bowl over to me – she's still wearing her nightie.

'Sugar?' I say from my beanbag.

'Didn't I? Oh, sorry dear.'

She takes the bowl off me again. Mum looks tired. Her cheeks are pale and clammy.

'I don't know why I didn't sleep well last night,' her eyes drift back. 'I was tired enough!'

It's okay. Sometimes Mum's vague for a day or two but then she comes right.

I devour half-squishy half-crunchy bix while watching the *Today Show*. They have a clock on the screen and every time it reaches 7:47 I sing 'Riding along in a seven forty-seven', which is a line from a cool country song Uncle Ken once played me. Every half an hour they have the news report where I cheer on

Gerhard Berger in the Formula One and Crystal Palace in the soccer because I like their names. It's good having someone or a team to go for so I even cheer on Falls Creek in the snowfall.

Blossum comes over and sniffs my empty bowl. I let him lap up the milk. The spoon dings against the bowl as he licks. I look around for Mum who'd normally have her breakfast now too.

'Mum?' I call out from the hallway. I hear the bed springs creak.

'Yep,' Mum appears, eyes startled. She breathes quickly through her nose. Her lips quiver into a smile.

'My apron?'

'Yes, I'll find it.'

She wanders off into the laundry, humming to herself. She wanders back and hands me the apron. I kiss her goodbye and head out the door.

It's a wet, claggy old day. I save Billy a seat in Maths but he doesn't turn up. It's weird without him. It means I have to make more of an effort to talk to the other members of the group at lunchtime. Ryan likes the new Nike Air Haurache running shoes I bought with my birthday money.

Ryan's tall with curly brown hair and an easy-going manner. His parents own Jointley's fish and chip shop and his older brother is in grade nine. Ryan likes Sarah, Bianca's friend, and they play mercy in MDT (manual arts), where you link fingers and have to try and bend the other person's hands back. Ryan pinned Sarah against the desk and her cheeks were all flushed. I didn't know you could be so rough with a girl.

After school I find the key still in the front door. Mum flies up from the couch the second I slam the screen door. She straightens her top and looks at the clock.

'Hello dear, is it that time already!' she says, scratching her head.

There are papers spread out on the table. I recognise the booklet with 'Personal Finance Co.' written in blue. I throw my bag down and announce my good news.

'I won two subject awards in assembly!'

Mum beams. 'Really? Two!'

'English and PE!'

'Oh Justin how wonderful. We'll have to go out for tea to celebrate.'

I get the certificates out of my bag and show her.

'And we get our reports next week.'

Mum takes a big breath and lets it out. She looks out the window, worried.

'Are you okay?'

'Oh yes, I've just got the damn car rego coming up. I might have to borrow some from Mum and Dad when they get back. I don't know Justin, no sooner does it come in my hand than it flies out again.'

Nan and Pop have gone away to visit Uncle Ken in Canberra and Pop's brothers in Queensland. They'll be away for a whole month so Sparky will come stay with me and Mum. It's the longest they'll have ever been away.

It's been a busy birthday patch with mine and Mum's and Nan's and Nigel's birthday's all happening within a month. Mum was in a flap organising Nan's present before she and Pop left for the mainland, even though Nan told Mum not to make a fuss.

'That naggy voice of hers. "Don't worry about a present for me",' Mum does a high pitched screech. I laugh.

'She gets on my nerves a bit sometimes.' Mum's eyes have a wild glint. 'Like how she was with you at Greens Beach. "We don't like white sugar!" There was no need for her to be like that.

She just likes to pick. She's always been like that. Pickin' at any little thing.'

Mum frowns while smiling, trying to look sympathetic. I don't laugh now.

'Nag nag nag ...' she says softly. She shakes her head and laughs. 'Sometimes I could clock her.'

Later in the night I'm comfortably curled up in my beanbag watching *A Country Practice*. Shirley Gilroy is sitting cross legged inside a white pyramid, meditating. She closes her eyes and says 'Ommmmm.' I hear Mum cackle behind me. I didn't think it was that funny.

'What is it? Mum?'

'Oh, just something silly I thought of. It'll soon be bedtime won't it?'

I normally stay up till 9.30.

'Have you had your tablet?' I ask.

Her brow scrunches.

'Have I? I don't think I have. I'd better take it.'

It's so hard to get up. My whole room is dark but apparently it's 7.25. The alarm keeps blaring so I turn and whack snooze. I don't care about school, I just care about bed. I can snooze three times and not miss the bus ... or is it twice? My hair is a fog helmet. The doona cocoon's too beautiful to leave. I rip it back and roll myself out of bed and upright. My legs are too tired to stand up in the shower. I melt down on my side in the tub as thick drops rain over my side.

I dry and spray and pull on my shorts. It's really getting too cold for bare legs but I hate wearing jeans. I open my curtains to the cloudy, empty yard. There's a gluggy, grey gloom in the air.

Get Up Mum

A clomping elephant of quiet that knows something's different.

Mum is in the kitchen with her bare ankles and squished toes peeking out from beneath her long white dressing gown. I can see little black hairs above the pale ankles. She spreads toast slowly with her head down. Her hair juts out. Her cheeks are flushed.

'Good moaning!'

It's what the policeman on *Allo Allo* says.

'There you go dear,' she says with a croak. The skin around her eyes is puffed. Her voice is thin and croaky. Her face looks sad and strained.

'Did you sleep better?'

'Yes thankyou dear,' she says, reaching an arm behind her. 'Except I've got a damn itchy back again. I might get you to rub some ointment after school.'

I'm already running late and it's drizzling, so Mum drives me up to Parklands. I watch two rain drops flutter and wobble down the window. I'm glad it's wet because it means there's no one waiting around as we pull up. The Volks tends to get a bit of attention.

'Thanks Mum.'

'Okay have a good day,' she says in a high pitch voice, smiling. I lean and kiss her cheek. It feels hard.

Locker, books, Billy's back! We're having a quiet joke in Social Science when Mr Jordan's magnified gaze fixes on me. He stretches out a finger and curls it back like an old worm.

'Come 'ere yew!'

My cheeks burn as I walk towards his desk. I'm never in trouble.

'What's your name sonny?'

'Justin,' I say quietly.

'And what school did you come from?'

'Montello.'

'Well Justin from Montello, I don't know what sort of standards they expected of you, but here at Parklands it's a very different game sonny. We might be studying the dark ages but there's no need for you to be living in them!'

I plod back to my desk. Billy's eyes are screaming at me.

'If you still think it's funny you can stay back at recess.'

My chest steams. I can't help it if Billy and I are hilarious and he's an old idiot.

Billy invites me to his place after school. We catch the Havenview bus uphill and along Old Surrey Road. Up this high there are impressive views of the Emu Valley and Dial Range. Billy's house is big and modern and tidy. There isn't a thing out of place, including his room, which doesn't even have any posters up on the wall. He shows me his Guns and Roses poster inside his bedroom cupboard. Billy's quieter and more uptight at home. He says we have to be quiet because his mum works nightshift at Lactos Cheese factory.

Billy just lives with his mum. His dad is often working down at the Savage River mine. His older brother used to go to Parklands but it sounds like he's a bit of a delinquent. Billy doesn't want to talk about him.

He shows me his IBM with a game called *Wolfenstein 3D*. It has the best graphics I've ever seen. It's set in World War II and you have to walk around a maze of corridors shooting German soldiers. It's played in first person so the perspective is from behind the soldiers eyes. There's better animation than other games and you can see blood coming out of the soldier's chests when they die. You can even save a game and come back to it later.

'It took me ages but I finished the whole game,' says Billy. 'At the end you take on Hitler, check it out.'

I've only just seen the game and already we're on the last level! I hear grinding footsteps like a tank in the distance as an angry Hitler stomps forwards in a robo-suit. He has two submachine gun barrels that rip away Billy's health in seconds.

Billy's tactic is to take pot shots while holding down 'Alt' and shimmying sideways, taking cover behind a block. Even when he's out of view I still hear the 'stomp-stomp-stomp' of Hitler's robo-suit. As long as Billy's in the room he never stands still or stops trying to kill him.

'Have a go!' Billy stands up and gives me the chair. I'm nervous. There are too many keys. I don't like Hitler coming at me. I die on purpose.

'Let me show ya how it's done son,' says Billy, taking over. He cackles away as he unloads rounds of bullets from his submachine gun. Hitler says something in German and disintegrates in a pile of blood and guts. It's so cartoonish and exaggerated but also quite realistic. The screen says 'Let's See That Again' and shows a slow motion replay in 'Death Cam'. I find the horror a bit full on.

I check my watch. My chest sinks as I tear out of the trance.

'Is it alright if I ring my Mum?'

'Yeah, the phone's in the lounge. Be quiet 'cos Mum's in bed.'

3. 1. 5. 2. 6. 0.

It rings. It rings for too long.

'Hullo?'

It's Mum, but it's not her hello. The notes are different. This ends in a question.

'Hi Mum, I'm at Billy's.'

There's space on the line.

'At Billy's …'

'Do you remember where he lives in Old Surrey Road?'

Thump. Thump. The room grows colder.

'Yep.'

Justin Heazlewood

'Can you come and get me?'

'Alright, I'll come now.'

I hang up. I look around Billy's lounge. There's a black soft leather couch and TV and photos in shiny silver frames. A black cabinet with plants and plush white carpet with a sweet laundry smell. It's a nice, comfortable, normal house.

Outside a plover squawks in the distance. The sun passes beneath a cloud, cloaking the room so it suddenly looks cold and unwelcoming.

I think Mum's getting sick again.

34

The next day Billy comes over to my house after table tennis practice.

'This is pretty cosy,' he says as he walks in.

I wish we didn't have Billy's younger cousin with us as well. Adam's in grade six with floppy hair and a nervous smile. He sits silently on the chair in the corner of my room. I'm not used to so many people in my room at once. There aren't enough chairs! I hope my stuff is cool enough.

Before they sat down in my room I pressed record on my tape recorder hidden under my desk. As long as I keep talking things will be okay.

'Billy do you want to mow my lawn for me?'

'Do you have to mow the lawns? Aww, let's go on the tramp. I'll beat you at the tramp.'

'I know you would.'

Billy starts a brawl with Adam on the floor. Billy declares he is the superior and goes in for the slam. Whenever there's a stacks on, Billy's usually the first to ground. In footy, Billy plays rover and can usually be found hugging the ball at the bottom of the pack. He's effortless at hitting and wrestling and getting in the fray. I get a bit jealous sometimes.

I don't like pretend fighting because it stresses me out. I'm never sure what the rules are or how hard to hit. In primary school we played 'Gang-ups', which basically involved chasing each other around and throwing gumnuts. Nick used to practice his wrestling moves on me like the figure four leg lock, until I'd get scared and yell 'submit.'

Billy does confident, controlled whacks on my arm and leg.

'Oh right, now it's squared all down to this, Bottles!'

I don't have anything to tease Billy about so I call him an egg.

'Don't call me an egg!'

Billy wants me to hold down Adam so he can fart on his head. The terrible smell reaches my nostrils. Billy cackles like a hyena.

'Go home Bill!'

'I think my Dad should be here soon.'

I don't want him to go.

'Ssssshhhh.'

I hear it through the walls.

A shard runs through me.

'Back in a sec,' I say. I turn and whip out the door and close it behind me. Billy and Adam keep up their wrestling – I don't think they heard. Mum's lying on her bed with twisted sheets and a crooked mouth.

'Mum!' I scream in a whisper. 'Billy's here!'

Mum pops her head up.

'Billy?'

'I can hear you swearing. Go out in the lounge if you have to.'

'No, I'll be alright.'

I hear a thump from my room and rush back in to find Billy holding my Tyrannosaurus Rex skeleton. I've assembled it from the parts that came in *Dinosaurs!* magazine.

'Justin if you drop this, your lifelong dream will be down the drain.'

'Alright, I trust myself,' I say.

'You do, but you don't trust me.'

He lobs the skeleton. I fumble it.

'He's a rough and tough dinosaur, he can take it.'

'Where's your mum?' Billy asks quietly. His face is serious.

'Oh, she's just having a rest.'

'Is she sick?'

'No, she's just … tired.'

'Yeah my Mum has to have naps during the day sometimes.'

Billy looks around my room. I'm nervous and don't want him to get bored so I show him my writing kit and koala money box and plastic tub with moss and bark I collected from bushwalks.

'I was a bit psychotic, so I did those sort of things,' I laugh.

Billy eyes my Surf Club medals. I have them arranged in gold, silver and bronze on a nail on the wall above my dresser.

'Oh look at the poppadom, he puts his bronze with his gold – what a loser!'

Some of the gold medals are a deeper shade and resemble bronze.

'Aww do you like David Boon?' He spits, scanning the poster.

David Boon is a great cutter and puller of the ball and chews gum and adjusts his box and scampers quickly between wickets and takes classic catches at short leg. I can't wait for one of the openers to get out because then Boony comes to the crease.

'Yeah.'

'He's a wanker.'

I feel the sting of being teased. I thought every Tasmanian loved Boony. Billy likes to act tough when there are others around and often I'm the one who cops it. Sometimes he confuses me. I have to keep figuring him out.

I pull out my old primary school class photos. It's good to see Billy laughing at people he knows. I have a red card from kindergarten with our class photo.

'Wasn't I the cutest thing?' I say, adding, 'Wasn't I the biggest knob?'

I'll tease myself before Billy can.

'The biggest square,' he grins. 'Can you pick the Coke bottles kid!'

'Look at my shirt.'

'Couldn't you just vomit on it.'

'I used to have that on my wall,' I say, 'I don't know why.'

'Did ya? What a knob.'

I'll impress Billy with my trick money box. It's a green cube floating in the centre of space. The coins disappear when you put them in the slot.

'How did they do it? I still haven't worked it out,' I say in a sarcastic voice.

'Justin, tell me …' says Billy with a frown.

'Can't you work it out?'

I like it when Billy needs me. In class I'm usually the one helping him. He looks at me with an embarrassed smirk.

I know I could tease him but what would be the point? I want Billy to like me.

'Fishing line?'

I laugh. 'How come it doesn't swing then?'

'There's a pane of glass running through it?'

He's getting warmer.

'Mirror …' I correct softly. 'Quite ingenious,' I beam.

I'm proud of my cube. Billy lobs it at me.

'Catch it!'

Billy picks up the Holy Bible on my bedside table. I'm shy because it's personal and I haven't mentioned being Christian.

'I might start readin' the Bible,' he says. 'That's why your life is running so smooth.'

'It's not running smooth, that's for sure.'

There's a toot from the street and Billy and Adam scamper out of my room, and out the door.

Mum peers from her bedroom door, running her thumb around the track pants' waist

'Did Billy go?' she asks foggily.

'Yeah.'

I trundle back to my room and press 'stop' on the stereo. Now it's just me in my room. I smooth over the bed and put away the photos and trinkets. I look around my room, which I recently rearranged. My certificates and medals and autographs. I pick up the kindergarten photo.

We're all sitting out on the grass at Montello, legs tucked or crossed. Half of us aren't looking at the camera and hardly anyone has their uniforms on. There's a cookie monster doll being held up in the air. I'm in the middle of the group, sitting up with my body to the side. I have short blonde-brown hair, glasses and a white T-shirt with brown arms. My mouth is slightly open. I'm not smiling or frowning, just looking at the camera, ready.

35

After school I go to Nick's house and then on to table tennis. We play in the social league Tuesday nights and school league on Wednesday afternoons. The table tennis hall is inside the Police Boys Club, which is a big sports complex next to the Burnie Pool. As we walk up the long, cold hallway I can hear the 'sss' of smacked punching bags from the boxing room and the echoes of shoe squeaks and basketballs from the indoor courts. The most comforting sound is the 'ka-dack, ka-dack, ka-dack' and bouncing table tennis balls.

Ka-dack. Ka-dack. Ka-dack.
Left. Right. Right. Left.
Forehand. Backhand. Backhand. Forehand.

Table tennis is my game. I've got a good serve, low and fast. Backhand is my strength, so much so that I jump right when I can, just to avoid a forehand. It never feels right, my elbow up in the air like a chicken wing. A high elbow is what they teach us at swimming training. Fingers pressed together, thumb cutting the water first. At table tennis my forehand feels weak, bat out of view. I like backhand because I can see the ball in front of me.

Get Up Mum

I play my best when I'm behind. There's more to fight for and nothing to lose. Sometimes if I'm way out in front I feel tight-chested and fuzzy-headed and start making mistakes. The longer the rally goes the more the pressure builds. I start to think about how annoyed I'll be if I stuff up until it's all I can think about. I get so desperate that I whack it harder so it's more likely the point will end and I can get back to scratch.

You can do it!
I can't.
You might!
I won't.
You should!
It's hard.
You're good!
He's better.
You're in front!
I suck.

Karl from Burnie High is my rival. I can get close but he manages to beat me every time. He's completely boring and never smiles or says anything. He floats his hand up at the end and rests it against mine with enough force for me to shake it once. Uncle Ken said to never trust anyone with a 'wet fish' handshake. After games I sit on the side and sip my Coke until someone asks me to umpire. It's a relaxing way to unwind after games, watching the ball go back and forth with no pressure at all.

Afterwards I pack up my bag and zip up my polar fleece and walk home in the cool evening. It's crisp but not cold with sweet wood smoke drifting in the air for my nostrils to draw in. I smell as far as the eye can see. I imagine the houses up on the hilly streets, lighting their fires and toasting their socks.

I walk the path behind the pool onto Terrylands and walk uphill and turn right onto Bird Street. Ours is one long street that runs dead straight past Montello Primary to the goat track, which big dumb cars like to hoon up and down. When I reach our place all the lights in the other units are on except ours. I knock on the glass next to the door. Nothing. I take the metal knocker and do three knocks. I listen out for steps.

The door opens slowly. I can't see Mum's face.

'How come it's dark?'

'Oh, I didn't notice. I must have forgotten to turn the lights on,' she says groggily.

I drop my bag and flick the light switch, the heater switch, the television switch.

I close the curtains and let in Blossum and open his can of jellymeat.

Mum glances at the clock and pours herself a glass of water. She's in pale track pants and a dark brown windcheater that she's been wearing for days. I can hear the noises in her neck as she swallows. She gulps the water down in one go and slams the glass down.

'Oh, I needed that.'

Mum doesn't say things like that.

'Justin if I give you the money can you go and get two McCains dinners.'

She's been home all day. What was she doing?

I head back out the door and walk around to the shop in the dark.

I don't want to be here, in this battle.

But there's nothing I can do.

I don't feel like crying.

I feel like disappearing.

Get Up Mum

At recess Elvis pulls me up in front of the canteen. His blond hair curls beneath his red Chicago Bulls cap. He has John and Rhett from Montello flanked either side of him.

'Guess what Hazelnut, I've got news for ya,' he grins. 'You can't run in the inter-high cross country! I told Mr St John about your birthday and he reckons you're too old for Under Thirteens. Sorry mate!' he cackles. I stand there, stunned. I've always been the oldest in my grade because I did Prep. I'll have to compete against the grade above me for the rest of high school, instead of racing with my friends.

What a twank! He won the cross country while I came third. I've known him since grade one. He's in my table tennis team. Elvis is a bully and a friend.

Today's a wet weather day so I head to A1 and join in a game of table soccer in the corner. When it's raining the whole of grade seven has to cram into two classrooms. It's loud and crowded and muggy. At least I'm sitting down, which means I get to hide my legs. My new jeans haven't gone well so far. They're stiff stonewash ones that Mum got from Fitzgeralds. They ruck up around the ankles and make my legs look like crinkle cut chips! Earlier in the day I was clomping along the basketball courts on my way to PE when a gang of grade eights started laughing.

'Nice boots coke bottles. Are you going for a hike?'

I decided to wear my bushwalking boots because the jeans didn't look good with black shoes. They're chunkier than Billy's fashionable Rossi ones with a buckle and flap.

'Check out them clodhoppers!'

It's so embarrassing. People will think I'm pov. Even Billy seemed ashamed when he saw me this morning.

The week is bad and getting worse. I lost my prescription goggles at swimming training, found out that Nick and his family are going to Queensland for three months AND I've got dandruff!

At least English with Miss Stones went well. She's passionate and engaged and I can tell she likes me because I'm the best writer in my grade. We've been working on descriptive pieces so I wrote about my bushwalk on top of Cradle Mountain with Nan. It's called 'Mountain Spirit' and my best writing so far. Miss Stones says she'd like to include it in the end of year anthology!

It's a relief when the bell goes. I get off the bus a few stops early and call into the Terrylands milk bar to play a game. The pool is abandoned for winter. They've drained the water so it's a cold cement hole in the ground.

I fight past the thick plastic strips in the doorway into the heat and sparkle of the milk bar. I can smell chocolate and cigarettes and the metallic heat from the video games. Jars of different mixed lollies line the counter including my favourite cobbers and freckles and the dreaded black cats. There's a dome of Chuppa Chups in cola and choc-banana and a rack of Hubba Bubba in strawberry and grape. The ice-cream sign features a giant new Paddle Pop 'Mud Puddle' flavour I'll have to try.

I wait while two little girls stand on tippy toes and put their collection of five cent pieces on the counter. They're very cute, asking what lollies they can get. Mixed lollies have gone up to two cents each! It gives me time to decide on fifty cents of choc rainbow balls. They're like Jaffas but in yellow, blue and green as well.

On the way home I pass the house where Jade, the weird doll girl, lives. You sometimes see her being shuffled along by her mum and Nan. She has bright red hair, pale skin and is always dressed like a porcelain doll with white stockings and frills. She went to Montello and was in the grade below me. I thought she might be pretty until I saw her up close one day. Her face was puffy and there were small red welts showing through her makeup. There's clearly something wrong with her but no-one knows what. You never see her anywhere without her Mum holding her arm. She's like a blind ghost.

A gust of wind pushes me from behind as I jump over 'MOLLY 86' scrawled in the cement. Dry leaves scrape and scuttle along the gutter. Montello Primary is quiet and empty. I think about Mr Burgess and how his new class is going. Are they still making the *Montello Times*? What new games are on the Macintosh?

When I arrive home Mum makes an effort to get up. I remind her that I need a clean uniform for tomorrow. She stands in the kitchen with a crumpled expression, scratching her head. Which way will her face go? Angry or laughing? Quiet or sad? It might depend on how many sets have come and gone during the day. She pulls open the fridge and stares while I wonder whether it's worth telling her about my terrible time at school. I'm glad it's almost the weekend.

She wanders back to her bedroom as soon as we've had our tea.

'Goodnight dear, sleep tight.'

'Yep,' I sigh.

Mum shakes and puts her hand to her mouth. She swallows a laugh like it's the hiccups.

'I'll be alright tomorrow.'

I lock the back door and slide the bolt across. I go to close the lounge room curtains.

'No, leave them open,' says Mum.

'Why?'

'So the neighbours won't know if we sleep in.'

I go to my room and read some more of my Bible.

Jesus is explaining the parable of the weeds.

'The man who sowed the good seed is the Son of Man; the paddock is the world; the good seed is the people who belong to the Kingdom; the weeds are the people who belong to the Evil One; and the enemy who sowed the weeds is the Devil.'

I'm trying to calm my heart down, but there's another set of sound waves.

'Sssssst … sshhhhhht.'

Ugh! Fury burns inside me. I could destroy that sound.

I spring up to close Mum's bedroom door.

'No, don't close it!'

Mum is a voice in the dark.

'Stop swearing, I can hear it.'

'Okay dear, I'll stop.'

My eyes are heavy as I pick up the Holy Bible again. I finish the page.

'Just as the weeds are gathered up and burned in the fire, so the same thing will happen at the end of the age: the Son of Man will send out his angels to gather out of his Kingdom all those who do evil things, and they will throw them into the fiery furnace, where they will cry and gnash their teeth.'

36

It's Friday night and Nick and I are in Danny's room going crazy. We've pulled out his huge chest of toys including Transformers and He-men and G.I. Joe's. I grab the G.I. Joe doll and hold his legs while twisting the top half around.

'Where am I? Where am I? Where am I?'

I feel a snap as the torso comes apart in my hand. I watch Danny's face change in slow motion. The happiness shrinks as his pale blue eyes shine with water. His brow turns to anger and his cheeks blush.

'You broke it!' he squawks.

A wave of shame burns over me. Nick's kneeling next to me. I let the pieces fall to the ground.

'It's okay Danny, I can fix it,' says Nick, kneeling next to me.

I stare down, mouth locked. Danny screws his face up like he's eaten a lemon.

'I'm telling Mum!'

I can't get in trouble can I? I'm a guest.

'Danny you were being rough with it too,' yells Nick.

'Ah, Nick! Is this true?' Nick's mum appears in the doorway.

Danny waits behind her. I can see two lines of tears running down his cheeks.

I have my leg tucked up, resting my chin on my knee. I pick up a toy car and fiddle with it. I have nothing to say. Nick's red cheeked and annoyed.

'I can fix it.'

'YOU BROKE IT!'

Danny's in grade five but now he seems like a baby.

'I didn't break it!' says Nick.

'Then Justin did!'

Danny dobs me in. Now I'm embarrassed. I've let Nick's mum down. It's all happened so quickly. I wasn't thinking, I was just being silly. Nick's mum crosses her arms and sighs.

'Alright, I don't want to know who broke it, I just want you both to say sorry to Danny!'

Nick's had more practice than me. I look in Danny's little kid eyes and mumble 'Sorry'.

After a hot Milo, Nick and I get back into our insane mood. We're playing chasings with Danny around the house. I'm flying around the kitchen table when I feel my bum brush something. I run off and hear a crash behind me. It doesn't seem like much but then I see Nick's mum crouched on the ground while a ceramic pot is in pieces on the floor.

'Oh no, my pot! I paid fifty dollars for that.'

I'm frozen.

'Sorry,' I say quietly. I don't want to say it too loud in case it annoys her.

There's a buzzing in my guts as my heart starts up a stomp. This might not all be happening. Not two things in one night. There must be a way it can end up okay. I stare at the clock on the wall. 10.45pm. This is Nick's mum's house. These are all her things, not Nick's.

Get Up Mum

He's quiet. He squats down next to his mum, watching. She picks up the biggest pieces and tries to fit them back together. She clicks her tongue in disappointment.

Click. Click. A wet match strike with no fire.

'Can you glue it?'

'Maybe?'

They speak calmly, to each other. Not to me.

My heart is beating hard as I collect up all the gloom. Our fun has gone cold and I don't want to be here anymore. I want to say sorry but my mouth won't move. I stand very still. It's the best I have. The overhead fluorescent light is on. The TV is screeching tyres and gunshots. It's late and I want a solution and I'm so tired.

Nick's mum is different this time. She stands and goes back in the lounge.

'I'll clean that up in the morning.'

She doesn't say anything to me. I'm not part of this family.

'It's alright, maybe we'll go play computer,' says Nick.

I go to the toilet. I close the door behind me. I stare in the mirror. My hair is flat. My eyes are small. My mouth is a straight line. I look like a dork. Now I have this memory and I can't get rid of it.

Justin Heazlewood

My mood is staying under
longer.
In my dreams I can breathe
underwater.

I hold my chest
until it
hurts.
I run on the spot
and fall down
in the deep
where nothing grows
and nobody knows.

Upside down

head first

in a hole.

stinging nettle
singing kettle
spinning top

Life is a bad dream that lives inside my chest.

Get Up Mum

It's Sunday. I wake up at Nan and Pop's. They're not here. Mum and I are housesitting for a bit. The house feels so empty without them. The garden looks restless through the window. Only the roses keep their colour. The canary's voices are hidden by the wind.

We missed the paperboy.

There's no soup and no toast and no radio.

I wander into the lonely lounge and eat breakfast alone.

'Sssssssstinkin' bag of shhhiiiiiiiiit.'

'Mum …! Stop it.'

There's a body on the recliner. Mum's pulled the handle and tilted it as far as it'll go. Her feet dangle over the foot rest. Her hands nurse her head as she stares upwards. From the kitchen her feet are the only part I can see. Her toes jammed together, her little toe a triangle. She's made the chair into a bed.

The hissing slices.

I stand up, desperate. The light in here is so gloomy. I can't stand Nan being away right now. Nan doesn't like Mum sitting like that.

'Mum you shouldn't sit like that.'

She doesn't respond. I can't be bothered. At least it's a bigger house than our place and I can escape up to Nan and Pop's room with two layers of doors closed.

Nan and Pop have a matches holder. It's a wooden rectangle that holds about eight boxes. I slide one out as another falls in its place. I slide open the packet. It's brimming with clean fresh heads. I take one out of the pack and scrape it against the side. It flares up and releases a sparkle of smoke. I hold the light before my eyes.

I watch the lovely flame creep down the stick. I let it burn as close to my fingers as I can before puffing it out. Now there's smoke and a pleasant wood burn smell.

Justin Heazlewood

'Is something burning?' Mum calls from the couch.
'I lit a match,' I say.
I crush the burnt head between my top and bottom teeth.
It tastes salty.

37

It's quiet and lonely when I come home after school on Monday. I'm sitting at the table staring at Nan and Pop's birthday card. It has a cartoon sausage dog on the front with a metal spring tail. It's a fold up card so the dog appears normal at first and then grows. It's a bit daggy with its waggy tail but I don't mind. It's all I have of them. There's pressure in my stomach. It's like I've eaten too much party food, but there's only air inside. My eyes are heavy but I'm not really tired. There's a swelling in my throat. The whole day is pressing down at once.

I stare at the dog and feel my storm of sorrow. I'm quivering like the waggy dog's tail.

'To Justin on your 13th year. We both love you and wish you a lovely day. Pop & Nan. Xx'

I imagine Nan sitting at the kitchen table, writing out the words just for me. Everything I have of them is in the past. What if something happened to them? How would I ever cope? How would I ever say goodbye? I miss them so much it hurts.

I'm feeling so much I'm lost. I'm sinking and fading. I need to talk. Part of me is holding on to all the feelings. I'm holding everything in. The lump in my throat is burning. There are too many days like yesterday. I'm kneeling on the kitchen chair, concentrating on the silly puppy dog and wanting Nan and Pop and I don't know what to do.

    I can't even call.
    They're so far away.
    I didn't know I could feel this sad.
    Oh.
    I burst into tears.
    There it is. All the upset.

There are large, warm sobs. More than I imagined. They drool down my cheeks. They pool around my nose. I take my glasses off as I sputter and swallow. I keep my sobs low. I'm so very, very down. I know it now. I don't care anymore. I push the card out of the way and hang my head and let it go.

    I imagine Pop picking out the sausage dog with a party hat on and thinking of me and loving me. It's a bit childish for someone my age but that only makes me sadder because I love it more. My daggy dog has all of Nanny and Poppy in it and I've never felt so much about anything before and now my tummy shakes as my chest heaves and my eyes burn and there's so much pain coming up from everywhere.

    It's so much love and pain – raw and complete.
    It was hidden deeper than I knew.
    I feel all of it now. I have to let it come out.
    I don't try and wipe. I just sit and shake and ache.
    My teeth bare as I breathe hot, heavy breaths.

    I'm so…

Get Up Mum

I moan as the giant sobs die down.
The storm has passed. Now there's stillness.
A quiet moves in because there's less pressure inside.

I wipe my lenses with my shirt and slide them back on. They're steamy and smeary but I can see fine. I feel comfortable and calm.

I stand up slowly because my foot is asleep. I hobble out to the backyard and sit on the step. There's a line of ants marching along the path below. Blossum hurries over with a groan. It's good to pat him. It's all I want. I stroke Blossum and I watch the ants. A light breeze dries my face.

I feel normal.

'Justin!'
Mum calls for me.
Her room is dark except for the glow of the green clock. It's flashing 12.00. The power went off and Mum hasn't fixed it.
She's sitting up in bed.
There's a square of light on the doona.
'Have a seat, dear.'
She pats the edge of the bed. I back myself onto the mattress.
'I'm sorry I haven't been well lately.'
I nod.
'I know it's hard on you.'
'I just want you to get well,' I say.
'I try dear, I really do. But sometimes I can't control the voices inside me.'
I stare at the floor.
'They tell me things.'
'About me?'

'No dear,' she softens. 'Never about you.'

'Have you had your tablet?'

'They don't always work,' Mum whispers. 'They leave me feeling like a zombie.'

All is quiet outside. There are no cars, no wind. We sit in silence for a long time.

'Sometimes I wonder if it might help you if I wasn't here.'

Mum's voice is calm and distant.

'What do you mean?'

'I could end it all.'

The back of my neck crawls.

'Mum, don't talk like that. I need you.'

There's a burning sensation under my arms.

'No. I need you!'

I lean forward and wrap my arms around Mum. I smell the faint flowers of her perfume through the darkness. I feel the warmth of her body as she sits perfectly still.

'Mum, I love you.'

I squeeze harder.

'I love you too, dear. I didn't mean to worry you. I'll keep going, for your sake.'

I don't believe it. I don't believe she'd do anything.

I lean back and let go. Mum rubs her hand on my back, takes a breath in and sighs. She sits up with her hands on either side of her, pressing down into the soft doona, dangling her legs over the edge of the bed. We both sit, facing forward. I have no idea what to say.

It's not the first time she's talked like this. When I was little she called me into her room and said that we could both lay down and go to sleep together. I said no and stormed out.

I think in slow motion now. I have to get out of this room. I fumble out into the hallway and go to the fridge top and lift the lid on the little ceramic pot. Inside are Mum's tablets. They're small and round and light green, the colour of a bird's eggs. I pour them into my hand and count thirteen.

'We'll have to put you in the other bed I reckon.'

'He can sleep in mine if he wanted,' mumbles Nan.

I always hope Nan will suggest this because I'm too shy to ask.

'I thought he might disturb ya.'

'Nuh. He only wants to cuddle up to Nan! Don't cha?'

Sometimes I sleep in Nan's bed when she's away. I like her sheets because they smell minty from her 'Methyl-Sal' ointment.

'Eh! You gotta be in with Nan and Pop!'

Nan and Pop let me sleep in between them. They have two single beds, pushed together. I find a little possie on the edge between both beds, covered with a bit of doona from each. I know I'm getting a bit old for it.

I tell them how some kids say 'grandfather' and 'grandmother' which makes them sounds too old and posh.

'Thanks very much Justin. I like Nan and Pop.'

Nan's face is buried in her pillow, her voice comes out muffled.

'Say Nan you old bitch and Pop you old bastard!'

I laugh.

'You can turn that recorder off darling cos I've gone to sleep. Goodnight.'

I ask what it's like to be back in her own bed. I mention the library book she borrowed off Merle.

Anything to keep her awake. I don't want her to go.

I listen until the tape runs out.

Static. Silence. Click. Stop.

I don't want them to go.

38

Sometimes we go for a drive to Table Cape lookout.
There's a short, craggy path to a big open view.
I lean over the rail and fill up on the space.
Vandals busted the binoculars, long ago.
But I can see all I need to see.
I can see the sea.

I gaze down at the clumps of rock and diagonals of green growing out of the cliff.
Postage stamp blue and papier-mâché moss. It hardly seems real.

This close to the edge, all I want to do is throw something off.
Including myself.

That bit of wood will do.
Flinging, spinning, shrinking.
I wonder how it feels to be a stick.
Free floating and falling.
Nothing to stick to.

Get Up Mum

Would I reach the water?
I heard you pass out halfway.

So I imagine being able to fly.
Climbing up on the railing and jumping off.
I dive bomb and pull up at the last moment
skimming the waves with my belly.
I'm invincible and invisible with no worries or cares.

I'd be nature's friend, hanging out with the birdlife.
Floating and soaring and gliding.
I'd be so far out that the shore
would look like the horizon
and the horizon
would look like home.

Light blue and dark blue.

Now where would I be?

I'm a bit depressed okay?

Justin Heazlewood

Thinking is drilling.

I'm drilling through the walls
of silence and confusion
looking for clues
looking for answers
looking for Mum.

I have a lot of
work to do.

So I sit and I stare
and I think so hard
I can cut through the moon
because I'm the sun.

Thinking is drilling.

I'm drilling up and out of the rubble.
Thinking is making air for myself.
A space to survive.

I can think into space
into outer space
into inner space.
I can drill inside
deep down and hide.
I can drill around in circles
so fast that everything's a blur
and I have rings like Saturn.

Get Up Mum

A drill is a weapon
with a pointy tip.
I leave it running
to rip the black pillows
when they come to smother me.

Thinking is drilling.

My mind is always moving.
There's work to be done
a maze to be dug
a tunnel of fun
somewhere deep
to bury my time capsule.

39

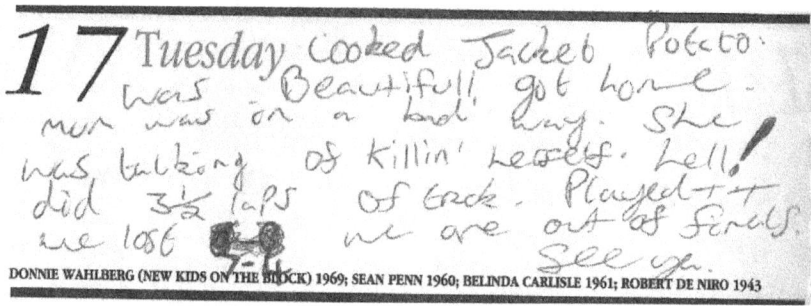

It's good to be back at school. Deep inside I know I'm quite down but it helps having plenty to keep busy with. Billy yaps away and draws me into his silly games so no one notices if I'm really quiet. After school Mum and I head downtown. I'm always a bit on edge being around so many strangers when she's sick. What if she started swearing or crying?

The Volks shudders its way down View Road with a view of the Burnie port and woodchip pile. We turn left past the cinema and towards the beach to find a park. We pass all the main places like the library and Kmart and Eye Biz where I go to get my glasses. Thursdays are always busy because it's pensioners' payday. I remember when Burnie was declared a city in 1988 and the Queen drove through the streets in her black Rolls Royce. There were crowds even bigger than the Christmas parade.

I watch Mum closely in the bank but she doesn't do anything worse than purse her lips. After looking at the computers and getting a thickshake at Fitzgeralds we head to the doctors for Mum's appointment. I counted her tablets last night and there was definitely one less one.

I flick through a *Woman's Weekly* (it comes out monthly ... der!) and stare at Claudia Schiffer because she's so pretty. Mum's flicking through a *New Idea*, turning the pages so forcefully I'm surprised they don't tear. She has her legs crossed in her light coloured jeans and I can see the purple socks I got her for her birthday as her foot taps away. She's angry at Charles for having an affair with Camilla.

'Gee people make ya sick with the way they carry on.'

'Who Mum?'

'Oh Charles and Camilla. Look at the sour face on her. Talk about muckraking. Gee they put a lot of crap in things nowadays,' she says crossly.

'What things?'

She throws the magazine on the pile.

'Sex and everything Justin. I don't know what's wrong with the royal family sometimes. Some example they're supposed to be setting for everyone. It's enough to drive you round the twist.'

'Maureen.'

Dr Gaylan appears. She's a pale woman about Mum's age with long brown hair.

Mum stands up and puts on a smile.

'Hello.'

I say a tiny prayer in my mind for Mum to tell the doctor everything.

Hopefully it's obvious that Mum isn't right. I can tell by looking at her so surely the doctor can too.

I stay in the waiting room while Mum walks off with Dr Gaylan. To my left is an old man with a white patch on his face that makes me shiver. A baby girl in a pram stares at me. She has piercing blue eyes and her face is perfectly still. I look away and wish she would look somewhere else. I peek back and now she's gazing up at her mum. *What's the matter, aren't I interesting enough?*

One of my favourite songs comes on the radio. Seal sings that we'll never survive unless we get a bit crazy.

I read about Tom Cruise and Nicole Kidman adopting a baby called Isabella. I've definitely won my bet now. In grade four I was excited that an Australian was marrying one of the best actors in the world but Nan disagreed and promised they'd be divorced within a year. I didn't like her being so negative so we ended up making a bet for fifty dollars. Now I can say I was right! I knew they were in love.

'I'm ready.' Mum appears, clutching her handbag. She wasn't very long! I look around, wondering if Dr Gaylan wants to say anything to me but she's talking to the old man with the patch. Mum and I wander back to the carpark where it's getting dark.

'What did the doctor say?'

'Oh, just to keep taking my tablets,' Mum says flatly.

'Did you tell her how you're not well and you've been crying?'

'She said I can take an extra one or have Panamax if I get a migraine.'

Mum's eyes becomes shadows as she stares downwards. She minces her lips and cracks her teeth. I stop dead on the spot as a car drives past. I cross my arms, watching the dumb back of Mum plodding ahead. She doesn't even notice. I can't stand being near her right now.

I stroll slowly behind, keeping out of earshot of her hissing and crunching. What would happen if I ran away? She wouldn't realise until she got to the car. I wonder if she'd even care? Where would I go? To the library? A Safety House?

Help! There's a stranger. It's my Mum.

Rain starts to fall as I catch up and climb in the passenger seat. I plonk down on our stupid familiar car seat covers. I've run my fingers over these a thousand times. My sitting and waiting chair. I click in the clunky, chunky seat belt that is a rough, thick band that doesn't retract like every other car. It just sits there, floppy and in the way. Even the horn on our uncool car broke so they put a hard black button next to the radio. I reach out and pull the red 'hazard' knob. The lights of the car start blinking on and off.

'Don't do that Justin,' says Mum, pushing it back in. 'That's only for emergencies.'

Mum calls into the drive-thru bottle shop. A young bloke bends down and peers in.

'Two stubbies of Boag's.'

He gives her the change and tells her to have a good night. Mum says she will in a croaky tone. I'm eying off the white station wagon parked next to us. I picture myself in the middle of the kids with another woman as my parent in the drivers seat. In my mind I'm not even saying anything because I don't need to. She is together and normal and understands me. The boy has his head down, playing a video game. The girl dances her arms to the radio. They're not worrying about anything at all. They won't have to. Not even once.

Look at all the company they get!

I get nothing with lonely on top.

Crack!

'Don't Mum!'

I don't know where to scream.

She ignores me, revving the car. It lurches forward and stops abruptly. My body judders forward, caught by the seatbelt.

'Buggar ya,' Mum growls through clenched teeth. I can feel the kids in the car staring at us. I shrink my neck and shoulders, shrivelling down in my seat. I don't get it. How is my life THIS UNFAIR?

Mum turns the key as the car farts back to life. I shift uncomfortably in my seat, careful not to shake up the stubbies.

'Shall we get takeaway for tea?' says Mum.

I think about the empty fridge at home. I like groceries.

'No, Mum, we need to do the shopping. Call into Roelf Vos.'

'I don't really feel like it now.'

'Please Mum, I want you to make tea. I can help. We can't afford to get takeaway all the time.'

Mum belts the indicator and swerves towards the supermarket. Once we're parked I stride ahead and grab a shopping trolley. Instead of zooming it around like normal, I start slowly down each aisle, looking left and right and thinking about the things Mum usually gets.

Cat food.

Beef German (what we call luncheon meat).

Bread.

Milk.

Toothpaste.

Margarine.

Frozen donuts.

I take the things and put them in my trolley. It's fun playing grownups and hiding from Mum. I'm in a maze while she's in a daze. I spy her at the opposite end of the aisle and whip ahead so she can't see me. I scan the cereals and instead of Rice Bubbles I decide to try Home Brand's 'Rice Pops' because they're cheaper. I'm sure Nan would approve. I pick out the orange and mango fruit drink and Butternut Snaps that Pop gets. This is good.

Mum finds me in the fruit and veg section. She places her Nescafe and pads in the trolley. I sample some grapes while ripping off a plastic bag for the apples and carrots. Mum orders ham from the deli.

'About eight slices,' she says with a strain.

I unload our things onto the conveyer belt.

'How's your day been?' asks the checkout girl. Mum's busy staring into her purse.

I nod and say 'good'.

It's getting dark as the car heaves up View Road. Spuds roll out of the shopping bags in the back as we skid a little on the wet road. I feel a spark of alarm.

'Mum!'

'C'mon damn ya,' Mum growls, grinding the gears.

View Road is always steeper than I remember.

When we make it home I unpack the groceries while Mum goes to lie down. I'm getting hungry so I ask if she can start on tea.

'In five minutes.'

I'm feeling inspired to try my own thing. Cooking has been one of my favourite subjects this semester and already we've made a Waldorf salad and jacket potato in class. I take a plate and squat down in front of the fridge and pull out everything that can be eaten raw.

I cut slivers of Beef German, open a tin of sliced beetroot, peel some lettuce leaves, spoon out some coleslaw, pinch some alfalfa sprouts, grate some carrot and even do a thin slice of orange to have on the side. I spread a fresh piece of bread with butter. I pour a glass of juice and sit down at the table. I look down at my plate made up of fresh things that I just picked out from the supermarket. I've made it as colourful as possible. My own rainbow salad.

40

It's Friday and Nan's back from the mainland! I'm catching the bus over after school. It's the first time I've travelled over by myself. I make sure to get a seat on the right so I can gaze out over the sea. There are train tracks that run all the way along the coast but never any trains. The bus passes Doctors Rocks and then turns right along the Old Bass Highway and past the golf course with rows of huge macrocarpa trees guarding the view. To the right is the wide flat, pale sea and Table Cape. Green to the left, blue to the right, yellow sun ahead and space everywhere. I feel better already.

Nan is just a bum poking up between two shrubs in the front garden. I say 'Hi Nan' from a distance so I don't scare her. I'm always worried about Nan's heart.

'Is that my Justin already?' she says my name out of breath in a kind of singsong.

'Where does the time go?' We hug carefully as she's holding a pair of secateurs. I smell her scent and feel her strong squeeze.

'I'm no lady,' she says, brushing strands of wispy hair back. 'See where my roses have attacked me!'

She slides up her sleeve to reveal a fresh red groove. I imagine an army of velvet warriors, petals pinched in a frown.

'They're mad at me for going away and neglecting them.'

I show her one of the latest scratches I got from Blossom when I put my hand near his belly.

'Ooh Justin, I'd get some metho on it.'

Pop's still up in Queensland with his brothers so it's a chance to spend time with Nan alone. She updates me on what's happening in the garden. She's been pruning jasmine and planting ranunculus and picking out rape (which isn't a good name for a weed). She says it's almost knock-off time so I drop off my bags, fill the birdbath and 'prune' the strawberry patch.

In the lounge room Nan has the jigsaw puzzle I got her for Christmas spread out on the orange card table. When she broke her ankle in the garden two years ago we spent the holidays working on one together. Like fishing, it's a relaxing way to pass the time and there's plenty of time to talk while you work. Every now and then a piece pushes into place and it's very satisfying. On the box is a painting of a young girl in a white dress reading a blue book to a brown dog. Nan's already worked out the book and the dog's face so they're floating inside the frame like little islands.

I give Nan an update on Mum. I'm careful with my words because I want to tell her how bad it's been without worrying her too much. I leave out the bit about Mum ending her life because I don't think she was being serious. Nan shakes her head and frowns. Nan can make sense of most things but she can't understand why Mum is still sick. Isn't she taking her tablets? Can't she see how much it upsets me? Why can't she pull herself out of it? I mention that Mum went to her doctor yesterday but nothing much came out of it.

'I don't think your mum tells her the full story,' says Nan. 'She's very independent your mum and very stubborn. She's been that way from the beginning. I'm sure she can be quite crafty when she wants to be. Perhaps you ought to go in there and let her doctor know what's really going on.'

That idea scares me so I change the subject. I tell Nan about my excellent school report with four OA's (outstanding achievement) and five HA's (high achievement). I won the subject achievement awards for PE and English. Miss Stones said I was intelligent and independent with a capacity for original thought and a willingness to help others! I even had perfect attendance with ninety-four out of ninety-four days.

'Oh, Justin,' Nan says slowly. 'Congratu-lations!'

Nan mentions how they came to Montello for grandparents' day last year and Mr Blazely told them what an outstanding student I was and how I showed great leadership potential. I'm beaming inside. Pleasing Nan is the best feeling.

I remind Nan about our bet over Tom and Nicole. She says she can't remember. We shook on it and everything! Nan says she'll put the money into a savings account for me. How boring. I was looking forward to that money.

Turns out today is Nan and Pop's anniversary. They have been married forty-five years! They met at the Wynyard Show after Pop got back from the war. Nan shows me photos of them in their younger days. It's strange seeing them like this – I've only ever known them to be old. There's a black and white photo of Pop with brown hair. He's carrying a lot more weight. Nan has hair like the old movie stars and her big 'Duniam nose' (this is Nan's maiden name and noses run in the family!).

'You were very pretty as a young woman.'

'Thanks very much, but I'm not now.'

'You're not bad for a sixty-seven-year-old.'

'Aww. You're a sweetheart.'

When Nan and Pop were young they moved from farm to

farm working odd jobs. They ran the local post office for a while. Nan knitted clothes to sell and Pop drove the school bus.

'Wherever we moved, the first thing I did was start a garden. I loved making gardens. Our first place at Takone, by god it was cold because it was in between two rivers. You couldn't stay in bed, Justin, because your breath would turn to icicles. Even our love couldn't keep us warm.'

Nan moves from one wild story to the next. I've heard most of them before. For each of Nan's kids there seems to be a story about how they nearly died. Max turned blue from asthma while Mum turned yellow from jaundice. Nigel was white as a sheet with his eyes rolling in the back of his head.

'I had to hold the lantern out the window so your Pop could drive our Model T Ford in the fog.'

'I grabbed your mum by the ankle and went "Choonk!" and shook her like a rabbit and all of this black bile came down off her lungs.'

Mum's ankles still click to this day.

'Then with Nigel I kept yelling "Nigel Nigel! Stay with me Nigel!" He'd been drinking Southern Comfort and his mates had delivered him to our doorstep paralytic. If I hadn't found him he would have drowned in his own vomit. Pop was trying to nurse you and you were screaming in his arms.'

'Mum always said I was a quiet baby.'

'Oh, you had a set of lungs on you when you needed it. Geez I nearly died that day.'

I join a corner piece up to the rest of the jigsaw. We have all the borders of our puzzle now. Now we just have to fill in the middle.

Nan was the second oldest of nine kids! As soon as she turned nine she had to learn to carry bags of spuds on her back and look after all her brothers and sisters.

'There was one kid after another and my mum had no time for me. I felt shut out my whole bloody life. Jesus, did she used to growl me. "Do this! Do that! Do somethin' else! Go and see to the young ones".' Nan's voice goes into a nasally pitch.

'I did not know a childhood,' she says sadly.

I fiddle with two puzzle pieces, trying to force them together.

'I know it's hard sometimes with your mum but if you start to get down you've just got to remind yourself, there's always someone else far worse off than you. Justin, there are children your age who are quadriplegics!'

I don't know any kids in wheelchairs. There are starving kids in Africa on TV all the time. I can't do anything about it.

'Justin, will you spring up on those strong young legs and pour your Nan another drink please! You might have to open up a bottle.'

I go to the fridge and take out a bottle of home-brew. The fan is on low and I can smell spuds and mint drifting from the steamer. There's a T-bone steak wrapped and waiting for me to cook in the cast iron pan like Nigel showed me. I get the carved Maori bottle opener with its green-blue reflective eyes and pop the cap. I get the glass jug and tilt it while pouring slowly from the bottle. I hold it up to the window so I can see where the cloudy sediment is and not let any out. I take Nan's glass and tilt it carefully while pouring slowly from the jug so it doesn't make too much head.

'How's that?' I ask.

'Not bad barman, not bad,' she says, taking a sip.

'Some people, Justin, dwell on the past and say "Oh woe is me, I've been so hard done by" but what's the use in that? It doesn't change anything. If you've got a problem, then talk it over properly, otherwise, get in and focus on the future and work towards your dream. That's what I've always done and that's what I hope you'll continue to do.'

'There's all sorts of ups and downs in life but you mustn't let things get to you. You tell yourself "Nan said to not to worry and to concentrate on my schooling so I can be a success." I don't know if you're going to be a vet or an astronomer.'

'Not sure yet.'

'You'll face a lot of ups and downs in this life Justin. You've got to learn to stay positive and remember – "the strong survive, the weak, they fall."'

Nan's voice is loud and clear. The words are simple and direct. She's counting on me. There's a reason to keep going.

I have two pieces of the girl's face joined up. I hover them around the table, searching for the right spot.

41

It's been another tough week at home with Mum. She's seemed especially agitated and is talking more about how people are against her and no-one cares about her. I'm in my beanbag when Nan rings up. We're supposed to be heading over there tomorrow. Mum answers the phone, listening with an angry face.

'Yep. Okay … Okay. No I don't need to … Yeah, if you like … Alright!'

Her volume goes up. She's ready for a fight.

'Yep, bye.'

Mum hangs up the phone and curls her lips into a snarl. Under her breath she whispers, 'Ya bag of shit.'

'Mum, what's wrong?'

'Oh, it's just Nan and the way she carries on.

'What about?'

'Oh she wants to know what time we'll be there tomorrow, and if we can bring our washing. Reminding me to bring Sparky back, what does she think I am?!'

'She's only trying to help.'

'They're not very nice people, Nan and Pop,' she says calmly.

Her voice sounds like her normal self. It makes the words even more worrying.

'Mum, don't talk like that.'

Mum stares into space. I have no idea what she's thinking.

After school on Friday Mum and I head over to Wynyard. While tea's cooking Nan and Pop and I watch *Gardening Australia*. Pop likes to make fun of Peter Cundall saying 'like that'. Mum sits by herself at the kitchen table.

'C'mon Maudie, why don't you come in and join us?' says Nan.

'I prefer the quiet,' says Mum forcefully.

On Saturday morning I sprawl in front of the heater to watch *rage*. Nan appears in the doorway with her hands on hips and eyes scowling.

'Your mum's not well. She's been up there doin' her hisssin' and shittin' all bloody morning.'

A smile starts to creep on my face. Nan saying it like that is funny. I nod and frown it away.

'I said "Maureen, maybe it's time you got up and joined us". She says she's "just resting".'

'Maybe she should sleep in,' I say.

'It's not good for her to be laying there like that. She's not sleeping, she's only swearing.'

'Hmm,' I say, flaked out by the heater. Nan needs to watch her volume. I don't like the idea of Mum overhearing us.

'I wish you'd go up there and say something – she might listen to you.'

I'd rather stay here and wait for my new favourite song, 'Killing In The Name', to come on *rage*. Last week it was number seven and they're already up to number nine. 'Informer' by Snow comes on. It's a crazy rap song with so many lyrics you have no idea what the guy is saying.

'I do hate that.'

Nan says it while looking at the screen. I'm not sure if she means Mum or the song.

'I don't bloody know,' she says, storming off. I wonder what Nan would like me to do? She sounds surprised that Mum's the way she is. I've been putting up with it all week. If I knew the right thing to say I probably would have said it by now.

It's still weird to think of Mum swearing and someone other than me hearing it. Nan and I are on the same team when Mum's like this. Pop's too deaf to notice. I stretch out on the floor and roll onto my stomach. This is my position for beach flags at Surf Club. You fold your hands and rest your chin and you spring up from your stomach, turn around and run towards the flags. I might not be the fastest runner or surf swimmer but I'm the best at getting up quickly.

I can hear raised voices down the hall. Uh oh. I whip up in a flash and dash over to the hallway. Mum's standing in her bedroom doorway while Nan faces her off.

'I know I'm a bitch, I'm only trying to help you Maureen. You've got a very worried son who wants to spend some time with his mum!'

'Perhaps you should just worry about yourself, Mother.'

I don't like Mum's tone. She's got her sarcastic, villain voice on. Her eyes are suspicious and honed in on Nan. She crosses her arms menacingly.

'Aren't you a picture of concern. Always so worried about everyone.'

I think Nan should ignore Mum when she's like this.

'Mum!' I yelp. 'You're not well.'

'Listen to your son Maureen, please.'

Mum keeps staring. Her expression softens. She makes a smirk and gently rocks from side to side. It's a look I've never seen before.

'Okay then, Mrs Heazlewood.'

Mum turns and goes back in her room.

Nan glances at me with a deeply puzzled look. She shakes her head quickly, as if trying to shake the scene out of her mind.

After the *rage* top fifty there's *Video Smash Hits*. I'm zonked out infront of Yothu Yindi's 'Treaty.' I remember Mum saying how she liked this one. She liked how it shows the Aboriginal people happy and doing backflips on the beach. At least someone somewhere is having a good time.

Nan appears muttering about Mum. Her beady eyes scan my scene.

'I think someone needs to go up there and try and get your mum motivated.'

I sit up on my elbows, careful not to spill my drink. I'm really not in the mood.

'C'mon, you can't be sittin' in front of TV all day. I thought we might all go for a drive or somethin' after lunch. I'd like to go and bag up some of that good leaf mulch at Oldina. It might do your mum good to get out for a while.'

A drive with sick Mum, there's not much to look forward to.

'Maybe we should just leave her?'

Nan puts her hands on her hips and takes in a shocked breath.

'God, leave her up there laughing to herself.'

Nan does an impression of Mum's laughing.

'Tee hee hee. Tee hee hee.'

It's so weird.

Pop walks over from the kitchen. He's holds out a freshly

peeled and washed carrot. Perfect and orange. Carrots are good for eyesight. They help you see in the dark.

'Thanks Pop.'

I crunch down Bugs Bunny style and wait for Nan to get distracted or change the subject. I'm trying to get out of worrying.

'*Treaty yeah. Treaty now.*'

She shakes her head and turns.

'I don't bloody know,' she says. 'I'm going out in the garden.'

I feel guilty and relieved. Girlfriend are being interviewed. I have a crush on Siobhánn. I crunch my carrot and gaze over her long, shiny blonde hair.

TV TV. What's on TV?

I run my hand over the glass and collect the static zaps. I lean back and play with the remote. I keep the sound down low. Even if it's *Healthy, Wealthy and Wise* or a boring movie. Silence would be too scary. TV means there's always someone in the room.

Tonight I'm in luck because my favourite movie is on – *Three Men and a Baby*. It has an excellent plot and lots of funny scenes. It's the only movie I've rewatched over and over again. I always liked Tom Selleck from *Magnum* but in this one he's strong and funny and tender with the baby. At first he doesn't want a bar of it. They have to go shopping for baby stuff and try to change nappies. By the end he bonds with Nancy and picks up her little pink construction hat. The baby is very cute and I love the scene where Steve Guttenberg slams the powder down on the pool table, sending a huge cloud in the air.

After that is *The Late Show*, where they do a brilliant parody of 'Informer.' It looks and sounds just like the real thing but is just a little bit off.

'Inform me if you can comprehend what I'm saying.'
I wake up on Sunday with the heavy grey day looming down on me. I get up and make breakfast and read the paper with Pop. Nan and Mum's voices are raised at the other end of the hall. They've been fighting all morning.

'... order me around like you do!'

'... don't spoil your teeth Maureen. You've got such a lovely smile.'

Mum wanders into the kitchen. She looks terrible. Her eyes are glaring. Her mouth is squashed. Her cheeks are flushed and greasy. Her hair is ragged from not showering. She hitches up the shoulder of a baggy old T-shirt and stands at the sink to make a cup of coffee. Nan follows her into the kitchen.

'Maureen, you know I'm only trying to help you.'

'Maureen, I'm only trying to help you!' Mum screws her face up and wiggles her head back and forth in a nasty impression. Her face drops and her cracked voice goes low.

'Some help.'

Pop looks up from his paper, his eyes searching blankly around the room. His mouth is closed. He breathes heavily through his wide, deep nostrils.

Mum brings up problems from when she was a teenager. She snuck over the fence at night to see a boy, Peter. When she got back Nan belted her with the kettle cord.

'Yeah you didn't mind laying into us when it suited ya.'

'Oh Maureen, be fair,' Nan lets a breath escape like a laugh. 'You think I took pleasure in punishing you? I cried tears of blood about that. I was so worried and I didn't know where you'd gone.'

Mum leans against the sink with her arms crossed. Her whole body ripples with anger. She narrows her eyes and speaks in a low growl.

'Yeah, you just watch yourself.'

She rears her body up and takes a step forward. Nan flinches and backs away.

'Mum!' I yell. 'Calm down!'

Mum makes her coffee and stirs her spoon furiously. She heads back into her room. To my relief, Nan doesn't say any more.

'I thought she was going to attack me there for a second,' whispers Nan.

'Gawd,' says Pop finally.

'You're not doing nuthin' to help?' Nan glares at Pop.

'What?' He says grumpily. 'What am I 'sposed to do?'

'Get up there and help your daughter,' Nan pours her glass of water into a pot plant.

'She doesn't listen to me,' grumbles Pop.

'Yeah, well, you won't try.'

I've read the same sentence in the paper three times. Carlton walloped Collingwood. Kernahan kicked seven. We're third on the ladder. I hate seeing everyone so miserable.

Pop shakes his head.

'I don't know me boy,'

I make a click with my tongue. I breathe out while saying 'No.'

I spend the morning playing basketball and helping Nan put the brew down. We line the sterilised bottles up and put in one spoonful of sugar per bottle. I hold each one under the long white nozzle coming out of the brew until they're filled. Nan places the capping machine carefully over the metal cap and wrenches down hard on the arms. Once all the bottles are filled we tip each one upside down. Then the bottles go in a carton with today's date on top. They won't be ready to drink for at least two months.

Inside Pop's in the lounge catching up on his diary.

'You been doodlin' in me diary,' he says, holding up the inside cover. I bought a spinning top with a texta built in that makes cool spirals.

'Ya twerp!' he chuckles.

Mum appears in the doorway.

'My son's not a twerp!'

'Oh Maureen, I'm just having a bit of fun,' he sighs. 'Justin knows I am.'

'I don't like you calling him names,' she says.

I stare at the carpet, waiting for Mum to pass.

At least there's lunch to look forward to. Mum and Nan argue about who's going to cut the roast lamb. I hover about, grabbing little morsels to test. I always get the bone. The meat is definitely more tender and there's lots of tangy, fatty, salty bits to get at. We take our places around the table. Nan keeps chatting away, trying to remain positive. Mum lowers her head and starts stabbing at the food.

'Mum, I thought I might say grace,' I say gently.

She looks up, surprised.

'Oh, I'm sorry dear, yes.'

I'm shy because it's not something we normally do. Now I feel heat in my cheeks as all the attention is on me.

'For what we are about to receive may the lord make us truly thankful. In your name. Amen.'

'Amen,' says Nan.

'We always used to say that in the army, "Two four six eight, now bog in don't wait,"' Pop chuckles.

'I like how Justin says it,' says Nan quietly.

'Who taught you that one?' Mum asks.

'I think I heard Ned Flanders say it.'

'Lovely,' she blurts and goes back to gobbling her meal.

'Who's Ned Flanders?' asks Nan. Her nickname is Ned.

Get Up Mum

I tell her he's off *The Simpsons*. She shakes her head and changes the subject. Nan talks between every mouthful. Sometimes it's like she's having a conversation with herself.

'You know, where I planted those broad beans last year and got absolutely nothing …'

Clink clink. Chew chew.

'… well this year the climbing beans I've had so much more luck with.'

'We're reading *To Kill A Mockingbird* in English,' I say. When I speak, everyone makes an effort to listen. Even Mum raises her head.

'It's set in Alabama during the depression and the kids say yessum and nome, instead of yes and no,'

'What's that one?' asks Pop.

'Yessum and nome!' Nan repeats in a loud voice. 'Turn your hearing aid up, Father!'

'That is supposed to be a good one,' says Nan, 'I have not read it.'

'It's a bit like *Tom Sawyer* I suppose. We read that in primary school. This one's a bit more serious.'

'You know, when I was a child in my family I was not encouraged to read,' says Nan. 'So I really tried to encourage my children. Your Uncle Max was alright with a motorbike magazine but there was no friggin' way I could get him to read a novel! "Untrue, just bloody falsehoods!" That was what Max would say.'

'Well you've always been an avid reader,' says Pop.

'Yes, Len, but only in later life. Ken was into dog and horse stories. Nigel, well, he'd pick up a book of any description – that kid was into it. He just read and read and read.'

Nan turns to Mum with a furrowed brow. Mum's demolishing the last of her spuds.

'I could never get to what you liked to read Maureen. It was a very strange thing.'

Mum looks up, wide eyed.

'I like to read,' she says flatly.

'I used to present you with books but you weren't into them. "No, I don't want them, no I don't like it."'

'I wouldn't say that,' Mum says, staring at Nan. I wish Nan wouldn't impersonate Mum right now.

'Yes, but you did …'

Mum purses her lips. She sits up in her chair.

Outside a gust of wind sends the plastic axeman on the lattice into a chopping frenzy.

Clack! Clack! Clack! Clack! Clack!

'I didn't always have to. I just did my own thing.'

'That's not what I was saying, Maureen.'

'Then what are ya saying?'

Mum voice grows wild, her eyes glare.

'Anyway, let's not worry …' says Pop.

Mum's eyes narrow. She slowly puts her cutlery down and folds her arms deliberately. She locks her gaze onto Nan. I rest my fork and keep my eyes on Mum. There's a fluttering and tightening in my ribs that sinks down into my tummy. The food jams mid digestion. My heart churns everything up.

Nan's fork hovers in mid-air.

'I was just saying I couldn't always get you into reading, Maureen.'

'I read when I felt like it. What the hell are you goin' on about?' Mum's head quivers. She wants to grit her teeth and speak at the same time. I can see her breathing as her chest rises and falls and snorts fast out her nose.

Nan lowers her eyes to her plate. She shakes her head quickly.

'Never mind,' she mutters.

Mum's foul eyes laser in.

'… ssssit there criticising me. Ya bitch,' she hisses.

'Yes Maudie, I know I'm a bitch,' Nan says solemnly.

'Mum, calm down!' I yell. I want her attention but she doesn't budge. There's pressure in my throat and it aches as my voice passes. The ache rises behind my eyes. I widen my eyes to fill up the room.

'Maybe if you'd've stopped pressurin' me.'

Mum's mouth is crooked. Her eyes are cold brown yolks. Nan puts down her knife.

'Maureen please, listen …' Nan's voice is tender. 'It was not my intention to pressure you …'

Mum's face is swarming. She can't settle on an expression.

'I know you were very independent as a teenager. It would be the same with this young fulla here. If he wasn't into reading, I'd be a fool if I kept trying to push it on him. Maureen, your mum, your own mum. I did not get into reading until I was forty!'

Nan talks normally. Mum lowers her eyes, finally.

I don't take mine off her.

After lunch I head outside to play a game of basketball. I need fresh air. I've made up a shoot-out game based on the cracks in the driveway. I have a league with teams based on my friends and imagine the other players in my mind. I used to do the same thing with football in the hallway. Nan knitted Pop a small grey cushion for him to kneel on at bowls. He never used it so it became my indoor football. I'd close all the doors and go mad in the hallway being all the players and kicking and marking it from one end to the other. The doorways were goal posts and Nan's sea urchin collection on the wall was definitely out of bounds.

It's a cool, overcast day with a few spits of rain, or is it mist from Nan's hose? My heart is on high alert and my ears are tuned for signs of trouble.

The basketball hits the backboard and flies to the side. It bounces off one of Nan's pea straw bales and over the fence. I hear it bouncing down the neighbour's driveway, then silence. It must have gone into a bush.

Sound shocks my chest.

'Ya trollop!'

'C'mon Maureen!'

I tear inside, ripping open the fly screen door.

I'm in the kitchen in time to see the back of Mum. She has one arm raised. Her hand is balled in a fist. Nan's eyes are wide. She holds up open palms.

'Caaamonnnn … fight me then!'

Mum's voice is rude and dirty.

'I won't! Maureen, please calm down.'

Mum leans in and swings her fist. It passes through Nan's hand and collects her in the side of the face.

I feel a shock of pins in my fingers.

Nan takes a step back. Mum swipes again.

'Do it again in front of your son!'

I step forward and grab both of Mum's arms. Mum pushes her right fist forward and it connects with Nan's jaw. I cuff my fingers around her wrists and pull her backwards.

'Mum stop it!'

'Listen to your son!'

Pop appears in the doorway of the lounge.

'Maureen, leave Mum alone!'

Mum flicks her head, distracted.

'Come on, ya bitch!'

Her voice is a gravelly growl. She surges forward like a beast.

Her muscles are rippling beneath my fingers. She's become something else.

'You're sick, Maureen!'

'Oh, you're the ssssick one,' she hisses in full tilt.

'Mum! You're going crazy!'

Her head turns. She takes a step back with me. Her arm is still raised for a strike but I have it secured. She slowly lowers her arms. I don't let go.

'I'm sorry, Maureen. Justin is right.'

Nan takes the moment to hurry past us, towards the hallway. I feel Mum heave towards her but I keep her pinned.

'Yeah …' Mum bellows. 'You run ya COWARD!'

This is pure rage. All trace of Mum is gone.

I've never been in a fight before. I feel strong. If Mum tries to attack again I'll stop her.

'Maureen, you're not right,' says Pop, standing in the lounge.

'Very well, Sergeant Major,' Mum sneers.

'What did you say?'

'If people don't love you, knife 'em and toss 'em aside.'

Pop presses his lips together hard and breathes hard through his nose.

'You must calm down.'

'I'm calm! I'm a peaceful person. When I'm not being attacked.'

Mum finally lowers her arms. I loosen my grip, but not by much. Mum hasn't said a word about me the whole time.

Three o'clock. The aftermath. The day feels stunned into silence. Mum's on her bed, lying quietly. Pop's watching the footy with the sound down low. It's another one-sided Swans game.

'It's not a game it's a shame,' he says.

'Do you know where Nan is?' I ask.

'I dunno, she's probably down in the garden somewhere.'

Sunday has never seemed sadder. My throat is swollen as an ache swells in my temples. My heart is pounding but there's still work to do. I've got to make sure Nan's okay.

Outside the light is steamy and gloomy. My head is a cloud, ready to rain.

'Plonk' goes the frog in the tadpole pond. A sudden gust rattles the trellis and sends the plastic woodchopper into another flurry of swings. He belts away, always missing the log.

Nan's garden is a sprawling maze. There are paths either side of the main lawn divided by garden. They run in a full semi-circle by the back fence and hot house. The caravan is folded up and parked behind the garage on the left, and next to that is the corrugated water tank. The vegetable garden blooms with carrot tops and climbing beans tied to stakes. Netting protects a row of sprouts and green shoots, popping up from the soil. The grass is plump and clean beneath my feet.

I find Nan huddled in the hot house where the exotic flowers live. The air is humid and salty from dried seaweed, which makes a scruffy bed on the floor. She nurses a glass of flat beer. Her eyes are wide and forlorn. She makes soft half sobs, like a little girl.

'Oooh, hoo hoo hoo!'

It's how someone might cry if they were pretending. She sniffs big through her nose and half-coughs half-shudders, all while doing her tragic whimpering.

I hover by the door and watch.

Nan. I have to protect Nan.

'Are you alright?'

'Justin, me lad,' she sniffs.

I've never seen Nan cry. It doesn't seem real.

'I'm sorry you had to see that.'

Nan looks small. In the light I can see strands of grey amongst the brown. I feel sorry for her. She was just trying to prepare a lovely lunch for her family. She never turns us away, no matter how bad Mum gets.

'She kicked my bad leg, before you came in, while I was sitting down. She went straight for me shinbone.'

Nan's glass is at a slant, almost spilling. She peers off to the side and sputters out a few sobs. I want to reach out but I'm frozen.

'Lucky I came when I did.'

'Justin, she was wild!' Nan glares up at me. 'My own daughter. You didn't see her face, her eyes! I thought she was gonna damn near murder me.' Nan's voice is nasally from her blocked nose. It softens her tone.

'I don't know, it must be the devil or something.'

'It doesn't matter what I bloody say. She flies off the handle and wants a fight. I'm getting too old Justin!' Her voice rises in panic.

'She's your mother Justin but she's MY DAUGHTER! I've been dealing with this for too many years now, well before you were born.'

I study the floor. Underneath the shelf are spare pots inside pots and a white bag of 'blood and bone.' I want to fix this. I need to! I can't stand to see my family suffer.

'Your Pop and I … well he's seventy-four. Doctors have said I could have a stroke at any time. We're getting too old Justin. You're grown, you can stand up to her. I saw her face when you grabbed her. She wasn't expecting you to be so strong.'

My chest blooms. I'm glad I shocked Mum.

'I think you should make an appointment with Dr Gaylan. You can just quietly ring up while your mum's outside, or do it from here.'

'I wouldn't be allowed, would I?'

'Of course you would! She's a doctor. You'd be seeing her on behalf of the family. There's nothing to say you can't make enquiries. You can tell her what's really going on.'

The idea makes me nervous. What if I got in trouble? It would be good to tell someone the full story. I know I'm capable. I can be a leader if my family needs me.

'You go inside now darlin' and keep an eye on her please. I'll sit here with my garden and my hippeastrum, isn't it beautiful?'

As I get up I admire the pretty red flower with a cream stripe, shaped like a megaphone.

I plonk down in the chair next to Pop. He's planted in his seat like a woollen tree with black sock roots.

'I don't know me boy,' he sighs, staring ahead.

I squint at the screen. I stare out the curtains at the neighbours' house. I wonder if they heard anything? What on earth would they think?

'Eh?'

He reaches an arm across and gives my shoulder a squeeze.

'I know it's hard on you.'

I don't move. Tears fill my eyes.

'We'll try and work in together and … sort something out,' he sighs. 'We'll get her right somehow.'

My throat is tight. A tear spills.

'Yep.'

I sit with Pop, watching the football, holding in.

Mum is packing her bag. She's decided to go home early.

'Are you coming too?' she asks. Her eyes are baggy, like a worn out owl.

'I'll stop here. Pop can bring me over in the morning.'

'Yes, alright.' She puts down her things and turns to face me. Her smile is faint – her eyes pained.

'I'm sorry if I upset you, dear. Really I am.'

'You hurt Nan.'

'Did I?' She nibbles her bottom lip. 'Maybe I'll go and apologise?'

'No, Mum, leave her be.'

Pop appears in the hallway. He speaks softly and quietly.

'Are you alright to drive?'

'Yep, I'll be right.'

'Maureen. You can't go upsetting Mum like that again. You know she's not well herself.'

'Yep.'

Mum is like a girl getting in trouble.

She puts her bags in the bonnet of the car. The Volks roars alive, reverses and fades into the distance. It's a good sound. I go to the fridge and spoon some yoghurt in a bowl. It's cool and creamy and sweet in my mouth. I sit on the lovely soft couch and let my toes have a play. It's quiet without Mum. Already there's more air.

I flick through the phonebook for Barbara's number. It's an easy one to find because it has '666' in it.

'Hello!' comes her high voice.

My words wobble because I've never rung her before. I stand up and focus and suck air into my voice.

I tell her how Mum had a fight with Nan and is now heading over to Burnie.

'Oh Justin, that's no good is it? She seemed well when she was here before, last week. Is your Nan alright now?'

'Yeah, she's in the garden.'

'Well you tell her not to worry and that I'll check in on Maudie when she comes home. I'll bring the cat food round like I normally do. I can give you a call and let you know she's arrived safe.'

'Thanks Barbara.'

'And don't you let it worry you, will you?'

'No.'

After I hang up, I wander into my room and close the door. It's dark so I have to turn the light on. I'm not sure what I feel like doing. I flop down on the bed. I bow my head and make a prayer with my hands.

I imagine Mum inside her car. She's driving safely. She doesn't crash.

I lean over and unzip my bag and take out my Bible. I read a few pages. A man comes in yelling at Jesus and he orders the evil spirit to leave the man.

'The evil spirit shook the man hard, gave a loud scream, and came out of him.'

I close my eyes and whisper a prayer asking Jesus to free Mum of all evil spirits and to keep Nan and Pop alive for as long as possible.

I stretch my arms across the bed and rest my head on the side. I think of bushwalking with Nigel. Blinking red lights. Nothing at all.

21 Saturday HAD an awful morning. Mum and Nan were going cook. Mum was really horrible! Listened to Footy- Carlton beat collingwood by 54. YES - we are in finals. Soo sure! yey yey yey.

22 Sunday TODAY WAS A HORRIFIC DAY. Mum/Nan arguing all day. Mum went phsycho. She hit nan a few times. Nan upset. Mum went home. I rang barbara. I staying here for night. Simpsons finished tonight. OKAY.

Notes

TABLETS HELP MUM

Sorry bout that

42

Nan appears after tea with her hair in a turban. She's doing her oiling routine where she coats her hair in castor oil which she keeps in a greasy plastic bottle by the heater. She says it's her mother's secret for keeping the colour in your hair. It seems to work because Nan's hair is still brown and she looks way better than other women her age. Her hair routine makes her seem girlish, more like Mum.

The Simpsons is on but Pop can't stand it so I watch it on the TV in Nan and Pop's room. Krusty the Clown's show gets cancelled and Bart and Lisa help him stage a comeback. Dylan from *Beverly Hills* is in it as 'Sideshow Luke Perry.' In the guide it says: '*The Simpsons* (Final).' I always get sad when the voice on the ABC says it's been the series final of something like *Fawlty Towers*. I don't like things ending.

Nan goes to bed early as usual so Pop and I sit up while I have an after-tea snack. Pop puts on Uncle Ken's tape. It's called 'Come From the Heart' and is his version of already known country songs. I find the music a bit daggy but I like Ken's voice. It's deep and rich and doesn't sound like anyone else.

Pop sits in his chair, arms on the armrests, staring forwards. Sometimes it feels like he could be waiting for something. He might be waiting for one of us to say something, I'm not sure.

'I've been reading the Holy Bible.'

Pop turns his head to me.

'Eh?'

'I'm still reading the Bible.'

'Oh yeah,' he says. 'It can be a comfort sometimes.'

'Have you read it?'

'Oh, bits and pieces. They used to make us at school.'

I take a bite of my Sao and vegemite and tap it like a cigarette. Crumbs fall onto the plate.

'Did you go to church much?'

'Aww, we used to go there for a while. Your mum'd come with me.'

'When was that?'

'Oh, long time ago now. Before you were born. She was only, oh, fifteen.'

'Do you still believe in God?'

Pop stares ahead. His head does a little shake, as if he's rattling a thought into place.

'I don't know, Justin. I like to think there's … something out there, more than just us.'

I reckon that counts as believing in God. Pop will be okay.

I nurse my silver mirrored pewter mug in my hands. Pop won it at bowls and because it said 'Carlton' he had it engraved for me:

JUSTIN HEAZLEWOOD
2-12-87

I like playing with my reflection. If I tilt it slightly my head stretches up making it look like I have a cone head. While this is happening another upside down head floats down from the top. The two reflections morph into each other until two sets of glasses melt into one. Now there are only frames with skin covering the eyes. I keep tilting until the nose gets swallowed and there's only a small head of hair and a single mouth, opening and closing.

On the stereo Ken is singing a sad ballad. I like the chorus. Lose your one and only … there's room here for the lonely. Broken dreams dancing in beams of a neon moon.

That night I lay back in my warm bed and listen to Pop shuffling about and switching off taps. A car swishes past but otherwise it's quiet. He goes into the bedroom and I can hear Nan talking to him. I wonder what her and Pop talk about when they're not arguing.

I imagine what it would be like.

If this were my room all the time.

In the morning Nan wakes me up by pressing the backs of her fingers against my cheek.

'Feel how cold Nan's fingers are!'

'Aaaah,' I groan, escaping under the covers.

'C'mon then up you get. We've got to run you over to home to pick up your uniform in time for school!'

Nan states the obvious. I follow the orders.

There's a burst of excitement and relief.

I made it through sleeping. I made it through yesterday!

It's over and it can't ever happen again.

I enjoy the dreaminess of being at Nan and Pop's on a Monday morning. I wash with the Imperial Leather soap and use Nan's flowery shampoo. I flick all the switches on their new IXL Tastic heater with its super bright lamps that coat the room in warmth and destroy the chill. I dab Pop's Christmas talc under my arms and a slap of Musk for Men aftershave on my chin for good luck.

Out in the hallway Pop leans back against the edge of the bedroom doorframe. He moves himself side to side, scratching his back like an old horse. I hear a low squeak.

'Pop went Pop!' he chuckles.

Outside the lawn is crisp and new. Pop reckons the frost will be good for the swedes. I'm happy the veggies are happy. With the heater going and the *Today Show* on TV the whole atmosphere feels light and normal. On the news it says *A Country Practice* has been cancelled! Sydney might be hosting the Olympics in 2000. I'll be twenty. I guess I'll be at university.

Nan packs my lunch. 'Remember what I said about Mum's doctor. And you know we're only a phone call away if things get bad.'

I nod. I have homework.

'You be careful Len because there's ice on the road and there's idiots about.'

'Yeah I know.'

'Will you go straight to Probus or come back here?'

'I'll come back here I reckon.'

I'd love to call in sick and go with Pop to his Probus meeting (whatever Probus is). I'd find a table up the back and get some bingo tickets and order a Coke and read the paper. Afterwards we could get a counter meal and call in and do some shopping. Then I could help Nan in the garden and mow the lawn for some pocket money. Then I'd be here at five o'clock when Nan and Pop knocked off and we could all sit together on the swing seat and I'd catch all the conversations I'd normally miss.

We load up the car and I buckle up as we back away. Nan waits at the porch and blows me a kiss. I catch it and blow one back. We turn and she waves and disappears from view. Now there's no-one in sight, only the road ahead and sky above.

The streets are clean and calm in the morning light. I wriggle myself comfortable in the seat. Pop squeezes a pellet of 'Juicy Fruit' into his mouth. He sees a mate he knows driving in the opposite direction. I know this because they both lift their pointer fingers from the wheel.

I fiddle about in the glovebox. There are four green travel cups where I hide my secret notes to Nan. She found my first one and now we write back and forth, sometimes over months.

The sun casts patches of twinkling glitter on the sea as we drive past. My eyes are a superhero skimming the diamonds, hurdling road markers and jungle swinging power poles. Clean white clouds are wispy and stretched out across the morning blue. They're spun like fairy floss and spread out like feathers. I can form the outline of huge creatures with my eyes. They're zooming across the sky. I make out a head and body and wings.

A lovely creature.

A woman.

A sky angel!

There's two of them, mid-step and prancing at light speed. Their gowns are flowing behind like comets. The picture is of them mid-warp as they dive-bomb into another dimension. The crisp light makes them glow and seem three dimensional. I picture myself out there in the blue grey steel, paddling away, alone.

The horizon line is constant in the distance.

No matter how far we travel or how fast we go, it's always the same.

We near the final bend into Burnie. On the right is a long concrete wall where the street rises up. I look out for my favourite graffiti.

1981 ALL YOU NEED IS LOVE ☮

43

Arriving at school in the Subaru is a bonus. I like getting dropped off in a car that doesn't make everyone stop and turn. I'm like any other normal kid! I lean over to give Pop a hug. It's not easy with the steering wheel and seatbelt in the way. I feel his fingers tap me on the shoulder. I'm careful not to kiss him.

'Alright, you enjoy your day. No use worrying about things.'

'Okay.'

My teeth are still chalky from using Nan and Pop's denture toothpaste.

It's good to stroll through Parklands blue doors into the corridors with the wood panel walls and brown carpets. I soon get lost in the stream of dark blue jumpers and grey shorts and stockinged legs and brown hair in scrunchies and yapping and yawns with fog coming out. First thing in the morning everyone's either dazed or energized, scurrying along and laughing at anything. Sleepovers and quad bikes and footy and boyfriends.

I blur my thoughts among the faces and wander down to the gym to see who's there. We're in second semester now. There's only one more week until holidays. I know where everything is and what I have to do and how to fit in.

She wanted to get at Nan.

But I wouldn't let her.

I'm worn out from yesterday, but already it seems further away.

After the bell goes I walk upstairs to Top C. The lockers are in order of grade so being grade seven, mine is on the bottom. I sink to one knee and twirl my combination back and forth while the legs of older girls and boys hover and dance on either side of me.

SLAM! goes the locker next to my head. I wish they'd do it gentler. Maths is first up, which gives me a sinking feeling. It's always hard work and if you don't concentrate you can miss a lot. At least it's cosy from the heaters and Billy's arrived first and saved me a plastic red chair in our usual spot up the back. It's really good to see him.

'Here he is! Didja get up to much on the weekend?'

'Nah. Listened to Carlton on the radio.'

'Yeah how good was it! Big 'Sticks' with seven goals. I went and saw my dad play footy for South Burnie. He bagged ten goals!'

'Yeah?' I say flatly. Billy's talking quickly.

'Did you hear what I said?'

'I didn't know your dad played footy.'

'Yeah I've told you that before.'

I stare at the scratches on the chair in front.

It was as bad as it gets.

It was the worst it's ever been.

Mr Dickenson comes in. He has a deep, steady voice that helps me to concentrate. We're doing geometry which is all about angles and lines.

Intersecting lines are lines that meet.

Parallel lines are lines that do not intersect.

Angles are made when two lines meet.

Angle looks like angel.

Mr Dickenson gives us a series of examples to work on. I take out my pencil. It's quiet now with everyone scratching away. The hum of the heaters and the murmuring of numbers and the shuffling of papers. The lights are bright and my eyes are aching. How tired am I? I don't really know how much sleep I got, but I definitely woke up early.

Lines and letters. Numbers and angles. My thoughts slow and hollow, like I'm not always here. My heart does a double beat and there's a prickly, tickly feeling around my skin. I open my mouth wider and take a deep breath. I don't know if I can stay here. My heart speeds up. I'm alone at my desk. I don't want to be here. I can't go anywhere else.

'Justin, help,' Billy says, leaning over. He peers at me with a goofy smile and scans my page and compares my answers to his. I don't mind, at least he's polite about it. I can feel his arm touching mine. I like the closeness.

Mr Dickenson goes on about Pythagoras' theorem. I watch the clock.

9.35.

9.40.

9.43.

'Next period' I tell myself. Next period I can switch off and take a break from thinking about anything. It's science with Mr Verze and that's always a bludge.

C'mon clock!

Mum didn't attack me.

She never does.

Out in the corridor in between classes it's mayhem as usual. A student highway with three lanes going in all directions. There's shrieking and shoving and slamming and dodging. I'm a fast walker with quick responses, so I make a game of steering myself through the obstacle course like I'm in a video game. I get a jolt as someone drags my shoulder backwards. I turn to see the ugly face of Wilkie with his monobrow and white spot where a bird could have crapped in his hair. Uh oh, what have I done?

'I heard you're collecting Lakers cards. I reckon I've got some you'll want.'

The grade eights aren't hassling us anymore and have become our basketball card dealers. American basketball is all the rage and you can't even take a shot for the bin without someone rebounding or swatting it away. NBA cards have all different brands like Upper Deck and Skybox and players with crazy names like Muggsy Bogues and Mookie Blaylock (who Pearl Jam first named themselves after). Every card is worth something, especially inserts and rookie cards, and their values are listed in a magazine called *Beckett*. I go for the Los Angeles Lakers because of Magic Johnson even though he's got AIDS.

Billy waits up for me, fending off Vanny who's trying to give him a horse bite.

'Hey are we still going down to McDonalds after school?' Billy squeals, as we outwalk Vanny's hands.

'Yeah, we can record some ambience on your recorder.'

Billy and I have written a hilarious monologue about McDonalds for speech and drama. We'll be performing it in front of the rest of grade seven on Friday.

In Science we're doing 'The body in question' with Mr Verze. We have to write out what's on the whiteboard. It's hard for me to see from up the back. I lean over to copy off Billy. He's squinting too and thinks he needs glasses! I get out my half plastic Rulex ruler that Billy snapped pretending it was a diving board. I rule up two columns. I haven't left much room to write. I only fit four words to a line.

'Explain that the human body is a complex living thing, which is made up of many systems and organs.'

I can't be bothered making it any better.

'Come on, ya bitch!'

She didn't ask to be let go.

She knew I was there.

Memories echo and sink.

More itching inside. I annoy Billy.

'Don't!' he says, still writing. He sounds irritated and fends me off with one arm.

Mr Verze presents us with a bag of skipping ropes. We're doing an experiment to check our pulse. Billy has his fingers pressed tight into my wrist staring at his watch. We have to take one resting pulse then one after skipping for ten minutes.

'Ah, don't go running off anywhere, please stay in the area outside the science block!'

My resting rate is 60 bpm.

My exercising rate is 102 bpm.

There are questions on the board:
- What has changed?
- Why?
- How long does it take for your pulse to return to normal?

Now Mr Verze passes out stethoscopes.

'Okay we're going to listen to your heart.'

I sing 'Listen to Your Heart' by Roxette with the stethoscope as a microphone. It gets a good chuckle from Billy.

I push the cold buds in my ears and slide the stethoscope under my shirt. I always forget which side my heart's on. It's making a dull 'whoomp-whoomp' noise. I remember having trouble getting to sleep on my side because the sound of my heartbeat in my ears disturbed me. As soon as I become aware of my heart I worry about it stopping.

Whoomp-whoomp.

Whoomp-whoomp.

Whoomp-whoomp.

You forget your heart is there until you listen to it. It's thumping away inside its cage.

The sound troubles me.

What if there's something wrong with it?

'What can you hear?' asks Mr Verze.

'A soft boom-boom noise in rhythm,' I write.

She didn't struggle.

I knew Mum was there.

In there, somewhere.

'Who's comin' to the canteen?' asks Billy at lunch. There aren't any other takers so he turns to me, frowning.

'C'mon,' he says, flicking his head.

The lunchtime lines are crazy as everyone races down the stairs to get in first. They only make one batch of hot chips, so if you don't line up before the first set of stairs you miss out. The roller doors haven't even gone up yet! Some people try Chinese swaps where you let someone in line and then swap places with them which just pisses everybody off.

Luke Whelan slides in for a sneak attack. He hunches his shoulders and whips his head around, as if it makes him less likely to be seen. He's got his floppy hair tucked back beneath his Charlotte Hornets cap to show off his shaved undercut. Luke wears an earring and looks pretty tough so no-one bothers him, except sometimes Elvis who doesn't seem to be scared of anyone.

'Marvelous effort that!' says Billy, doing an impression of the Twelfth Man doing an impression of Tony Grieg.

Billy mimes slapping a pie in my face.

'Pyyyyye-thagoras!'

'Hey, lemme try on your glasses!' asks Luke, grinning.

'They'll blow your mind,' says Billy.

I hand them over cautiously. My eyes relax as my focus slips into a soft fuzz. I never see the reactions, only hear them.

'Fuck they're thick!' cackles Luke. 'I feel like I'm drunk! How do you see through those things?'

Everyone asks the same thing. I don't know how to explain that I see fine. I guess I'll never know what they see either. Nan says I shouldn't let others try on my glasses because it'll put them out of plumb. I'm still enjoying the notoriety, even though it's a long wait for them to return.

'Does anyone else want a go?'

At least they impress people. I'm first in blindness.

And I'm next in line! I order a chocolate dessert because I've already brought my lunch. They've started charging ten cents for the spoon! Billy shouts me.

'I should start charging twenty cents to try my glasses on!'

'Yeah,' he laughs.

We park ourselves at a bench near the music rooms. I take out Nan's sandwich wrapped in foil.

Everything was normal

Except for the monster at the table.

The sandwich is like the ones I usually have when we're bushwalking. It's ham, lettuce, beetroot, alfalfa sprouts and apple. The bread is slightly soggy but I don't mind. I think about Nan making it just for me and the pain swells as I wonder if she's okay.

Get Up Mum

I won't see her until the weekend.
   'Has that got apple in it?'
I'm in two places at once.
I blink the places together.
'Yeah.'
'Ya freak, doesn't it go brown?'
I shake my head.
'Who made that for ya?'
'Nan.'
'Little Justin, with his apple sandwich!' he teases.
'Don't Billy.'

I liked holding onto her.
I was the one in control.

44

After school I find the front door open and Mum on the couch. She's grinning away and eating a plum. She's wearing her cream windcheater with 'Vive La Marine' in big letters and drawings of three little sailors with white caps. Below them it says 'New young French style.' She's had it for years and I've always liked the cartoons.

'Oh, you're home?' she asks.

She lets out a laugh and starts coughing and choking.

'You okay?'

Mum nods and squints while sitting up and patting her chest with a hand.

'Oh, dear,' she says. 'It went down the wrong way.'

For a moment she seems normal.

I go to my room and take out my carousel of cassettes. I've had an idea for a cool project where I dub all the best bits of each tape onto one super tape and call it 'Heazlewood Highlights.' I can include all my favourite segments from Nigel breaking a beer bottle to Yahtzee and 'Doing a Heazlewood' New Year's Eve.

That way I won't have to sit through the dull bits or listen to another one of Nan's serious lectures. On the south-west walk tape there's a pretty heavy section where she goes on about sex and marriage. It starts off funny but she soon gets worked up about my future wife and how I should listen to her. While I've got that tape in the player I might as well tape over it. I'm allowed if I want. I make up the rules. The red light glows – I'm live. I lean down and talk into the mic.

'Nan means well but sometimes she goes overboard a bit, doesn't she, with a bit of graphical detail. I mean, I know all about that stuff. It's not that it shocks me at all. It's just, our tapes are supposed to be funny and fun and I don't need this traumatic stuff on it, you know what I mean?'

I press stop and play, making sure I haven't erased any good stuff. It's Nan's voice, as usual.

'Yes and you've got it on tape and I hope you'll learn to read it over and listen to it because I speak the truth!'

Ha, sorry Nan. Not this time.

I start making a list of which tapes and sides have the best sections. I have thirteen now, dating back to 1988. That was on my old red recorder so the quality wasn't as good. Crayfish Creek '93 is easily my favourite. Nan's going berserk with the mozzies while Nigel and Ken chime in like Norm and Cliff from *Cheers*. I'm cool and cheeky and getting told off like Bart Simpson.

I slot in the grey 'Yahtzee' tape and press play. I love handling the neat rectangles. I whip them out of their cases and into the cassette door like a gunslinger. I switch buttons from 'reverse' to 'stop' to 'play' like an expert pilot controlling an F-14. The atmosphere pours through the black grills. I can hear dice being shaken as Pop rolls a Yahtzee and we all bellow and shriek and wail. Nan says 'wow wow wow wow wow!' I emit a long siren noise. It's the perfect time for Nigel to do his line.

'I hope this is just a passing phase for this family.'

'Mum'll shoot me,' laughs Nan. 'She'll say "Won't you bloody grow up Mum?" Nuh, can't, sorry.'

'Can't grow up?'

'Aaah. you've gotta have a bit of fun of some sort,' says Pop, trying to add up.

'Oh, I give up.'

'Pop, you gave up years ago,' says Nan. 'I can't understand this game.'

'Me either,' says Nigel.

'I know he's got the tape on that's why I'm performing. That's all I'm performing for you little shit!'

I laugh when the me on the tape laughs.

'Who's that?' Mum appears in the doorway.

I press stop, startled.

'Oh it's us playing Yahtzee at Christmas.'

I still get embarrassed about my tapes.

'What did Nan say about shooting someone?' My heart jumps. Did Mum hear?

'Oh, she was just ... being silly. She was talking about my Super Soaker.'

Jeez, I never lie. Will I get Nan in trouble?

'Hmmm.' Mum says with a breath, bending the note. Her eyebrows are raised. Her eyeline is sideways at my bed. She steps forward and hands me a small picture in a frame. 'I thought you could have this.'

It's an old religious picture. It has a young boy in a white robe with a halo around his head. A woman in a shawl and a man with a beard gaze lovingly down on him from above.

'It's boy Jesus with Mary and Joseph,' says Mum, matter-of-factly.

I like it. I can put it on my bedside table.

'Thanks Mum.'

She turns and wanders back to her room.

I turn back to my other family.

I slide the volume down and swap tapes. There's another Crayfish Creek one from when I was in grade four and Uncle Ken was here. There's a bit where I'm off doing a wee but the characters talk about me.

'He's cheeky,' says Pop.

'He hasn't got that bloody tape on again has he … he's got a couple more tapes of Nan at home …' says Nan.

'He is, he's cheeky,' says Uncle Ken.

'… he said Nan, when you are gone, I'll be able to play that and I won't ever be lonely.'

A furry head brushes my bum as I squat by the kitchen cupboard. I stroke the top of Blossum's head, stand and pull open the left kitchen drawer. This is the messiest drawer where Mum sticks all the bills and newsletters and brochures and everything else like bits from Mastermind and Matchbox cars and multicoloured note pads from my tour of the pulp mill. Most envelopes are covered in numbers and lists and doodles.

I was trying to find the latest Hydro and Telecom bills and something that might say when the rent is due. Nan's asked me to get in and check what bills need paying so I can let her know and help Mum stay ahead of the finances. Nan said I could even look in Mum's handbag if I needed to. That feels like a pretty naughty thing to do, but I know I'd be doing it for the right reasons.

'What are you looking for?' says Mum, appearing behind me.

'Oh, just a packet of stamps.'

'Put everything back where you found it. I won't know where anything is.'

'Yep. Have you had your tablet?'

'No, I was just about to take it.'

I hear the chink and rattle as Mum fishes a tablet out of the jar on top of the fridge. She stands at the sink, her back to me. She puts her right hand up to her mouth and uses her left to drink water. She swallows and I hear the sound in her neck. She puts the glass down and waits at the sink a moment, staring out the window. She turns to look at the stove. Her hand goes up and her fingers start waggling.

'Mum, we didn't even use the stove. We got McDonalds.'

'Okay dear, I think I'll get an early night.'

Her fingers keep waggling.

'Are you going back to your doctor soon?'

'She said I don't have to see her until next month.'

'Shouldn't you go back soon and tell her about what happened with Nan?'

Mum's fingers stop. She turns to me.

'Oh Justin, I won't let anything like that happen again. I don't know what got into me. I mustn't lose my temper like that again and upset everyone.'

She gives me a quick hug and says goodnight.

I'm still a bit shy and chicken to ring Mum's doctor. I feel guilty because I want to do what Nan says. But I figure if I take care of the bills Nan'll be happy enough with that. I go to the fridge, grab the jar that Mum's just put back and count the tablets. There seems to be one less in there. I hope she swallowed it.

I close the hall door and sit at the kitchen table. There's a postcard from Nick. He's in Queensland where the weather is twenty-six degrees in winter and there are four TV channels! He's at a school with 1400 kids in it and in grade eight for some reason.

Mum's handbag is hanging on the chair. I place it on the table. The material is cool and soft like a dress. It's a bit like Mum's drawer – messy and full of papers. I fish around and find a roll of film, Tattslotto wallet, small silver watch and a booklet marked 'Personal Finance Co'. That's where Mum went to get a loan to pay the car rego. I open up the leaflet. There's an amount of $300 at the top and then each week it goes down by $25. Mum's paid about half off. There's a payment due on Thursday.

I take out Mum's floral clasp purse and check inside. It's exciting seeing all the money.

I remember a time in grade three when I took some money from Mum's purse. I was obsessed with the video games at the local milk bar and wanted to play them every day after school. Mum said she couldn't afford any pocket money. I fell in with a tough freckle faced kid Dwayne who was a year older and lived up the road. He came to my house and knew Mum was in bed and said I should just steal the money out of her purse.

I grabbed a few coins and headed up to Joyce Street to play games with Dwayne. I was worried that Mum would notice and tell me off but she never did. The next time I took a two dollar note and now it was fun because I was getting away with it and playing games whenever I wanted. I could be like the teenagers who always had a row of twenties lined up along the bottom of the screen and a crowd of young kids watching them play.

My favourite game was a space one with a weird name – *Xain'd Sleena*. At the start you have to choose which of the planets to travel to. My heart would race as I smashed the buttons and wrenched the joystick and battled to stay alive. Parts of the game were scary like the molten lava and floating pharaoh's head, and the cliff where you'd fall into the void and lose a whole life. At the end of each round you'd fly back into space and take on the mothership.

Xain'd Sleena was hard. Even if I put a whole dollar's worth of twenties in, I usually struggled to make it past the first two stages.

I'd start to panic when it said 'CONTINUE ?' with the timer counting down. I'd have to make a hurried decision about whether to put in more money (pretty easy when I'd run out). Still, there was a chance my man could come back to life.

I loved the game so much I thought about giving someone else lots of twenties to play it so I could watch them get to the end! If you completed all five planets there was a final metal planet, but I'd only seen someone get up to it once. I've never seen anyone get to the end of any video game.

One day I decided to take Mum's fifty dollar note. I was a bit scared because it was the most money I'd ever had in my life but by this stage Mum was always on the bed and I was starting to feel angry at her.

I impressed Dwayne when I told him that I'd share it with him and his friends and buy everyone lollies. That's when he dared me to hold up the Joyce Street shop. The next thing I know I was walking into the shop at about seven o'clock with a bread knife.

I asked the woman for money.

'Give me that.'

I handed her the knife.

'Does your mum know where you are?'

I shook my head. I was so worried that I'd be in trouble. Instead she gave me a hotdog and a packet of multicoloured chewing gum – for free! She said I should go home because my mum would be worried. I walked home in the dark and put the rest of the money back in Mum's purse.

The next time I saw Dwayne he had a new friend with him. He pushed me over on the footpath for a joke. Dwayne laughed. I stopped seeing him after that.

Mum started to get well and eventually noticed there were two twenty dollar notes instead of a fifty. It was a relief to tell her about everything (except the knife). She said it wasn't safe to be hanging around milk bars late at night and if I needed money to play games I should just ask.

It's so weird thinking about those days. It was me but I didn't know what I was doing. I was drifting along like a dream.
    I close the clasp on the purse.
    At the bottom of the bag is a roll of blackcurrant jubes.
    I'm not sure why but finding them makes me sad.

45

It's the last day of term! I've been in a good mood all day because of my dream last night. I was flying high up over the sea and sunset clouds. The water was a soft navy blue and the sun was a glowing orange marble. There were shades of purple and gold tinged in the clouds. I was just sailing along effortlessly with nothing else around me. It was one of the best dreams I've ever had.

Now I'm a bit nervous because I'm reading over my comedy speech 'A Guide to McDonalds' that we're presenting in double Speech and Drama in a few minutes. This year Burnie got their first McDonalds. It was such a big deal that people were lining up around the block! I haven't seen anyone do that since *Milo & Otis* was on at the pictures.

I'll be the narrator while Billy does the actions. It's a good set up because not all the focus is on me and I can't forget my lines. I got the idea from a video of Rowan Atkinson we watched called 'How to Behave at a Restaurant'. There's also a similar sketch on *The Late Show* where Tom or Jane guide you through a dinner party conversation.

Get Up Mum

I've written most of the script and we've been rehearsing for the past couple of weeks. The teacher, Miss Mcfadzean, has been encouraging Billy to amplify and exaggerate his movements. I feel confident having him out front because he's already funny and everyone likes him. He knows how clever and funny I am and wants to be on my team!

Billy and I peer out at the crowd gathered on the library floor. The whole of grade seven is here including our mates and Sarah and Bianca. Billy gawks at me with a pale smile. I jiggle my legs as my resting heart rate feels like my exercising one.

'We'll be good,' I whisper, holding up my piece of paper.

This will be my first drama performance since I played the role of Dick Whittington in grade five. Last year our guitar class sang 'Way Out West' in front of Kmart, but that was in a group.

When I look out over a crowd I remember how I got lost at the Heybridge Country Music Festival when I was six. I wandered around a maze of legs until a man in a big hat took my hand and walked me up onto a huge stage. He led me between the microphones and I got a great view of a sea of people. The man asked everyone to wave at me and they did. I waved back. I was shy but also excited. Mum soon came and got me but I liked it up there with the men.

There are a few pairs performing before us but I hardly pay attention. I've brought along my black stereo and have a tape of ambience that we recorded at McDonalds. It was pretty funny – Billy and I had to sit there eating and not talking. As soon as we're introduced by Miss Mcfadzean I crank up the volume and press play. Billy stands in position. Already people are giggling. This is good.

I remember to force my voice out of my mouth. I tend to speak quietly. Miss Mcfadzean told me to aim for the back of the room.

'McDonalds, the biggest fast food chain in the world, designed to take the wait out of service and the money out of your wallet, can get to you. But the following should make your next trip a little easier. Place your hands on the bar, take the strain and heave!'

For the first action Billy squats his legs, sticks out his bum and exaggerates having a tug of war. The doors at McDonalds are ridiculously heavy. There's a flutter of laughter from the crowd. Gold butterflies fill my tummy with hope.

'Next you'd better get yourself in the queue and let's face it, you'll be there a while so take note of the people in front of you, say, the seventy-year-old who's fiddling with his hearing aid.'

'Can I take your order?' I say.

Billy acts like Grandpa Simpson.

'What? Allan Border? What a guy!' he roars.

'Sir, can I take your order please?'

'Huh? I gotta disorder with my knees?'

People are laughing. A lot. More than I expected. It feels fantastic.

'And how can we leave out the woman who forgot her glasses.'

'Can I take your order please?'

Billy scrunches up his eyes while adopting a posh high pitch.

'I'd like a sleazeburger, a large poke and a chocolate Saturday.'

I can see Bianca sitting near the front. She has her eyes closed and a happy smile on her face as her shoulders shake with giggles. Now Billy is starting to laugh, which makes me want to laugh. I start to talk but not everyone has finished laughing, so I stop and start again and that sets people off again. Billy's cheeks have gone from pale to flushed red. My insides are electrified.

'By the time you've ordered, you're probably dying to stuff your face. So quick, find a seat. Oh oh, there he is. The guy that's finished eating, ready to leave, but insists on pondering the meaning of life with his cookie box. So by the time you've picked out the gherkin, got chips everywhere except in your mouth and are giving that acne a bit of a kick along, spare a thought for that struggling party beside you.'

For this part I do the voice of a posh mother. Billy has to play all the different kids she's yelling at. It's a lot of characters to do in a short time.

'Charles dear, stop vomiting on Grimace's feet.'

'Tabitha! The waitress is not a dart board.'

'Quentin! You cannot declare war with the other tables.'

'James! How many times have I told you about ear wax on the table?'

'Butch! I told you not to bring your studs, leather jacket, Mohawk and rifle, you're scaring little Egbert.'

'Egbert! Get off the back of that semi at once!'

By the end Billy can't keep up with my lines, he just flails his arms in the air while racing from one side of the stage to the other. Everyone is cracking up.

'After you've made the decision of never having kids, you'd better tackle the burger. As your teeth push past the bread, meat and lettuce you feel a presence. An evil demonic mind at work beyond the comprehensions of man. Oh no! It's the gherkin!'

Billy pinches his fingers and holds them aloft, his eyes wide in horror. Everyone picks out the sliver of slimy gherkin.

We finish up by mentioning how the thickshakes are too thick, the apple pies are tough and the bins are really hard to find.

'The kids are leaving, the mothers are yawning and Ronald McDonald is flat on his back on the floor. So once you've dumped the trash, struggled your way through the screaming parents and that seventy-year-old guy who still hasn't ordered. Well done, you've survived. But after all, it was only McDonalds.'

I'm blasted by a wild choir of 'wooooooo!' that hurts my ears. I don't care. Without the script I'm not sure where to look. Billy nods slowly and smiles with his mouth closed. The applause keeps going. They really, really loved us!

Afterwards lots of people come up to Billy to tell him how great it was.

'Oh my god that was hilarious. You guys could go on TV,' says Ryan.

'Aww, it was mostly this guy,' says Billy, nodding towards me. 'He's the brains of the operation.'

Bianca drifts over, arms by her side. She peers up with bright blue eyes.

'That was really funny Justin.'

'Thanks,' I smile. 'Do you go to McDonalds?'

'Aww, we're not allowed,' she laughs. 'At least I know now what to expect.'

Billy and I are suddenly the unexpected stars of grade seven. I feel cool and liked and popular. The magic feeling carries me up the stairs and out the door towards home and school holidays. On the bus even Elvis is impressed. His cheeky eyes light up underneath his blond bowl cut.

'You're a crack up Hazelnut! I'll shout you a Happy Meal!'

As the other kids joke and shout and swear I stare out the window. The Montello streets whir by – the pool and police boys and Terrylands followed by Bird Street and Montello Primary. I'm heading back to my neighbourhood that I've walked around a hundred times before. Safety houses and milk bars and starry eyes and scary dogs and 'MOLLY 86'.

A shadow of tiredness passes through me.

My sinuses are tingling and my ears feel hot.

My bowels twinge as I press the bell.

I think I'm getting sick.

Mountain Spirit
— By Justin Heazlewood (Grade 7)

Slowly the mist emerges and scowls beneath me, partially covering the serenity below like a huge white blanket. The ferocious wind fresh off the snow, pierces my body like a thousand daggers. I shudder, both at the cold and the loneliness of my surroundings.

The jagged rocks seem to have been savagely bitten off by some huge mouth. The bushes sway to and fro uneasily as if in slow motion. The whole area seems restless as if it has been frozen for a hundred years and is agitated by its first intruder.

I peer over the rugged cliff at the sea of trees below. They have almost vanished from sight. I feel isolated from the rest of the world as if the mountain is trying to make me feel unwelcome. I sit down and close my eyes hoping for comfort but the howl of the wind reminds me of where I am. 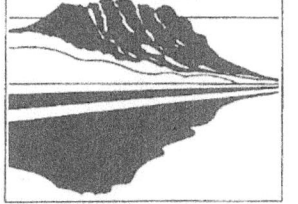 Somewhere in the distance I hear the cry of an eagle forlornly floating amongst the clouds like a lost spirit.

Suddenly the wind is as still as death and the chill of the mountain diminishes until everything is motionless; as if put on pause. Sunlight punctures the thick cloud and streams through warming my dampened body and soul. I look up at the great heavenly body and squint; the power of the sun is too much for my humble eyes. The cloud and mist now shrink and disappear. I take in the pure beauty of the mountain bathed in sunlight. The god of the sun wraps its great arms around the land killing the darkness and chill. The pleasant wind gently brushes my face. The whole land appears to have been given new life as all is calm on top of the massive rock. Among the celebrative chorus of the birds, the forest beams as I make my descent down the mountain.

AFTERWARDS

It's a sunny Saturday so Mum and I are heading down to Burnie Park for a barbie. The atmosphere at the park is always relaxed and lovely. The grass is a thick rich green and there are weeping willows that cast soft, spidery shadows. The top of the grassy slopes overlooks the sparkling sea with Table Cape resting on the side like a sentinel. The steep, spongy grass is perfect for roly-poly's, but I haven't done one of those in a while. I watch Mum crab walking carefully downwards.

I'm taking everything in. The shriek of the peacock. The excitement of little kids playing. The sky turning to mist overhead.

Something is missing.

'Mum look – the tyre swing!'

The tyre swing used to be perched up high on the slope, away from all the other equipment. It was comprised of three wooden poles arranged in a triangle. There was a chain at the top attached in three places to a tyre with a dirt dugout beneath. I'd sit with my feet inside the rim holding onto the chains. Mum would pull me back up the hill as far as she could go. Finally the tyre would be way up over her head. She'd stretch and flex her arms and fingertips until finally letting go.

The tyre would sail forwards and swing around as air whistled through my hair. It was a big swing, always going higher and faster than I'd planned and dizzying me with danger. I'd lean back and hang my head upside down as the grass became blue and the blood rushed to my head. I never made any sound or called out. I just hung on with all my strength.

Now it's gone. There's just a bare patch of dirt.

There's something else missing.

Mum and I had a favourite swing. It was a metal twin carriage where you sat facing each other. There was a bar in the middle where you could gently swing yourselves back and forth. We'd sit in the warm shade, chatting away. Mum would tell me about her life as a young girl and I would ask her questions about everything.

'When will I do swimming lessons again?'

'Where do butterflies sleep?'

'Why can we see the moon in the day?'

'How come Mummy didn't marry?'

At home we have lots of packets of photos of me at the park. Posing by a tree in my brown skivvy. Chewing my finger in my red parka near the yellow climbing caterpillar. But there aren't any of our swings.

'They must be replacing all the old ones,' Mum says sadly.

Burnie Park has a small creek running through it and an animal enclosure. It's fenced off with a walking path. Mum and I used to come all the time with stale bread to feed the ducks. The main attractions were and still are the peacock and the emu. When I was little I poked my finger through the fence and the emu bit it and I bawled. I'm still scared of the emu but I love watching him because he's so funny looking. He looks like a person inside a costume.

The rippled reflection wobbles across the surface, keeping the water alive. It forms a mini waterfall where the ducks gather. Mum and I walk over to the little jetty and gaze out. It's a pretty scene with the weeping willows cascading down over handsome brown ducks with their metallic green necks. I lean against a post and drift off with the sighing gust of wind coming from all around. My gaze is still but my thoughts are moving. This is a meeting point for all my memories. Peace and warmth and Mother Nature. They twinkle in my mind's eye.

I feel the most true me. The one inside that knows.

I add this moment to my collection of time.

Get Up Mum

At least they've left one bit of the old play equipment. We stroll over to the steam train, parked between the animals and the barbecues. It's a black locomotive with a big smokestack and a cabin with lots of cold steel bolts and levers and a fireplace that I used to throw leaves inside to power the engine. The bigger boys would climb up on the turret or the roof but I'd be too afraid. Looking at it now it wouldn't be that hard.

Mum takes the camera out.

'Climb up on the train and I'll take a photo.'

It feels a bit daggy having my photo taken now. My hair's flat today. Someone might see.

Mum picks a dandelion and hands it to me.

'Make a wish!'

I takes a deep breath and blow. The tiny white parachutes scatter into the wind. I turn it round in my fingers and finish it off. I can't remember the last time I did that.

I don't have to think about what to wish for.

I always wish for the same thing.

Mum plonks the eski on one of the picnic tables and starts unpacking. I settle in a seat in the sun. I wear contact lenses now so that has improved my looks. When I first put them in I spent ages staring at my giant hand. My whole life I'd been seeing the world much smaller than it actually is.

Mum forgot to bring the can opener.

'Oh well. We won't worry about pineapple.'

There's a tickle on my elbow. I glance over to see a gorgeous set of triangles. Dark orange with black lattice frame and cream pearl drops. I concentrate all my energy on making my arm bone completely still. My skin is a home now for this butterfly. I was so far inside my thoughts my mind had stopped for a second. I wasn't quite here. The butterfly brought me back.

What was I worrying about? Something. Quick! Don't remember. I distract myself as my skull shivers and the blood runs slow. The colour drains cold. I've been here before? The picnic. Mum forgetting pineapple. A butterfly. It's a moment and a replay of the moment. It's like there are two slides over the top of each other. The feeling lasts a second and it's enjoyable, like legs jumping in bed. The feeling fades. Who knows when it'll be back.

Mum puts oil on the plate and places two patties down to sizzle. She sits down opposite me. The barbecues are free now, you just push a silver button. There's still a red light inside a hole that tells you when there's heat. Mum jokes how everything's becoming computerised. At the library they scan a barcode with an infra-red pen now. Mum misses the stamp.

'I was thinking, Justin, next year you might want a bigger room, so you could have mine.'

My heart jumps and I shift position. I forgot about the butterfly! It loops away, frame by frame.

'You mean we'd swap rooms?'

'Yep.'

'Would you be okay in my room?'

'Yes Justin, I'll be alright, I don't need that much space, really. It makes sense seeing as you're about to start grade twelve. You know it only seems like last week that Nigel and Ken were here.'

'Time flies, money flies and blow flies' is one of Pop's sayings. Plus butterflies!

In May it was Nan and Pop's fiftieth wedding anniversary. Nan was very emotional and Ken and I performed songs in the lounge room. I played my new original 'The Volks' because Mum is thinking of selling the car, finally. It was great getting to stay up drinking and smoking with my uncles.

Earlier in the night Nigel starred with an impersonation of my football coach who'd been swearing at us at half time. Mum joined in too and for a while she and Nigel were improvising scenarios for the coach to be in like trying to find a loo and sleeping in. It got awkward when we'd all moved on but Mum kept going on about the coach and laughing uproariously. She was so hyper. I'd never seen her like that. I couldn't work out if she was well or sick.

It felt special to get it on tape. That was the first time I'd recorded my family in yonks. I've got a Walkman with a lapel microphone now so it's easy to go undercover. I use it mostly to record my own songs. I've made two albums that I'm extremely proud of.

I'm excited about having a bigger room, but also cautious. I don't want Mum stressing before Christmas.

'When did you want to swap? After Christmas?'

'Yes, we could do it in January.'

Mum still gets sick and then well every few months. She seems to take her tablets so Nan and I still don't know what's going on. She makes her sounds and I get so angry I scream and swear. I feel terrible afterwards but I can't help it.

This horror is my job.

At least I have a wonderful girlfriend – Erin. She's the first person I've told that Mum has schizophrenia.

'I'm sorry I haven't been myself sometimes lately,' Mum says suddenly as she flips the patties. 'I wish I was stronger but I don't know, these damn voices …'

Mum's been growing her hair longer. It's light and curly and wisping off at the sides. She's forty-three but looks much younger. I'm sure she could still have a boyfriend if she wanted. I can just never picture how it would happen.

'My mind wouldn't walk up a mountain like some people's can.' Her hazel green eyes gaze off to the side, gathering shadows as she squints. There are fine creases in the corners. Her cheeks are pink and soft. Poor Mum – she's still pretty.

'I tell you I'd rather have a broken jaw, at least you can set that into place, but not your mind.'

She dabs at a crumb on the table.

'I try and control it but it just sits there, like a clamp that won't let go.'

Mum makes a claw with her fingers and holds it on her head like a funny creature.

She's never really talked about her illness to me like this. I want to draw her out.

I'm nervous about what to say. I have a lot saved up.

'Nan says that the problems started when you were in Norway and you rang up saying you had some very exciting news, then you never mentioned it again. Do you remember what that was?'

Mum's head jerks slightly, wide eyed.

'I don't know, I don't remember that.'

'Nan thinks you could have been … pregnant, or something.'

I stare hard at the table, my heart beating fast. Someone has scratched their name into the wood. I run my fingers over the grooves and take a sip of ginger beer. I hope I don't offend Mum somehow.

'Oh no, nothing like that,' she says, smiling. 'I would have always told you if there was anyone,' her voice goes quiet '… other than you.'

I'm relieved.

'No the problems began when I started babysitting for Anne and Fred. Fred had a band and I used to go along to his concerts but they had their damn amplifiers turned up way too loud for such a small space. He played that screeching electric guitar and perhaps I had a little bit of marijuana, but it was all too much for me. If Fred hadn't played his damn music so loud, I might have been alright.'

Sometimes Mum complains about ringing in her ears. She's worried about my hearing when I go to Hobart to see Silverchair.

'I was unwell and I needed help but no-one was there to help me Justin. People can be very selfish. There are a lot of cold-hearted people in this world. I hope you never come across them like I did. So I had you and you were a dear little thing,' she smiles. I feel the warmth of her words.

'I just did my best to cope on my own.'

'With help from Nan and Pop.'

Mum takes a big breath in and raises her eyebrows. She looks sad and hopeful.

'Yes, where would we be without them.'

She goes to check on the hamburgers. I watch the kids across the park playing on the new equipment. They've knocked down the wooden fort and built a colourful metal climbing frame with a flying fox and dizzy slide. The bottom is covered in black spongy padding. We had sawdust when I was little.

Nan's stories and Mum's stories don't match up. I wonder who's telling the whole story.

'It's hard for us to help you when you get sick,' I say quietly.

'Well, Justin, I can't afford to get sick, not with everything we've got going on. I've got my Avon work to do and you'll be busy with your final year.'

I nod and frown. It hurts to be mad at Mum.

She dishes up. Open-cut bun, lettuce, cheese, beetroot, Nan's tomato sauce and a flat patty from the hotplate. I make sure to compliment her on our lunch.

'They cook up well those frozen patties.'

I gaze out to the sea behind Mum as we eat. The clouds on

the horizon are banked up in a long tube. I used to pretend it was a broken tidal wave, crashing towards us.

Bruisy clouds are gathering overhead. It's starting to spit, tapping the tin roof of our shelter. The sound of cooling and expanding, like the Volkswagen engine parked in the carport.

Mum laughs suddenly.

'Crikey dickens!' she says, looking up.

A duck family waddles by the creek edge behind us. I turn and watch the little baby ducks tottering along. They're so cute it makes me sad. Their heads are so small they can't see all the dangers. They have no defences. All they know is their mother is in front of them and they have to follow her to survive.

'It's a good day for ducks!' says Mum.

Praise for *Get Up Mum*

'… goddamn wonderful and heartbreaking. Justin's writing voice is so phenomenal – such a perfect combination of funny and whole-hearted without being syrupy, woe-is-me and sentimental. I have a feeling a lot of people will find relief in this book, especially if they grew up with parents who were dealing with any kind of mental illness.'
Amanda Palmer

'*Get Up Mum* is a warm, humorous memoir about coming of age, and the deep love between two individuals who need each other equally. Littered throughout the novel are lines of poetry that almost startle, asking to be read and re-read.'
Caitlin Cassidy, Readings

'Justin Heazlewood has written something so bloody important and special with this book. One of the most big-hearted – and heart-bruising – books you'll read.'
Benjamin Law, author of *The Family Law* and *Gaysia*

'Heazlewood's writing has extraordinary power and captures the world of a twelve-year-old living through an extremely alienating and difficult time.'
Paula Keogh, author of *The Green Bell*

'Equal parts heart-warming and heart-wrenching, this book is a funny time capsule of one year in a teenage boy's life, mixed with a very adult and very tragic tale of severe mental illness. Essential reading from an often forgotten perspective – that of the child caring for the adult. This book broke my heart into many pieces.'
Myf Warhurst

www.ingramcontent.com/pod-product-compliance
Lightning Source LLC
Chambersburg PA
CBHW021142160426
43194CB00007B/661